W9-BLT-863

THE OLD FARMER'S EVERYDAY COOKBOOK ALMANAC

THE OLD FARMER'S EVERYDAY COOKBOOK ALMANAC

A guarantee of goodness every day!

The Old Farmer's Almanac Books

Group publisher: John Pierce
Publisher: Sherin Pierce

Editor: Janice Stillman
Art director: Margo Letourneau
Copy editor: Jack Burnett
Editorial staff: Mare-Anne Jarvela, Martie Majoros, Sarah Perreault,
Heidi Stonehill; Fact-checking assistance: Carol Loria

compiled by Margo Letourneau

Production director: Susan Gross
Production manager: David Ziarnowski
Production artists: Lucille Rines, Rachel Kipka,
Janet Calhoun, Sarah Heineke

Web site: Almanac.com
Web site editor: Catherine Boeckmann; Designer: Lou Eastman
Programming: Reinvented, Inc.

color photography:

Food photography: Laurie Vogt
Food styling: William Smith; Prop styling: Robin Tucker
Photography assistant: Adam Lejak

Cover illustration: Kim Kurki

For additional information about this and other publications from
The Old Farmer's Almanac, visit Almanac.com or call 1-800-ALMANAC.

distributed in the book trade by Houghton Mifflin

Yankee Publishing Inc., P.O. Box 520,
1121 Main Street, Dublin, New Hampshire 03444

ISBN-13/EAN: 978-1-57198-463-0
second edition

Printed in the United States of America

Contents

A guarantee of goodness every day!

With *The Old Farmer's Almanac,* we aim to make every day special with our traditional wit and wisdom as well as advice on cooking and the home.

With the *Everyday Cookbook,* we aim to make every meal special—and folks are eating it up! Thanks to them (people just like you), we are delighted to present the second printing of this book.

Whether you are hosting a holiday feast or a special event, feeding the family, or fixing a snack for yourself, you'll find recipes here for nutritious food that isn't too fancy, is easy to prepare and put on the table, and tastes just like what your parents and grandparents used to serve. Only better.

The entire collection—425 recipes and 180 time- and money-saving tips—is by and for everyday people. In every chapter, you'll find winners of recent *Old Farmer's Almanac* reader recipe contests. Most of these dishes are family favorites, adapted and passed on through generations. Other recipes are kitchen classics, specially selected from our vast collection and updated for today's tastes and busy times. With each and every one of them comes a guarantee of goodness. Every day.

This is the kind of promise that we have been making every year with *The Old Farmer's Almanac* since 1792. You can learn a lot more about the Almanac, dig into its contents, and buy a copy at Almanac.com. While you're there, you may wish to subscribe to one of our free newsletters or tell us what you think about this cookbook (just use Contact Us).

The Old Farmer's Almanac has long been America's most trusted reference. We hope that you will make this your most trusted cookbook, to be used and enjoyed every day.

The Editors of *The Old Farmer's Almanac*

CHAPTER

1

Breakfast and Brunch

The 1994 Old Farmer's Almanac *Recipe Contest:*
"Best Original Main-Dish Recipe Featuring Eggs"

BREAKFAST AND BRUNCH

Chives-y Eggs

1 tablespoon butter, melted

4 ounces cream cheese, cut into 4 equal
portions

4 teaspoons chopped fresh chives, divided

4 large eggs, divided

½ teaspoon salt, divided

½ teaspoon white pepper, divided

4 tablespoons half-and-half, divided

6 tablespoons shredded sharp cheddar
cheese, divided

2 tablespoons chopped fresh parsley,
for garnish

1 large tomato, seeded and chopped, for garnish

1 medium avocado, chopped and combined with
1 tablespoon lemon juice, for garnish

Preheat the oven to 350°F. Brush four 6-ounce custard cups with melted butter. Place one portion of cream cheese in each cup and sprinkle with 1 teaspoon of chives. Add one slightly beaten egg and season with ⅛ teaspoon salt and ⅛ teaspoon white pepper. Gently pour 1 tablespoon of half-and-half over the egg and top with 1½ tablespoons shredded cheese.

Fill an 11x9-inch baking pan with 1 inch of hot water. Set filled cups in the pan. Bake for 20 minutes, until eggs are set. Remove the egg cups from the water and garnish the tops with parsley, tomato, and avocado. **Makes 4 servings.**

–Nikki Peden, Winter Park, Florida

HARD-BOILED FACTS

- Eggs boiled in salty water are easier to peel.

- To keep egg whites from seeping out of the shell during boiling, add a teaspoon of salt or a few drops of lemon juice or vinegar to the boiling water.

- To determine which eggs in your fridge are hard-boiled, spin them on their pointed ends. A hard-boiled egg will spin like a top; a raw egg will wobble and fall over.

FIRST PRIZE

The 2005 Old Farmer's Almanac *Recipe Contest: "Oatmeal"*

Swedish Oatmeal Pancakes

2 cups old-fashioned rolled oats

2 cups buttermilk, plus more as needed

½ cup all-purpose flour

2 tablespoons sugar

1 teaspoon baking powder

1 teaspoon baking soda

2 large eggs, lightly beaten

¼ cup (½ stick) unsalted butter, melted

1 large pear, cored, peeled, and thinly sliced

¼ cup lightly toasted sliced almonds

In a large bowl, combine the oats and 2 cups of buttermilk. Soak for at least 30 minutes. In a medium bowl, combine the dry ingredients. Stir them into the oat mixture. Mix in the eggs and melted butter. The batter should be thick; add 1 or 2 tablespoons more buttermilk if it is too thick to pour. Heat a nonstick skillet or griddle and grease with vegetable oil. Pour the batter in ¼-cup portions, allowing space for spreading. Place a few pear slices and almonds on each pancake. Cook for 2 to 3 minutes, or until the bottoms are golden brown. Gently turn the pancakes over and cook for 2 to 3 minutes more, or until brown. Repeat with the remaining batter, pear slices, and almonds, greasing the griddle as needed. Serve with butter and maple syrup. **Makes 12 (6-inch) pancakes.**

–Diane Halferty, Corpus Christi, Texas

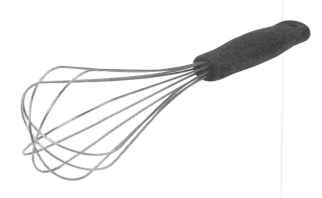

The 1994 Old Farmer's Almanac *Recipe Contest:*
"Best Original Main-Dish Recipe Featuring Eggs"

Creamy Smoked Salmon Tart

5 sheets phyllo pastry

3 tablespoons unsalted butter, melted

4 large egg yolks

1 heaping tablespoon Dijon-style mustard

3 large eggs

1 cup half-and-half

1 cup heavy cream

¾ cup (6 ounces) smoked salmon (lox), diced

4 scallions, chopped

1 to 2 tablespoons chopped fresh dill or 1 teaspoon dried dill

salt and pepper, to taste

parsley sprigs, for garnish, or use thin lime or lemon slices

Preheat the oven to 350°F. Generously grease a deep 9½-inch pie plate. Place one phyllo sheet on your work surface (cover the remaining pieces with a damp towel). Brush the sheet lightly with butter. Cut crosswise into four equal sections. Place one section in the buttered pie plate, covering the bottom and letting it hang over the edge of the plate. Place the next quartered sheet crosswise to the first. Repeat with the remaining quarters and the four phyllo sheets, making sure that the bottom and sides of the plate are covered. Fold under any overhanging pastry to make an edge flush with the edge of the pie plate. (This can be prepared a day ahead, if covered and refrigerated.)

Whisk the egg yolks and mustard in a medium bowl to blend; beat in the 3 large eggs, half-and-half, cream, salmon, scallions, and dill. Add salt and pepper to taste (remember that the salmon is quite salty). Pour the mixture into the prepared crust and bake for 50 minutes or until a knife inserted in the center comes out clean. Transfer to a rack and cool. Add garnish. **Makes 6 to 8 servings.**

–Diane Halferty, Corpus Christi, Texas

THIRD PRIZE
The 1994 Old Farmer's Almanac *Recipe Contest:*
"Best Original Main-Dish Recipe Featuring Eggs"

East Texas–Pennsylvania Ranch Eggs

6 small (6-inch) flour tortillas
2 cups Molé Sauce (recipe below)
6 large eggs
2 cups shredded cheese (Monterey Jack,
   Colby, cheddar)

Preheat the oven to 350°F. Lay the tortillas flat in a large greased casserole (try not to overlap). Cover each tortilla with ⅓ cup Molé Sauce. Crack one egg on top of each sauce-covered tortilla. Cover with the cheese and bake for 30 minutes. **Makes 6 servings.**

MOLÉ SAUCE:

1 small onion, chopped
1 small red bell pepper, chopped
1 tablespoon vegetable oil
2 cups chopped fresh or 1 can (14.5 ounces)
   diced tomatoes
1 tablespoon chopped fresh parsley
2 tablespoons chopped fresh cilantro
½ teaspoon cinnamon
½ teaspoon cumin
½ teaspoon oregano
1 square (1 ounce) semisweet chocolate
⅛ teaspoon ground cayenne pepper, or to
   taste

Sauté the chopped onion and red bell pepper in oil; add the remaining ingredients in order. Cook for 15 minutes over low heat. **Makes 2 cups.**

–David Rheinauer, Macungie, Pennsylvania

OLD-FASHIONED ADVICE

TESTING
AN EGG
FOR
FRESHNESS

▪ Put the egg in a pan of cold water. The fresher the egg, the sooner it will fall to the bottom; if rotten, it will swim at the top.

*–Roberts' Guide for
Butlers & Other Household
Staff, 1827*

TIPS FOR MAKING A PERFECT OMELET

■ Use an omelet pan or a similar pan with low, sloping sides to allow for easy stirring and turning. For a 7- to 8-inch pan, use two eggs.

■ Grease the pan with about ½ tablespoon of butter. Preheat the pan and cook the omelet over medium-high heat.

■ Pour the mixed eggs into the heated pan, tilting it to ensure that the eggs cover the bottom. When the eggs begin to set, use a spatula to gently lift the edges of the omelet all around, so that any uncooked egg runs underneath to cook. Within about 1 minute, the eggs should be cooked.

■ Turn the heat to low and add the fillings, gently spreading them down the center of the omelet. (Vegetable fillings, such as asparagus or peppers, should be precooked and warm. Cheese should be grated and at room temperature.)

■ With a spatula, gently fold one-half of the omelet over the other, covering the ingredients in between. Give the pan a shake (or use the spatula again) to dislodge the omelet if necessary, then slide it onto a plate.

Orange Dessert Omelet

3 large eggs, separated
2 to 3 tablespoons sugar
3 tablespoons frozen orange juice
    concentrate
1 tablespoon butter
fresh orange slices, as garnish

Beat the egg yolks with the sugar in a large bowl. Add the orange juice concentrate and stir. In a separate bowl, beat the egg whites until stiff. Melt the butter in a nonstick omelet pan or skillet on medium-high heat. Gently fold the whites into the yolk mixture. Pour the batter into the heated pan. Do not stir as it cooks. After 1 minute, fold the omelet and place it on a serving platter. Arrange the garnish. **Makes 4 servings.**

Strata

This dish can be made with crumbled bacon or shrimp, sautéed mushrooms or leeks, and just about any kind of bread, including raisin or a mixture of white and whole wheat or rye. Prepare it a night ahead. To feed a crowd, double this recipe and prepare it in a large baking dish.

14 slices bread, crusts removed

1 cup diced cooked ham

2 cups shredded Swiss or cheddar cheese

⅓ cup finely chopped shallots

2 tablespoons chopped fresh basil or parsley

6 large eggs

3½ cups milk

salt and pepper, to taste

Cut the bread into cubes. Generously grease a 13x9-inch baking dish. Make a layer with half of the bread cubes, arranging them so that they cover the bottom of the dish. Sprinkle the ham, cheese, shallots, and basil over the bread. Cover with the remaining bread cubes. Beat the eggs and milk together in a large bowl, and season with salt and pepper. Slowly pour the mixture over the top bread layer, saturating it evenly. Cover and refrigerate overnight; the bread will soak up the liquid as the mixture stands.

Preheat the oven to 325°F. Uncover the strata and bake for 1 hour, or until puffed and lightly browned. **Makes 8 to 10 servings.**

MAKIN' BACON

■ Are your bacon slices stuck together? Roll up the entire package crosswise. Unroll it and the slices will separate.

Baked Eggs

A ramekin is a small, individual baking dish. If you don't have one, use a 6-ounce custard cup. The ingredients listed are for a single serving, but you can bake multiple cups at the same time.

1 tablespoon chopped fresh dill

1 tablespoon cubed cheddar cheese

1 tablespoon diced cooked ham

2 large eggs

1 tablespoon sour cream

salt and pepper, to taste

Preheat the oven to 400°F. Lightly grease a ramekin or 6-ounce custard cup. Put the dill, cheese, and ham in the cup, then break the eggs over the contents of the cup. Add the sour cream, and season with salt and pepper. Place the filled cup in a baking pan and add enough hot water to the pan so that the water level reaches halfway up the side of the cup. Place the pan in the oven and bake for 15 minutes. Remove the cup from the water. **Makes 1 serving.**

Spinach Mushroom Quiche

Quiche is always a welcome choice for a lunch, brunch, or light supper. Some crusty bread and a mixed green salad is a perfect accompaniment.

3 cups sliced mushrooms

¼ cup chopped onion

2 tablespoons butter or margarine

1 unbaked (9½-inch) deep-dish pie shell

1 cup shredded Swiss cheese

4 large eggs

1 cup milk or heavy cream

**1 package (10 ounces) frozen chopped
    spinach, thawed and squeezed dry**

salt and pepper, to taste

⅛ teaspoon nutmeg

2 tablespoons grated Parmesan cheese

Preheat the oven to 400°F. Sauté mushrooms and onion in butter in a large skillet for 10 minutes or until soft; set aside to cool. Sprinkle the bottom of the pie shell with Swiss cheese. In a large bowl, lightly beat the eggs, then add the milk, spinach, mushrooms and onion, salt, pepper, and nutmeg; stir well. Gently pour the egg mixture over the Swiss cheese in the pie shell and sprinkle Parmesan cheese on top. Bake at 400°F for 10 minutes, then reduce heat to 350°F and continue baking for another 30 to 40 minutes, or until a knife inserted into the center comes out clean. Allow it to stand for 15 to 20 minutes before cutting. **Makes 6 to 8 servings.**

Salmon Quiche

1 unbaked (9½-inch) deep-dish pie shell

**1 can (6 ounces) skinless, boneless salmon,
    drained, or ¾ cup flaked, skinless,
    boneless, cooked salmon**

½ cup chopped fresh parsley

½ cup shredded Swiss cheese

4 ounces cream cheese, softened

**2 teaspoons chopped fresh dill, or
    ½ teaspoon dried dill**

½ cup heavy cream

3 large eggs

¼ teaspoon salt

¼ teaspoon white pepper

1 tablespoon lemon juice

1 tablespoon capers, drained and rinsed

⅛ teaspoon paprika

Preheat the oven to 425°F. Prebake the pie shell for 10 minutes. Allow it to cool. Reduce heat to 350°F. Spread the salmon in the pie shell. Sprinkle it with parsley and top with Swiss cheese. In a medium bowl, beat the cream cheese with the dill and heavy cream until smooth. Add the eggs, salt, pepper, and lemon juice, and beat until well combined. Pour the egg mixture over the salmon and cheese. Top with capers and sprinkle with paprika. Bake for 40 to 45 minutes, or until a knife inserted into the center comes out clean. Allow it to stand for 10 minutes before serving. **Makes 6 to 8 servings.**

This is one of the most popular recipes at Almanac.com/food. Reviewer comments at the site include: "Easy and delicious"; "Everybody loved it"; "WOW!"

A Hungry Man's Quiche

1 unbaked (9½-inch) deep-dish pie shell
3 small potatoes, mashed
¼ cup cubed cooked ham
2 cups shredded cheddar cheese
5 large eggs
1 cup milk

Preheat the oven to 325°F. Prick the bottom of the pie shell with a fork in several places and prebake for 15 minutes; remove from the oven, then increase the oven temperature to 375°F. Layer the potatoes, ham, and then cheese into the shell. In a medium bowl, beat the eggs and milk together, and pour the mixture into the shell. Bake for 30 minutes at 375°F. Reduce heat to 350°F and bake for an additional 10 minutes. **Makes 6 to 8 servings.**

EGG-QUIVALENTS

■ The number of whole eggs, whites, and yolks needed to make 1 cup are as follows (approximately, depending on egg size):

	JUMBO	EXTRA-LARGE	LARGE	MEDIUM	SMALL
WHOLE EGGS	4	4	5	5–6	6–7
WHITES	6	6	7–8	9	10
YOLKS	12	12	13	14	16

■ In recipes that call for eggs, use large eggs or adjust according to the following equivalents, based on egg size:

JUMBO	EXTRA-LARGE	LARGE	MEDIUM	SMALL
1	1	1	1	1
2	2	2	2	3
2	3	3	3	4
3	4	4	5	5
4	4	5	5–6	6–7
5	5	6	7	8

■ An egg is approximately ⅓ yolk, ⅔ white. The yolk of a large egg is about 1 tablespoon plus 1 teaspoon; the white is about 2 tablespoons.

■ There is no difference in the quality or nutritional value of white and brown eggs. Discard eggs of any color that have an odor, discoloration, or crack; using them is not worth the risk of salmonella poisoning.

Honey Date Granola

4 cups quick-cooking rolled oats

1 cup chopped nuts, your preference

1 cup shredded coconut

½ cup wheat germ

½ cup honey

⅓ cup vegetable oil or melted butter

½ teaspoon salt

1 cup chopped dates

Preheat the oven to 300°F. Place the oats, nuts, coconut, and wheat germ in an ungreased 13x9-inch pan and stir to combine. Stir the honey, oil, and salt together in a bowl and drizzle over the oat mixture. Bake, stirring several times, for about 30 minutes, or until the oats are golden. Remove from the oven and stir in the dates. Cool completely. Store in an airtight container in a cool place. Serve with milk or yogurt as a breakfast cereal or snack. **Makes 7 cups.**

Buckwheat Pancakes

1 package (1 scant tablespoon) active
    dry yeast

¾ cup all-purpose flour

1 cup buckwheat flour

¼ cup cornmeal

1 teaspoon salt

2 tablespoons molasses

¼ teaspoon baking soda

2 tablespoons butter, melted

The night before you are planning to serve, mix the yeast with 2 cups of lukewarm (105° to 115°F) water in a large bowl. Add the flours, cornmeal, and salt. Stir to a smooth batter. Cover the batter bowl with a cloth and let it stand in a warm place overnight.

In the morning, stir in the molasses, baking soda, and melted butter. The batter should be of a thin consistency; add a little lukewarm water, if necessary, to thin it. Heat a well-greased griddle. Drop 1-tablespoon portions of batter from the tip of a spoon, allowing space for spreading. Cook for 2 to 3 minutes, until bubbles form on the surface and the cakes are dry around the edges. Gently turn the pancakes over and cook until the bottoms are golden brown. Repeat with the remaining batter, greasing the griddle as needed. Serve with butter, maple syrup, warm honey, fresh fruit, or yogurt. **Makes 18 to 20 (3-inch) pancakes.**

MAPLE YOGURT SAUCE
Mix together ¼ cup maple syrup and 1 cup plain yogurt until smooth. Use on pancakes, baked apples, or plain cakes. Makes 1¼ cups.

SPICE

■ Combine 1 cup sugar,
3 tablespoons ground cinnamon,
1 teaspoon ground nutmeg or
mace, and 1 teaspoon ground
cardamom in a shaker. Store in
a cool, dry place. Sprinkle on
pancakes, toast, or oatmeal.

German Apple Pancakes

Instead of using this griddle-then-oven version, you could simply add ½ cup peeled, cored, and chopped apple to regular batter and cook the pancakes on the griddle.

1½ cups all-purpose flour

⅓ cup sugar

¾ teaspoon salt

5 large eggs

1¾ cups milk

¼ cup (½ stick) butter, melted

5 apples, peeled, cored, and thinly sliced

3 tablespoons butter, for dotting

butter, melted, for brushing on pancakes

1 tablespoon each, cinnamon and sugar, combined

Preheat the oven to 400°F. Sift together the flour, sugar, and salt in a large bowl. In a medium bowl, beat the eggs with the milk; pour into the flour mixture. Add the melted butter to the batter and beat until smooth. Heat a 10-inch skillet over medium heat, brush well with butter, and pour ¾ cup of the batter into the pan, tilting it so that it flows evenly over the bottom. When the pancake is set (2 to 3 minutes), cover with a layer of sliced apple, dot with butter, and sprinkle with cinnamon and sugar. Continue to cook for 1 to 2 minutes, making sure that the bottom doesn't burn. Using two spatulas, fold the pancake in half and transfer it to an ungreased 14x10-inch baking dish, placing the fold of the pancake against the 10-inch side of dish. Butter the skillet and repeat with the remaining batter and apples, arranging the folded pancakes in a stepped, overlapping fashion across the baking dish. Brush the tops with butter and sprinkle with more cinnamon and sugar. Bake for 12 minutes, or until puffed and the edges are crisp. **Makes 6 servings.**

Vermont Maple Pancakes

1 cup sifted all-purpose flour

1½ teaspoons baking powder

½ teaspoon salt

1 tablespoon maple syrup

1 egg, beaten

1 cup milk

3 tablespoons melted shortening or butter, or vegetable oil

Preheat a cast-iron skillet or griddle. In a large bowl, sift together the flour, baking powder, and salt. Combine the maple syrup, egg, and milk in separate bowl and gradually add it to the dry ingredients, mixing only until smooth. Add the shortening. Grease the hot griddle. Pour the batter in 3-tablespoon portions, allowing space for spreading. Cook until bubbles form on the surface and the cakes are dry around the edges. Gently turn the pancakes over and cook until the bottoms are golden brown. Repeat with the remaining batter, greasing the griddle as needed. **Makes 10 (4-inch) pancakes.**

Strawberry Pancakes

2 cups all-purpose flour

3 tablespoons baking powder

1 tablespoon sugar

½ teaspoon salt

5 tablespoons butter, melted

3 large eggs

1½ cups milk

½ cup chopped strawberries

Preheat a cast-iron skillet or griddle. Sift the dry ingredients together. Beat in the butter, eggs, and milk. Grease the hot griddle. Pour the batter in 3-tablespoon portions, allowing space for spreading. Scatter some strawberries onto each pancake. Cook until bubbles form on the surface and the cakes are dry around the edges. Gently turn the pancakes over and cook until the bottoms are golden brown. Repeat with the remaining batter and strawberries, greasing the griddle as needed. Serve with maple syrup or yogurt and more strawberries. **Makes 12 (6-inch) pancakes.**

HOT GRIDDLE TEST

Sprinkle a few drops of water on a well-greased hot griddle. If the water sputters, the griddle is ready.

Corn and Pepper Pancakes

These pancakes can also be served at dinner in place of potatoes, bread, or rice. For lunch, top them with creamed vegetables, a cheese sauce seasoned with hot peppers, or sour cream and salsa.

1 cup all-purpose flour

½ teaspoon salt

1 teaspoon sugar

2 teaspoons baking powder

1 large egg, lightly beaten

¾ cup milk

2 tablespoons vegetable oil

½ cup well-drained corn kernels

¼ cup minced red and green bell pepper

Preheat a cast-iron skillet or griddle. Sift flour, salt, sugar, and baking powder into a bowl. Combine the egg, milk, and oil, and stir into the dry ingredients. Just before cooking, mix in the corn and peppers. Grease the hot griddle. Pour the batter in 3-tablespoon portions, allowing space for spreading. Cook until bubbles form on the surface and the cakes are dry around the edges. Gently turn the pancakes over and cook until the bottoms are golden brown. Repeat with the remaining batter, greasing the griddle as needed. **Makes 12 (6-inch) pancakes.**

French Toast

4 eggs

1 cup milk

1 teaspoon vanilla extract

pinch of nutmeg

pinch of sugar

8 slices bread

confectioners' sugar for dusting

In a shallow bowl, whisk together the eggs, milk, vanilla, nutmeg, and sugar. Spray a large skillet with nonstick cooking spray and preheat the pan over medium heat. Dip as many pieces of bread as will fit in the skillet into the egg mixture, coating both sides. Cook for 3 to 4 minutes on each side, or until golden brown. Repeat with remaining slices of bread. Lightly dust with confectioners' sugar and serve. **Makes 4 servings.**

Banana Cinnamon Waffles

1¾ cups all-purpose flour

1 tablespoon baking powder

¾ teaspoon cinnamon

¼ teaspoon salt

2 large egg whites, beaten slightly

1½ cups skim milk

⅔ cup mashed banana

½ cup applesauce

Preheat the waffle iron. Combine the dry ingredients in a bowl. In another bowl, combine the egg whites, milk, banana, and applesauce. Add the dry ingredients to the wet, and mix briefly. When the waffle iron is ready, spray or brush lightly with vegetable oil. Pour the batter into the center of the waffle iron and close the lid. Cook for 3 to 4 minutes or until almost all of the steam has escaped from the sides. If the top resists and seems to stick, cook for an additional minute. Remove the waffle with a fork. Brush or spray the iron and repeat with the remaining batter. **Makes 6 (7-inch) waffles.**

Whole Wheat Buttermilk Waffles

1 cup whole wheat flour

1 cup unbleached all-purpose flour

2 tablespoons sugar

1½ teaspoons baking powder

½ teaspoon baking soda

½ teaspoon salt

2 large eggs, separated

2 cups buttermilk

1 apple, peeled, cored, and shredded

6 tablespoons (¾ stick) butter or
    margarine, melted

Combine the flours, sugar, baking powder, baking soda, and salt in a large bowl and whisk together to blend completely. In a separate bowl, whisk together the egg yolks, buttermilk, shredded apple, and melted butter. Make a well in the dry ingredients and pour in the egg mixture. Combine with a few quick strokes, using a wooden spoon. Do not overmix; the batter will be lumpy. Set the batter aside and preheat the waffle iron. In a separate bowl, beat the egg whites until soft peaks form, then fold them into the batter, which will be thick. When the waffle iron is ready, spray or brush lightly with vegetable oil. Pour the batter into the center of the waffle iron and gently spread it over the waffle grid with a knife. Close the iron and cook for 3 to 4 minutes or until almost all of the steam has escaped from the sides. If the top resists and seems to stick, cook for an additional minute. Remove the waffle with a fork. Brush or spray the grids and repeat with the remaining batter. **Makes 4 (7-inch) waffles.**

GET OFF TO A SMOOTH(IE) START

■ Combine 1 cup (8 ounces) vanilla yogurt, 1 cup fresh blackberries, 1 cup fresh blueberries, and ½ cup grape or cranberry juice in a blender and process until smooth. Serve immediately. Makes 2 servings.

Experiment with seasonal fruits such as strawberries, peaches, or raspberries and juices that you have on hand such as orange juice or orange juice blends. Use frozen fruit when fresh is not available.

DELICIOUS FRUIT PLATES

1 ripe cantaloupe or honeydew melon
4 ripe kiwis
1 lime
sprigs of fresh mint, for garnish
fresh raspberries, for garnish

Slice the melon into quarters, seed, and place the quarters on dessert plates. Peel the kiwis, and carefully slice into four to six crosswise slices. Fan out the pieces across the top of each melon section. Cut the lime into four sections and squeeze the juice from each onto the melon and kiwi. Garnish with mint and dot the plates with fresh raspberries. Makes 4 servings.

HINTS FOR HEAVENLY HASH

■ The finer a raw ingredient is diced, chopped, or shredded, the more rapidly it will cook.

■ Taste and adjust seasonings only after adding all ingredients and sautéing for a minute or two. (Leftovers are likely to be seasoned.) For a change, vary the spices and herbs used for seasonings.

■ Sauté with different cooking oils to create a new dish from the same main ingredients. Consider sesame, apricot, almond, walnut, peanut, or coconut oil, all available in health food or specialty stores.

■ Sauté the hash ingredients in clarified butter or in fat skimmed from the pan drippings of a roast.

■ Turn almost any hash into a crusty "pancake" by adding puréed or thickened ingredients to the chopped ones. Good binding ingredients include leftover mashed potatoes, puréed squash, leftover stuffing thinned with a little milk or cream, bread crumbs soaked in milk, gravy, leftover oatmeal, an egg beaten into a little milk, and grated hard cheese.

Roast Beef Hash

2 tablespoons butter

1 medium onion, chopped

2 cups leftover mashed potatoes, or 3 medium potatoes, peeled, cooked, and chopped

3 cups chopped cooked roast beef

1½ cups gravy, warmed

salt and pepper, to taste

Preheat the oven to 400°F. Melt the butter in a large oven-proof skillet and stir in the onion. Sauté over medium heat for 5 minutes. Add the potatoes and beef, and top with the gravy. With a fork, stir the mixture together gently and mash it lightly to smooth the top. Season with salt and pepper. Transfer the skillet to the oven and bake for 20 minutes. **Makes 4 to 6 servings.**

Red Flannel Hash

¼ cup (½ stick) butter

1 large onion, chopped

3 medium potatoes, peeled, cooked, and
    diced into ½-inch cubes

3 medium beets, cooked (see below) and
    diced into ½-inch cubes

2 cups chopped cooked corned beef

salt and pepper, to taste

¼ cup heavy cream

Preheat the oven to 400°F. Melt the butter in a large oven-proof skillet. Add the onion and sauté over medium heat until translucent. Stir in the potatoes, beets, and corned beef. Season with salt and pepper and gently mash the mixture down with a fork or potato masher. Drizzle cream over the top and cook for a couple of minutes. Transfer the skillet to the oven and bake for 20 to 30 minutes. **Makes 6 servings.**

HOW TO COOK BEETS

Select unblemished roots with diameters no larger than 2 inches and fresh, leafy tops. To prepare beets, wash them thoroughly and remove the leafy tops (reserve for a salad), leaving 1 to 2 inches of stem and keeping the root ends intact—this will reduce bleeding. Place the cleaned beets in a stain-resistant saucepan, and add enough water to cover them. Bring the water to a boil, reduce the heat, and cook (covered) for 30 to 40 minutes or until tender. Drain and run cold water over the beets. Cut the stems and root ends; the skins will peel off easily. Use according to recipe. Caution: Staining may occur on wooded cutting boards, porous surfaces, fabrics, and skin.

Turkey Hash

A great brunch dish when baked in ramekins or 6-ounce custard cups and topped with a poached egg.
Serve with fresh grapefruit and orange slices garnished with mint leaves.

2 cups diced cooked turkey

2 cups diced cooked potatoes

3 tablespoons finely chopped green bell
    pepper

½ cup finely chopped onion

1 tablespoon minced fresh parsley

½ teaspoon salt

pepper, to taste

1 cup turkey gravy

Preheat the oven to 350°F. Grease a large casserole. In a large bowl, combine all of the ingredients. Turn into the casserole and cover. Bake for 45 minutes. In the last 15 minutes of cooking, remove the cover to allow the top to brown. **Makes 4 servings.**

Ham Apple Hash

Here's a good breakfast dish that can stand alone or become the filling for a hearty omelet. Use hard winter apples such as Idared or Red Rome that hold their shape during cooking or see "The Best Baking and Cooking Apples in North America" table on page 244 for other suggestions.

1 tablespoon olive oil

2 cups finely diced cooked ham or roast
    pork

2 large cooking apples, peeled, cored,
    and diced

scant ¼ cup apple cider, or ¼ cup apple
    butter, apple jelly, or applesauce

cinnamon, to taste

Heat the oil in a large, heavy skillet. Sear the meat until well browned. Reduce the heat, add the apples, and sauté over moderate heat until lightly browned. Pour the cider over the ham and apple mixture, sprinkle with cinnamon to taste, and continue cooking over very low heat until the liquid is nearly evaporated. **Makes 4 servings.**

Nut Hash

Here's an elegant, crunchy, winter salad alternative. For a main dish, add 2 cups diced cooked chicken or turkey when you add the pears.

1 cup coarsely chopped nut meats, any
 kind
1 tablespoon light cooking oil, such as
 almond or walnut
1 large sweet onion, minced
2 firm, ripe pears, peeled, cored, and
 diced
2 navel oranges, peeled and cut into
 bite-size pieces
2 small stalks celery, diced
1 roasted red bell pepper, peeled, seeded,
 and cut into thin strips
½ teaspoon ground cardamom,
 or to taste

If using raw nuts, toast them in a deep, heavy skillet over moderate heat, stirring constantly for several minutes, until they give off a rich aroma. Remove the toasted nuts from the pan and reserve. Heat the oil in the skillet. Sauté the onion over moderate heat until translucent. Add the pears and sauté for 3 minutes, or until lightly browned. Reduce the heat and add the orange pieces, celery, red pepper strips, and toasted nuts. Cover the skillet and cook just until the celery is heated through. Sprinkle with ground cardamom. **Makes 4 servings.**

SHELLS 'N' ALL

If nut shells get mixed in with the meats, put the whole mixture into a bowl of water. The shells will float and you can just scoop them out. Then drain the water and blot the nut meats dry before using them.

Zucchini Sausage Squares

2 large zucchini

1½ cups (12 ounces) ground pork sausage

¾ cup finely chopped onion

4 large eggs

½ cup grated Parmesan cheese

½ cup bread crumbs

1 teaspoon dried basil

½ teaspoon dried oregano

¼ teaspoon salt

⅛ teaspoon pepper

2 cloves garlic, minced

1 cup shredded sharp cheddar cheese

Preheat the oven to 325°F. Grease an 11x7-inch baking dish. Wash and trim the zucchini (do not peel). Grate them and set aside. Sauté the sausage and onion in a skillet until the sausage is completely cooked. Drain off the fat and set the mixture aside. In a large mixing bowl, beat the eggs until frothy, then add the Parmesan cheese, bread crumbs, basil, oregano, salt, pepper, garlic, sausage mixture, and shredded zucchini. Spread the ingredients evenly in the baking dish. Bake for 25 minutes. Remove from the oven, sprinkle cheddar cheese on top, and continue baking for 15 minutes. Cool slightly and cut into 1½-inch squares. **Makes 35 squares.**

Sugar and Spice Doughnuts

3 tablespoons vegetable shortening

1¾ cups sugar, divided

2 large eggs

4½ cups all-purpose flour

4 teaspoons baking powder

1 teaspoon salt

1 teaspoon nutmeg

1 cup milk

vegetable oil, for deep-frying

2 tablespoons cinnamon

In a large bowl, cream the shortening with 1 cup of sugar, then beat in the eggs. In a separate bowl, sift together the flour, baking powder, salt, and nutmeg and add to the creamed mixture alternately with the milk, stirring into a soft dough. Roll out the dough on a lightly floured board to a ½-inch thickness and cut with a doughnut cutter. Heat the vegetable oil in a deep pan over medium heat. Add enough oil so that doughnuts will float in the pan as they cook. When the oil is hot (about 375°F), carefully lower the dough into the pan and fry for about 3 minutes on each side, turning only once. Cover a cookie sheet with paper towels and place the doughnuts on the sheet to drain.

Combine the remaining sugar and the cinnamon in a small, clean paper bag. Put the warm doughnuts into the bag, a few at a time, and shake until coated with the cinnamon mixture. **Makes 24 doughnuts.**

English Muffins

Cook in a cast-iron skillet.

1 package (2¼ teaspoons) active dry
   yeast
1 cup milk
¼ cup (½ stick) butter
3 tablespoons sugar
1 teaspoon salt
5 to 6 cups all-purpose flour
cornmeal

Dissolve the yeast in 1 cup of lukewarm (105° to 115°F) water and set aside. Pour the milk into a saucepan, heat to scalding, then add the butter, sugar, and salt, stirring until the butter melts. Cool to lukewarm. In a large bowl, combine the milk mixture with the yeast. Mix in the flour, 1 cup at a time, to form a soft dough. Knead the dough gently in the bowl and shape into a ball. Place in a greased bowl, turn to grease the top, cover, and let rise until doubled in size. Punch down the dough and divide into two portions. On a board sprinkled with cornmeal, gently pat or roll each half out to a ½-inch thickness. Using a biscuit cutter or English muffin ring, cut the dough into 3- to 3½-inch circles. Place the muffins 3 inches apart on ungreased baking sheets and let rise until doubled. Lightly grease a cast iron skillet and heat it over medium heat. Cook the muffins, starting with the cornmeal side, 10 to 12 minutes per side, or until puffy and brown. Cool on racks. **Makes 14 to 20 muffins.**

INSTANT MUFFIN CUTTER

A clean 6-ounce tuna can with straight sides makes a 3½-inch cutter, or ring, if you carefully remove its top and bottom.

For breakfast baked goods, turn to "Breads, Muffins, and Pastries," beginning on page 203.

Real Hot Chocolate

How this sweet treat is supposed to taste!

1½ cups milk

½ cup light cream

3 tablespoons brown sugar

½ teaspoon ground cinnamon, plus a
    pinch to garnish

1½ teaspoons vanilla extract

pinch of salt

3 ounces semisweet chocolate, roughly
    chopped

whipped cream, for topping

Combine all of the ingredients except the whipped cream in a saucepan. Cook over medium heat until the chocolate melts, stirring often. Pour into mugs, top with whipped cream, and sprinkle with cinnamon. **Makes 3 servings.**

GOT FAT?

■ Sometimes it's helpful to know the relative fat contents of dairy liquids:

MILK	FAT (GRAMS) PER 8 OUNCES
Whole	8
2% Reduced-fat	5
1% Reduced-fat	2½

CREAM	FAT (GRAMS) PER 2 TABLESPOONS
Heavy	6
Whipping	5
Light	3
Half-and-half	2

CHAPTER

Appetizers and Snacks

Salmon Wontons With Dipping Sauce

1 can (6 ounces) skinless, boneless salmon, drained, or ¾ cup flaked skinless, boneless, cooked salmon

¼ cup shredded carrot

4 scallions, chopped

½ cup alfalfa sprouts

1½ tablespoons soy sauce

1 to 2 teaspoons peeled and grated fresh ginger, or ½ teaspoon ground ginger

2 cloves garlic, crushed

vegetable oil, for deep-frying

30 wonton wrappers

Dipping Sauce (recipe below)

In a medium bowl, combine the salmon with the next six ingredients and toss together until crumbly. Heat the oil in a deep fryer or deep heavy pan to 375°F. Working in batches, lay six wonton wrappers on a dry work surface. Moisten the edges with a few drops of water, keeping the unused wrappers covered with a damp towel to prevent them from drying. Drop 1 teaspoon of the salmon filling on the center of each wonton wrapper and fold diagonally to make triangles; press and seal the edges. Still working in small batches, deep-fry the wontons in hot oil on one side until golden brown; then flip them over and fry on the other side. Drain on paper towels. Serve with Dipping Sauce. **Makes 30 wontons.**

DIPPING SAUCE

Combine 1 cup sweet-and-sour sauce, plum sauce, or duck sauce with 1 to 2 tablespoons soy sauce, 1 teaspoon hoisin sauce, and a dash of chili oil.

–Anne Dirksen, Hastings, Minnesota

SECOND PRIZE

The 1997 Old Farmer's Almanac *Recipe Contest: "Best Appetizers"*

Tuscany Cheese Tortas

3 tablespoons olive oil

½ cup diced red onion

1 clove garlic, minced

¼ cup chopped sun-dried tomatoes
    (not in oil), softened in warm water
    for 10 minutes and drained

2½ cups shredded zucchini

5 large eggs, lightly beaten

⅓ cup Italian bread crumbs

1 teaspoon dried oregano

¼ cup chopped fresh basil

1½ cups shredded cheddar cheese

1½ cups shredded Monterey Jack cheese

½ cup freshly grated Parmesan cheese

½ teaspoon salt

pepper, to taste

¼ cup toasted sesame seeds

Preheat the oven to 325°F. Grease a 13x9-inch baking dish. Heat the oil in a large skillet over medium-high heat. Add the onion, garlic, and tomatoes and sauté for 3 minutes. Add the zucchini and cook for 3 minutes, or until crisp-tender. Remove from the heat. In a large bowl, blend the eggs with the next eight ingredients, add the zucchini mixture, and toss until combined. Spread evenly in the baking dish. Sprinkle sesame seeds on top. Bake for 30 minutes, or until set when lightly touched in the center. Cool on a rack for 15 minutes. Cut into 1-inch squares and serve warm or at room temperature. This can also be refrigerated and served cold. **Makes 9 to 10 dozen tortas.**

–Kathy Lee, Valley Center, California

The 1997 Old Farmer's Almanac *Recipe Contest: "Best Appetizers"*

Clam-Stuffed Mushrooms

24 large, fresh mushrooms, stems removed

4 or 5 slices bacon

2 teaspoons reserved bacon drippings

½ cup finely chopped onion

½ cup finely chopped green bell pepper

1 clove garlic, minced

1 tablespoon minced fresh parsley

1 teaspoon dried oregano

salt and pepper, to taste

1 can (6.5 ounces) chopped clams, drained

⅓ cup grated Parmesan cheese

Preheat the oven to 350°F. Wipe the mushroom caps clean with a damp paper towel. Fry the bacon in a skillet until crisp. Drain and crumble the bacon into a large bowl, reserving 2 teaspoons of drippings in the skillet. Add the onion and green pepper to the drippings in the hot skillet and sauté for 3 minutes. Remove from the heat and stir in the garlic, parsley, oregano, salt, and pepper. Mix well and add to the crumbled bacon in the bowl. Stir in the clams and cheese. Using a spoon, mound the filling into each mushroom cap. Place the caps top down on a lightly greased baking sheet and bake for 20 minutes, until the mushrooms are tender. (Or microwave, covered with a paper towel, at medium power for 8 to 10 minutes.) **Makes 24 mushroom caps.**

–Susan Straney, Saline, Michigan

Mini-Meatballs

MEATBALLS:

1 pound lean ground beef

1 pound ground turkey

1 cup bread crumbs

2 large eggs, slightly beaten

1 medium onion, minced

1½ teaspoons salt

1 teaspoon dried basil

½ teaspoon pepper

1 tablespoon Worcestershire sauce

SAUCE:

1 can (16 ounces) cranberry jelly

1 bottle (12 ounces) chili sauce

2 tablespoons firmly packed brown sugar

1 tablespoon lemon juice

1 large round loaf of Italian bread, for
    serving

For meatballs: Combine all of the meatball ingredients in a large mixing bowl. Mix well and shape into 1-inch balls. Place the meatballs in a 13x9-inch baking dish. Preheat the oven to 350°F and make the sauce.

For sauce: In a saucepan on medium heat, whisk together all of the sauce ingredients and bring to a simmer, stirring often. Reduce the heat to low and cook, uncovered, for 10 minutes, stirring often. Pour the sauce over the meatballs. Bake uncovered for 30 minutes, or until the meatballs are nicely browned.

To serve: Slice the top from the Italian bread and scoop out the inside, leaving a 1-inch-thick shell. Fill the bread with hot meatballs, and place on a platter with toothpicks for spearing. (This recipe can be adapted for a main dish or buffet supper by making the meatballs larger.) **Makes about 50 meatballs.**

IS THE SNAP OUT OF IT?

■ To put the snap back into crackers, corn chips, or other crispy snacks, spread them on a baking sheet, bake at 250°F for 15 minutes, cool, and serve. Place cooled leftovers in an airtight container.

■ Keep a few clip clothespins or binder clips in the kitchen drawer to seal up bags of chips and the inner bags of crackers to keep them crispy.

Santa Fe Salsa

½ cup chopped scallions (white part only)

¼ cup finely chopped cilantro

3 large ripe tomatoes, diced

¼ cup freshly squeezed lemon juice

1 red bell pepper, minced

1 tablespoon white rice vinegar

½ tablespoon canola oil

¼ teaspoon hot sauce

½ teaspoon salt

¼ teaspoon freshly ground black pepper

Combine all of the ingredients in a bowl and chill for 1 hour. **Makes about 2 cups.**

QUICK CRISPS

Flour tortillas make a great last-minute hors d'oeuvre. Spray each side with vegetable cooking oil; sprinkle with curry powder, chili powder, Chinese five-spice, or your favorite seasoning blend; and cut into wedges or strips with kitchen shears. Place the pieces on a baking sheet sprayed with vegetable cooking oil and bake at 375°F for 5 to 6 minutes. These are also good with soup or salad.

Boiled Shrimp With Dipping Sauce

Allow about 1 pound of shrimp for every four guests. The sauce brings out the shrimp's flavor without overwhelming it.

3 pounds unpeeled fresh or frozen raw
   shrimp

1 to 2 tablespoons salt

Dipping Sauce (recipe below)

In a stockpot, bring 2 to 3 quarts of water to a boil. Add salt and the shrimp. Cook the shrimp in boiling water for 2 to 3 minutes. Drain and rinse with cold water. Peel the shrimp (devein, if necessary), place them in a serving dish, and chill. **Makes 12 servings.**

DIPPING SAUCE

Mix together ½ cup soy sauce, 2 tablespoons minced garlic, 1 tablespoon sesame oil, and 4 teaspoons balsamic vinegar. Serve in a small bowl, with the shrimp. **Makes about 1 cup.**

Rich Cucumber Dip

6 shelled walnut halves

1 clove garlic

1 tablespoon olive oil

1 cup plain yogurt

¾ cup peeled, seeded, and diced cucumber

1 tablespoon lemon juice

salt, to taste

Combine the nuts, garlic, and oil in a food processor or blender. Add the yogurt, cucumber, lemon juice, and salt. Blend until smooth. Serve this dip with crackers or raw vegetables. **Makes 1 cup.**

Blue Cheese Dip

4 ounces cream cheese, softened

¼ cup minced fresh parsley

2 tablespoons butter, softened

2 tablespoons chopped fresh basil

2 teaspoons minced fresh rosemary

1 clove garlic, minced

1 teaspoon chopped fresh thyme

2 teaspoons Worcestershire sauce

1 tablespoon lemon juice

¼ cup (1 ounce) crumbled blue cheese

Combine all of the ingredients except the blue cheese, and process or whip until smooth. Gently stir in the blue cheese. Refrigerate and serve on crackers, or add to a baked potato. **Makes 1 cup.**

Fiesta Dip

8 ounces cream cheese, softened

16 ounces sour cream

1½ cups salsa

2 cups shredded lettuce

2 medium tomatoes, diced

2 cups shredded cheddar cheese

tortilla chips for dipping

Combine the cream cheese and sour cream in a medium bowl and blend until smooth using an electric mixer. Spread the mixture over the bottom of a pie plate or other shallow dish. Refrigerate for 30 minutes. Remove from the refrigerator and layer (in this order) the salsa, lettuce, tomatoes, and cheddar cheese over the cream cheese mixture. Keep refrigerated until ready to serve. Provide tortilla chips for dipping. **Makes about 10½ cups.**

This is one of the most popular recipes at Almanac.com/food. Reviewer comments at the site include: "Made this for a potluck buffet, and it VANISHED!"; "Easy to make, always gets rave reviews"; "Everyone loved it!"

APPETIZERS AND SNACKS

Crab Dip

This is easy to prepare and can be made ahead and frozen until needed. Serve with crackers.

½ cup (1 stick) butter, softened
8 ounces cream cheese, softened
2 cups shredded mild cheddar cheese
1 pint (2 cups) sour cream
1 heaping tablespoon minced dried onion
14 to 16 ounces frozen crabmeat or imitation
    crabmeat

Preheat the oven to 350°F. Mix all of the ingredients in a large casserole. Bake, uncovered, for 45 to 60 minutes, or until the mixture is bubbling and the top is browned. Stir before serving hot, with crackers. **Makes about 7½ cups.**

Baked Pepper Cheese Dip

1 cup mayonnaise
1 cup shredded sharp cheddar cheese
1 large onion, grated
1 tablespoon minced fresh parsley
1 clove garlic, minced
¼ teaspoon freshly ground black pepper

Preheat the oven to 400°F. Blend all of the ingredients in a bowl. Put in a greased baking dish and bake for 15 minutes, or until puffy and golden brown. Serve with toasted pita bread triangles or with raw vegetables. **Makes 2 cups.**

QUICK FIX

When cheese dehydrates in the refrigerator, grate it to use in cooking or as a topping.

Deviled Egg Spread

5 large, hard-boiled eggs, peeled and finely chopped
¼ cup mayonnaise
2 teaspoons lemon juice
1 teaspoon Dijon-style mustard
½ teaspoon Worcestershire sauce
2 tablespoons minced chutney
1 tablespoon minced fresh chives
¼ teaspoon salt
⅛ teaspoon freshly ground black pepper

Mix all of the ingredients together. Spread on crackers or small squares of pumpernickel bread. **Makes 2 cups.**

Tuna Tapenade

Tapenade is a Provençal hors d'oeuvre of olives, mashed to a paste with olive oil and spices. This variation uses tuna.

1 can (approximately 6 ounces) tuna packed in oil, drained
1 clove garlic, minced
1 tablespoon lemon juice
2 tablespoons chopped fresh parsley
½ cup pitted black olives
3 tablespoons olive oil
2 tablespoons capers, drained and rinsed
salt and pepper, to taste

Combine the first five ingredients in a food processor and pulse until roughly chopped. Slowly add the oil through the feed tube, stopping when the mixture is still slightly chunky. Add the capers and blend them into the mixture. Season to taste. Serve with crackers, crusty bread, or slices of fennel. **Makes 2 cups.**

Cheese Sticks

1 cup shredded cheddar cheese
1 cup all-purpose flour
1 teaspoon baking powder
1 teaspoon salt
1 large egg, beaten
3 tablespoons milk, or more

Preheat the oven to 450°F. Combine the cheese, flour, baking powder, and salt in a bowl. Add the egg and enough milk to make a stiff dough. Roll the dough on a floured surface into ¼- to ½-inch-thick logs. Cut into 4-inch-long segments. Place the logs on a greased baking sheet and bake for 10 minutes, or until golden brown. **Makes 2 dozen.**

Dilly Cheese Puffs

Serve these quick and tasty snacks hot from the oven or cooled to room temperature. Store leftovers in the refrigerator.

5 tablespoons butter

½ teaspoon salt

¼ teaspoon freshly ground black pepper

1 teaspoon dried dill

1 cup all-purpose flour

1 cup shredded Swiss or cheddar cheese

5 large eggs, at room temperature

Preheat the oven to 425°F. In a medium saucepan, combine the butter, salt, pepper, dill, and 1 cup of water. Bring to a boil and stir until the butter melts. Reduce the heat to low, and add the flour all at once. Cook over low heat, beating constantly with a wooden spoon for about 1 minute, until the mixture pulls away from the sides of the pan.

Remove from the heat, add the cheese, and beat with a wooden spoon until well blended. Add four eggs, one at a time, beating until well blended after each is added. Continue beating until the mixture is shiny and smooth.

Drop the batter by half teaspoons (for bite-size puffs) or heaping teaspoons (for larger puffs) onto a lightly greased baking sheet. Beat the remaining egg with 1 teaspoon of water and brush the egg wash over the tops of the puffs. Bake in the upper third of the oven for 15 minutes, or until puffs double in size and are golden. **Makes 3 to 5 dozen, depending on size.**

Sesame Chicken Wings

36 chicken drumettes (bottom part of chicken wing)

2 cloves garlic, crushed

1 piece (1 inch) fresh ginger, peeled and chopped

1 onion, coarsely chopped

1 teaspoon red pepper flakes

2 teaspoons ground coriander

3 tablespoons reduced-sodium soy sauce

3 tablespoons fresh lemon juice

2 tablespoons sesame oil

2 tablespoons sugar

½ cup sesame seeds, divided

Rinse the chicken drumettes and pat them dry with paper towels. Combine the rest of the ingredients, except the sesame seeds, in a blender and purée. Put the drumettes in a gallon-size zipper-seal plastic bag and add the purée, coating them well. Seal the bag. Marinate the drumettes in the refrigerator for at least 2 hours, turning the bag over periodically.

Preset the oven to broil. Arrange the drumettes on a broiler pan with a rack and sprinkle with half of the sesame seeds. Discard the marinade. Place the pan under the broiler for 5 to 6 minutes. Remove and turn over the drumettes. Sprinkle them with the remaining sesame seeds and broil for 5 to 6 minutes more. **Makes 36 pieces.**

Spicy Beef Turnovers

FILLING:

1 tablespoon vegetable oil

1 pound lean ground beef

½ cup finely chopped onion

¼ cup finely chopped green bell pepper

2 cloves garlic, minced

½ teaspoon salt

1 teaspoon chili powder

¼ teaspoon ground cumin

½ teaspoon ground coriander

½ teaspoon dried oregano

PASTRY:

2 cups all-purpose flour

½ teaspoon salt

2 tablespoons butter

1 tablespoon shortening

1 large egg yolk

½ cup cold water (approximately)

1 large egg yolk, for egg wash

1 tablespoon milk, for egg wash

For filling: Heat the oil in a large skillet on medium-high heat. Add the ground beef, stirring and cooking until browned. Drain the fat. Stir in the onion, pepper, garlic, salt, and spices, and continue cooking until the vegetables are soft and begin to brown. Set aside to cool.

For pastry: Preheat the oven to 400°F. Combine the flour and salt in a large bowl. Cut the butter and shortening into the flour mix. Add one egg yolk and stir to blend. Using a fork or your hands, work the dough until it is smooth and fairly stiff, sprinkling it with water (1 tablespoon at a time), if necessary. Knead the dough on a lightly floured surface for 1 minute, or until it is no longer sticky.

Divide the pastry into four equal portions and wrap three in plastic or waxed paper to keep them from drying. Roll the remaining portion into a square roughly 12 inches on a side and ⅛-inch thick. Cut the rolled dough into quarters, then cut each quarter diagonally to make eighths. Moisten the edges with water. Place 2 teaspoons of filling on each wedge and fold pastry over to form a triangle. Press around the filling to seal the edges. Repeat with the remaining dough and filling. Prick the top of each turnover once with a fork. In a small bowl, whisk the remaining egg yolk in the milk. Brush the pastries with the egg wash. Place the turnovers on an ungreased baking sheet and bake for 15 minutes, or until light brown. Serve hot. **Makes 32 turnovers.**

Oven-Baked Barbecued Spareribs

5 pounds country-cut spareribs

¼ teaspoon pepper

½ cup firmly packed brown sugar

⅓ cup soy sauce

⅓ cup orange juice

¼ cup cider vinegar

¼ cup Worcestershire sauce

½ cup ketchup

1 teaspoon ground mustard

2 cloves garlic, crushed

Preheat the oven to 350°F. Season the ribs with the pepper and place them in a roasting pan. Bake, uncovered, for 40 minutes. Drain the fat drippings. Whisk the remaining ingredients in a bowl and pour the mixture over the ribs. Cover with foil and let the ribs marinate for 3 hours in the refrigerator, periodically turning them so that they are well soaked on all sides. Reheat the oven to 350°F and roast the ribs, uncovered, for 1 hour or more, basting frequently with sauce. Serve when ribs are nicely glazed, browned, and a little crisp. **Makes 6 servings.**

TOO GOOD TO LEAVE OUT

Popcorn Granola Munch

8 cups popped corn

1 cup wheat germ

½ cup shredded coconut

1 cup quick-cooking rolled oats

½ cup sesame seeds

½ cup creamy peanut butter

1 tablespoon vegetable oil

½ cup molasses

2 tablespoons honey

Preheat the oven to 300°F. Grease a 15x10-inch jelly-roll pan or 13x9-inch pan. In a large mixing bowl, combine the popped corn, wheat germ, coconut, oats, and sesame seeds. Put the peanut butter, 1 tablespoon of water, oil, molasses, and honey in a saucepan on medium heat, stirring to combine. Drizzle the peanut butter mixture over the popcorn, stirring to coat well. Spread the munch on the prepared pan and bake for 30 minutes, stirring often. **Makes 10 cups.**

CHAPTER

Soups, Chowders, and Stews

SECRETS OF GOOD SOUP

■ The basis of good soup is good stock, preferably homemade (make a large batch and freeze in pint or quart containers); store-bought may not be as flavorful, but it has saved many a meal.

■ Otherwise "useless" inhabitants of the refrigerator such as tired parsley, wilted carrots, and limp celery or the (clean) base of a bunch of it, add flavor to a stock and may be strained out at the end. Even clean vegetable parings will enrich your homemade stock.

■ Homemade stock needs to simmer for at least an hour, but cooking for too long can bring out unwanted bitterness.

FIRST PRIZE

The 1992 Old Farmer's Almanac *Recipe Contest: "Best Homemade Soups"*

Hungarian Garden Vegetable Chicken Soup

1 whole chicken (3½ to 4½ pounds)
10½ cups chicken broth
1 large onion, chopped
1 bunch scallions, sliced (white and light
  green parts only)
2 large carrots, peeled and thinly sliced
2 stalks celery, thinly sliced
4 or 5 parsnips, peeled and thinly sliced
1 medium zucchini, thinly sliced
1½ cups chopped cabbage
2 medium tomatoes, skinned, seeded,
  and finely diced
¼ cup minced fresh parsley, or
  2 tablespoons dried
1 tablespoon minced fresh dill, or
  1 teaspoon dried
1 teaspoon freshly ground black pepper
1 tablespoon Hungarian paprika
1 cup fine, dry egg noodles

Rinse the chicken thoroughly and place it in a stockpot. Pour the broth over the chicken and completely submerge it, adding water if necessary. Cover the stockpot and bring the broth to a boil, then reduce the heat and simmer until the chicken is tender, 45 to 60 minutes. Remove the chicken from the broth and store the broth (in its pot, if you wish) in the refrigerator, preferably overnight. Separate the chicken skin and bones from the meat and discard or use to make a lighter stock for other uses (if not doing right away, be sure to freeze or refrigerate skin and bones properly). Shred or dice the chicken meat. Remove the broth from the refrigerator and skim off the top layer of fat. Return the broth to the stockpot and add the chicken meat and all remaining ingredients, except the egg noodles. Stir, and bring to a boil. Reduce the heat and partially cover the stockpot with the lid. Simmer for 30 minutes, or until the vegetables are barely tender. Add the noodles and simmer for 5 minutes, or until tender. (Note: This soup freezes well.) **Makes 15 to 20 servings.**

–Julie DeMatteo, Clementon, New Jersey

The 2001 Old Farmer's Almanac *Recipe Contest: "Best Soups and Chowders"*

Sweet Potato Chowder

4 slices bacon, chopped

½ cup chopped onion

¼ cup chopped green bell pepper

¼ cup chopped red bell pepper

2 cloves garlic, minced

3 cups chicken broth

1 can (15 ounces) diced sweet potatoes,
   drained

1 large baking potato, peeled and diced

1 can (14.5 ounces) stewed tomatoes, undrained

2 cups milk

1 teaspoon curry powder

¼ teaspoon freshly ground black pepper

Sauté the bacon, onion, peppers, and garlic in a large Dutch oven. Add the broth. Purée the sweet potatoes in a food processor or blender, and whisk them into the broth mixture. Stir in the potato and tomatoes. Cover and simmer for 45 minutes, or until the potato pieces are tender. Whisk in the milk, curry powder, and pepper; heat, but do not boil. **Makes 6 servings.**

–Liz Barclay, Annapolis, Maryland

The 1992 Old Farmer's Almanac *Recipe Contest: "Best Homemade Soups"*

Spicy Veggie Nut Stew

1 to 2 tablespoons vegetable oil

1 medium yellow onion, chopped

4 to 6 cloves garlic, minced

1 teaspoon peeled and chopped fresh
    ginger, or ½ teaspoon ground ginger

1 to 2 dried red chiles, seeded and chopped,
    or 1 teaspoon crushed red pepper
    flakes, or to taste

1 tablespoon ground cumin

1½ teaspoons curry powder, or to taste

3½ cups chicken broth

1 can (6 ounces) tomato paste

1 package (16 ounces) frozen mixed vegetables

⅓ cup fresh cilantro leaves

¼ cup peanut butter, creamy or crunchy style

salt and pepper, to taste

chopped green onions, for garnish (optional)

chopped peanuts, for garnish (optional)

In a stockpot, heat the oil and sauté the onion, garlic, and ginger for 3 to 4 minutes. Add the chiles, cumin, and curry powder; stir and cook for another minute. Stir in the broth and tomato paste and bring to a boil. Add the frozen vegetables and bring to a boil again. Add the cilantro, reduce the heat, and simmer, uncovered, for 10 minutes. Add the peanut butter and stir to dissolve; simmer 4 to 5 minutes more. Season with salt and pepper, to taste. Garnish individual portions with green onions and peanuts, if desired. **Makes 4 to 6 servings.**

–Sara Perkins, Dallas, Texas

CHILI vs. CHILE

■ "Chili" is a prepared dish. A "chile" is a hot pepper, fresh or dried.

Jambalaya Bowl

4 slices bacon (for garnish) and drippings, divided

6 spicy sausage links, cut into 1-inch slices

2 chicken breast halves, boned, skinned, and cut into ½-inch pieces

3 teaspoons Cajun seasoning, divided

1 cup cubed, cooked ham (½-inch cubes)

1 medium onion, diced

1 large green bell pepper, seeded and diced

4 stalks celery, diced

½ cup long-grain rice

1 can (14.5 ounces) chicken broth

1 can (14.5 ounces) tomato sauce or seasoned diced tomatoes, undrained

3 to 4 cups tomato juice

6 to 8 drops hot sauce, to taste

½ pound small raw shrimp, shelled and deveined

salt and pepper, to taste

fresh basil sprigs, for garnish

Sauté the bacon in a large Dutch oven until crisp. Remove the bacon, drain it on paper towels, crumble, and reserve. Keep 2 tablespoons of the bacon drippings in the pan; pour off the remaining drippings and reserve. Add the sausage to the pan and sauté for 3 to 4 minutes, or until lightly browned. Remove the sausage and drain it on paper towels. In a bowl, toss the chicken with 1 teaspoon Cajun seasoning; add to the pan along with the ham; sauté for 3 to 4 minutes, or until golden. Transfer the chicken and ham to the plate with the sausage. Add the onion, peppers, celery, and 1 teaspoon Cajun seasoning to the pan, along with the reserved drippings as needed to sauté. Cook, stirring, for 3 to 4 minutes, or until the vegetables are soft. Add the rice and remaining teaspoon of Cajun seasoning, cooking and stirring for 3 to 4 minutes, or until the rice is translucent. Stir in the broth, cover the pan, and increase the heat to medium-high. Cook for 10 to 12 minutes, or until the rice is soft. Stir in the tomato sauce, 3 cups of tomato juice, and hot sauce to taste; reduce the heat and simmer, uncovered, for 5 minutes. Add more tomato juice, if necessary (the soup should be the consistency of heavy cream). Return the cooked meats to the pan and add the shrimp. Cook, uncovered, for 4 to 5 minutes, or just until meats are hot and the shrimp is pink. Taste and adjust the seasonings. Garnish individual portions with bacon and basil sprigs. **Makes 8 servings.**

–Marilou Robinson, Portland, Oregon

Russian Soup With Pickles

2 tablespoons medium barley

4 cups beef consommé

2 cups chicken broth

2 cups peeled and diced potatoes

3 tablespoons butter or margarine

1 large onion, minced

1 veal kidney (or 5 lamb kidneys),
   trimmed and sliced

1 tablespoon all-purpose flour

2 small dill pickles, thinly sliced

½ cup sour cream, at room temperature

2 tablespoons minced fresh parsley

freshly ground black pepper, to taste

In a saucepan, cook the barley in 3 cups of water for 1 hour or until all the water is absorbed; drain and reserve. In a stockpot, combine the consommé and broth, add the potatoes, and cook until half-tender. In a large skillet, heat the butter and cook the onion until soft but not browned. Add the kidneys to the skillet and cook, stirring constantly for 3 minutes. Stir in the flour and cook for 3 minutes more. Transfer the kidney mixture to the stockpot and add the pickles and barley to the soup. Bring to a boil, then reduce the heat and simmer, covered, for 15 minutes. (Skim fat, if needed.) Pour the sour cream into a large soup tureen or bowl. Temper, or gradually warm, the sour cream by adding a few teaspoons of hot soup to it and beating vigorously to prevent curdling. Pour the remaining soup into the tureen. Sprinkle with parsley and pepper. **Makes 6 to 8 servings.**

–Melanija Wozniak, Vernon, Connecticut

QUICK FIX

■ If you accidentally oversalt your pot of soup, add a peeled raw potato to the soup and boil for about 5 minutes. The potato will absorb some of the salt and can then be removed.

■ If your soup is too greasy, wrap several ice cubes in a plastic bag and drag it slowly through the surface of the warm soup. The fat will harden and cling to the bag. Wipe the bag and repeat as necessary.

SOUPS, CHOWDERS, AND STEWS

> ## STOCK ANSWERS
>
> ■ Stock is made by simmering bones (or shells) and vegetables in water.
>
> ■ Broth is made by simmering meat and vegetables in water.
>
> ■ Bouillon is similar to stock and broth but is reconstituted from a dehydrated form (usually a cube).
>
> ■ Consommé is a clear soup made from strained meat or vegetable stock and is served hot or cold (as a jelly).

THIRD PRIZE

The 2001 Old Farmer's Almanac *Recipe Contest: "Best Soups and Chowders"*

Spicy Pumpkin and Potato Soup

3 tablespoons olive oil, divided

1 medium onion, chopped

2 cloves garlic, minced

2 medium potatoes, peeled and diced

½ teaspoon chili powder

½ teaspoon ground cumin

6 cups chicken or vegetable broth

¼ cup chopped fresh cilantro

1 jalapeño, seeded and minced

1 cup solid-pack canned pumpkin

¼ cup half-and-half or light cream, heated

6 fresh cilantro sprigs, for garnish

Heat 2 tablespoons of oil in a Dutch oven over medium heat. Add the onion, garlic, potatoes, chili powder, and cumin and sauté for 5 minutes. Stir in the broth and cook for 15 minutes, or until the potatoes are tender. Process the soup in a blender, along with the chopped cilantro and jalapeño. In a separate bowl, whisk together the pumpkin, half-and-half, and remaining tablespoon of oil. Ladle the potato soup into six bowls. Swirl ⅙ of the pumpkin mixture into each bowl, creating a marbling effect, and garnish with a cilantro sprig. **Makes 6 servings.**

–Roxanne E. Chan, Albany, California

Indian Mulligatawny Soup

2 tablespoons butter

1 small onion, chopped

1 cup peeled, seeded, and diced butternut
squash

1 small red apple, unpeeled, cored, and
diced

2 teaspoons curry powder

5 cups chicken broth

1 pound boneless, skinless chicken thighs
or breasts, cut into 1-inch chunks

½ cup instant rice

salt and pepper, to taste

1 small red apple, unpeeled, sliced paper-thin, for garnish

In a Dutch oven, melt the butter over medium heat. Add the onion and cook for 3 to 4 minutes, or until golden. Add the squash, diced apple, and curry powder. Cook for 2 to 3 minutes, stirring occasionally. Add the broth, chicken, and rice. Bring to a boil, then reduce the heat to low. Cover and simmer for 5 minutes, or until the chicken is no longer pink inside and the rice is tender. Season with salt and pepper. Garnish individual portions with the apple slices. **Makes 4 servings.**

–Jean Roczniak, Rochester, Minnesota

KITCHEN TRICKS

■ Never put salt into soup until it has been cooked and skimmed; salt prevents the fat from rising.

■ Using fresh parsley in soups will lessen the need for salt.

■ For a more flavorful soup or stew, sauté onions in butter or oil before adding other ingredients.

■ To prevent formation of a "skin" when cooking milk or cream soups, cover the pan.

Mexican Chicken and Bean Soup

2 tablespoons vegetable oil

1 large onion, finely chopped

1 large clove garlic, minced

4 jalapeños, fresh or pickled, seeded and
    chopped

1½ teaspoons chili powder

1 can (14.5 ounces) diced tomatoes,
    undrained

2 cans (15 ounces each) pinto beans,
    drained and rinsed

6 cups chicken broth

4 cups chopped cooked chicken breast

2 tablespoons chopped fresh cilantro

6 corn tortillas, for topping

¼ cup vegetable oil, for frying

1 cup shredded cheddar cheese, divided

½ cup sour cream, for topping

In a stockpot over moderately low heat, combine 2 tablespoons of oil and the onion, garlic, and jalapeños. Cook, stirring occasionally, until the vegetables are soft. Add the chili powder, and cook and stir for 15 seconds. Add the tomatoes, beans, broth, chicken, and cilantro, and simmer for 10 minutes. While the soup simmers, cut the tortillas in half, stack them, and then cut them crosswise into ¼-inch-wide strips. In a skillet, heat the ¼ cup of oil over moderate heat; fry the tortilla strips in batches, stirring constantly, for 15 seconds, or until crisp and pale golden. Drain the strips on paper towels. Divide the cheese among 4 soup bowls and ladle the soup over the cheese. Top with tortilla strips and dollops of sour cream. **Makes 4 servings.**

–Michael and Tami Flannery, Keymar, Maryland

HONORABLE MENTION
The 2001 Old Farmer's Almanac *Recipe Contest: "Best Soups and Chowders"*

Alan's New England Clam Chowder

**3 slices bacon (for garnish) and drippings,
divided**

1 medium onion, finely chopped

1 celery stalk, finely chopped

6 tablespoons (¾ stick) butter

6 tablespoons all-purpose flour

salt and pepper, to taste

**3 cans (7 ounces each) minced clams,
drained, with juice reserved**

**1 can (5 ounces) whole baby clams,
drained, with juice reserved**

1 bottle (8 ounces) clam juice

**3 or 4 medium new potatoes, unpeeled,
cut into ½-inch cubes**

1 teaspoon hot sauce, or to taste (optional)

2 cups heavy cream or half-and-half

In a large Dutch oven over medium heat, fry the bacon until crisp. Remove the bacon, drain it on paper towels, crumble, and reserve. Sauté the onion and celery in the bacon drippings for 5 to 10 minutes, or until soft. Reduce the heat and add the butter, stirring until melted. Stir in the flour, salt, and pepper. Cook, stirring constantly, for 4 minutes to make a roux. Add the reserved and bottled clam juices, and cook and stir until thickened. Add the potatoes and simmer, uncovered, for 15 minutes, or until tender, stirring frequently. Add the hot sauce, if desired. Add the cream and simmer for 5 minutes. Add the clams and cook for 10 minutes, until very hot but not boiling. Garnish individual portions with crumbled bacon. **Makes 4 servings.**

–Alan Stewart, Wabash, Indiana

For more on how to make a roux, turn to page 128.

Cream of Broccoli Soup

For once, a vegetable soup that is not puréed! If you prefer stronger flavor, substitute a sharper variety for all or part of the cheese.

10 ounces chopped fresh or frozen broccoli

¾ cup finely chopped onion

2 cups shredded American cheese

2 teaspoons salt

2 teaspoons white pepper

1 teaspoon garlic powder

1 cup milk

1 cup light cream

¼ cup (½ stick) butter

⅓ cup all-purpose flour

½ cup cold water

In a stockpot, bring 6 cups of water to a boil. Add the broccoli and onion; boil for 10 to 12 minutes. Add the cheese, salt, pepper, and garlic powder. Cook over medium heat, stirring constantly, until the cheese melts. Add the milk, cream, and butter. Heat to boiling, stirring constantly. In a small bowl, whisk the flour and cold water together until smooth. Drizzle slowly into the hot soup, stirring rapidly. Continue to cook, stirring constantly, until the soup is the consistency of heavy cream. **Makes 8 to 10 servings.**

Spinach and Pasta Soup

1 pound bulk turkey sausage, or links with casings removed

1 medium onion, chopped

1 large clove garlic, minced

1 can (28 ounces) whole, peeled tomatoes, drained

4 cups chicken stock

1 pound uncooked farfalle (bow-tie pasta)

1 bag (10 ounces) fresh spinach, cleaned and finely chopped

1 can (15 ounces) cannellini beans, drained

salt, to taste

In a large stockpot over medium-high heat, brown the sausage, breaking it up with a spoon. Add the onion and garlic, and sauté for 3 minutes. Stir in the tomatoes, breaking them up with the spoon. Stir in the stock and 4 cups of water. Increase the heat to high and bring to a boil. Stir in the pasta and cook for 5 minutes. Add the spinach, beans, and 4 cups of water. Cover and simmer until the spinach is tender, stirring occasionally. Add salt to taste. **Makes 10 to 12 servings.**

SOUPS, CHOWDERS, AND STEWS

Red Bean and Rice Soup

2 cups dried kidney beans, picked over and
  rinsed

1 ham bone

2 medium onions, chopped

2 sticks celery, chopped

2 carrots, peeled and chopped

2 cloves garlic, minced

1 bay leaf

1 tablespoon brown sugar

½ teaspoon dried thyme

½ teaspoon ground cumin

1 can (14.5 ounces) diced tomatoes, undrained

1 cup cooked rice

½ teaspoon salt

¼ cup cooking sherry

2 hard-boiled eggs, finely chopped, for garnish

¼ cup minced fresh parsley, for garnish

Soak the beans to prepare for cooking. (See "When You Don't Know Beans About Beans," page 82, for advice.)

In a stockpot, combine the soaked beans with 8 cups of water, the ham bone, and the next eight ingredients, and bring to a boil. Reduce the heat and simmer, covered, for 3½ to 4 hours, or until the beans are tender. Stir occasionally. Add the tomatoes and juice, rice, and salt. (If the soup is too thick, add more water or broth of your choice.) Simmer for 5 minutes and remove from the heat. Just before serving, add the sherry. Garnish individual portions with chopped egg and parsley. **Makes 6 servings.**

Vegetable Barley Soup

8 cups vegetable stock

2 tablespoons chopped fresh parsley

2 stalks celery with leaves, chopped

1 cup barley

2 tablespoons butter

1 cup chopped leeks (white and tender green
  parts only)

6 cups (1 pound) sliced fresh mushrooms

4 to 6 carrots, peeled and sliced

freshly ground black pepper, to taste

In a stockpot, bring the stock to a boil. Add the parsley, celery, and barley, and return to a boil. Cover, reduce the heat, and simmer for 1½ hours, or until the barley is tender. Meanwhile, melt the butter in a frying pan. Add the leeks and mushrooms and sauté. When the barley is tender, add the leeks, mushrooms, and carrots to the soup. (Add 1 to 2 cups of water, if you prefer a lot of broth.) Cook for 20 to 30 minutes, or until the carrots are tender. Add pepper to taste. **Makes 8 to 10 servings.**

Traditional Dutch Split Pea Soup

1 pound dried split peas, picked over and
    rinsed

2 pounds smoked pork hocks

½ cup chopped leeks (white and tender
    green parts only)

½ cup chopped celery

¾ cup chopped onion

1 bay leaf

2 teaspoons dried savory leaves

2 cups peeled and diced potatoes

1 cup peeled and diced carrots

1 teaspoon salt

¼ teaspoon freshly ground black pepper

1 cup cooked, sliced, Dutch or Polish sausage

Soak the split peas overnight in a stockpot with 10 cups of water, or use the quick-soak method. (See "When You Don't Know Beans About Beans," page 82.) Add the pork hocks, leeks, celery, onion, bay leaf, and savory. Simmer for 1½ hours. Add the potatoes and carrots and continue cooking for 30 minutes. Strain the soup, discarding the pork hocks and bay leaf, and purée in small batches in a blender or food processor. Return the soup to the stockpot and season with salt and pepper. (If the soup is too thick, add water or broth to thin it.) Add the sausage and simmer for 10 minutes, or until the sausage is heated. **Makes 8 servings.**

Onion Soup

¼ cup (½ stick) butter

2 tablespoons vegetable oil

7 cups (about 2 pounds) yellow onions,
    sliced thin

1 teaspoon salt

3 tablespoons all-purpose flour

8 cups beef, chicken, or vegetable stock

freshly ground black pepper, to taste

French bread slices or cubes, for topping
    (optional)

grated Parmesan cheese, for topping
    (optional)

Melt the butter in a large, ovenproof soup pot or Dutch oven. Add the oil, onions, and salt. Sauté the onions over medium heat for 20 minutes, or until browned and tender. Sprinkle the flour over the onions and cook a few more minutes, stirring occasionally. Remove and reserve the onions. Deglaze the pan, by adding the stock and stirring to loosen any browned bits of onion stuck to the bottom and sides. Heat the stock to a simmer. Return the onions to the pot and simmer for 30 minutes. Add pepper to taste. Just before serving, toast the French bread and add it to the soup. Sprinkle grated cheese on the bread, or on the soup itself. Set the soup pot under the broiler to melt the cheese, if desired. (Watch it carefully; the cheese will brown quickly.) **Makes 6 to 8 servings.**

Granny's Best Chicken Soup

Any winter day is a great time to make this invigorating, traditional soup. You can use canned chicken stock—but it won't be quite the same.

16 cups (1 gallon) cold water

1 chicken (4 to 5 pounds), quartered

1 bay leaf

4 to 5 sprigs fresh parsley

2 medium carrots, peeled and chopped

2 stalks celery, chopped

2 cloves garlic, crushed

1 medium onion, peeled and quartered

2 teaspoons salt, or to taste

½ teaspoon freshly ground black pepper,
    or to taste

Pour the water into a large stockpot and add all of the ingredients. Slowly bring the soup to a boil over medium heat, then immediately reduce the heat and simmer for 3 hours. Skim the fat off the soup's surface, using a spoon. Remove the pot from the heat and cool. Skim the fat from the surface and strain the soup, reserving the stock, vegetables, and chicken separately. Wash the pot and return the strained stock to it. Remove and discard the bay leaf and parsley. Mash the carrots, celery, and garlic and stir them into the soup. Separate and discard the skin and bones from the chicken meat. Chop the meat and add it to the soup. Heat and season the soup with salt and pepper, to taste. **Makes 8 to 10 servings.**

SOUPS, CHOWDERS, AND STEWS

BROTH CAN-DO'S

No time to make a homemade stock or broth? Reach for a prepared variety in a can or carton. Consider these guidelines when measuring:

2 (scant) cups = 1 can (14 ounces) stock or broth

4 cups (1 quart) = 1 resealable carton (32 ounces) stock or broth

6 cups = 1 large can (48 ounces) stock or broth

Autumn Vegetable Bisque

2 pounds butternut squash, halved lengthwise

3 pounds acorn squash, halved lengthwise

7 tablespoons unsalted butter, divided

5 leeks, thinly sliced (white and tender green parts only)

6 sprigs fresh thyme, chopped

4½ cups chicken stock

4 tablespoons chopped fresh chives

2 carrots, peeled and finely diced

2 parsnips, peeled and finely diced

2 red bell peppers, seeded and finely diced

1 stalk lovage, finely diced

1 cup heavy cream

1 tablespoon sugar

1½ teaspoons salt

freshly ground black pepper, to taste

Preheat the oven to 350°F. Spread some butter or margarine on the cut surfaces of the squash halves, place them cut side down on baking sheets, and bake for 35 to 40 minutes, or until tender. When the squash is cooked, remove and discard the seeds. Scoop out the pulp and set aside. Discard the shells. In a stockpot, melt 5 tablespoons of the unsalted butter and add the leeks and thyme, cooking until translucent. Add the stock and the squash pulp and simmer for 15 minutes. In a skillet, melt the remaining 2 tablespoons of butter and sauté the chives, carrots, parsnips, peppers, and lovage for 5 minutes. Set aside for a garnish. In a food processor or blender, purée the squash mixture until smooth. Return the purée to the stockpot, reheat it, and whisk in the cream. Add the sugar, salt, and pepper to taste. Garnish individual portions with the diced cooked vegetables. **Makes 8 servings.**

Vegetable Chowder

1 cup carrots, peeled and sliced

½ cup green peas

⅓ cup chopped celery

½ cup chopped cabbage

1 medium onion, sliced

1 medium potato, peeled and diced

boiling water

1 chicken bouillon cube

¼ teaspoon freshly ground black pepper

2 tablespoons butter

2½ cups milk

1 cup heavy cream

Put the vegetables into a stockpot. Add barely enough boiling water to cover. Cook on medium heat for 15 minutes, or until tender. Add the bouillon cube and pepper. Stir to dissolve the cube and add the butter and milk, stirring to blend. Heat to near boiling. Stir in the cream and heat through, but do not boil. **Makes 6 servings.**

Corn Chowder

4 cups chicken stock

4 potatoes, peeled and cut into ½-inch cubes

1 sprig fresh thyme

1 teaspoon celery seed

2 tablespoons butter

1 medium onion, chopped

2 cups heavy cream

3 cups cooked sweet corn kernels, fresh or
    canned

salt and pepper, to taste

Combine the chicken stock and 4 cups of water in a stockpot. Add the potatoes, thyme, and celery seed and bring to a boil. Reduce the heat, cover, and cook for 15 minutes, or until the potatoes are tender. Melt the butter in a skillet. Add the onion and cook until transparent. When the potatoes are tender, add the onion, cream, and corn to the stock. Season with salt and pepper. Heat, but do not boil. **Makes 6 to 8 servings.**

Maine Potato Chowder

8 cups beef, chicken, or vegetable broth

1 pound Maine potatoes, peeled and cut
    into ½-inch cubes

2 carrots, peeled and diced

3 medium tomatoes, diced

3 leeks, thinly sliced (white and tender
    green parts only)

3 sprigs fresh parsley

1 small bay leaf

1 teaspoon dried thyme

½ teaspoon salt

freshly ground black pepper, to taste

4 slices bacon, for garnish

4 slices pumpernickel bread, cut into
    ½-inch cubes, for croutons

4 tablespoons sour cream

Bring the broth to a boil in a stockpot and add the potatoes, carrots, and next 7 ingredients. Reduce the heat and simmer, covered, for 30 to 40 minutes, or until the vegetables are tender. In a skillet, fry the bacon until it is partly cooked, then add the pumpernickel cubes and fry until the bacon is done and the bread is crisp. When the soup is ready, remove the parsley and the bay leaf and discard. Blend in the sour cream, starting with one tablespoon and stirring to combine, and simmer for another minute. Garnish individual portions with croutons and crumbled bacon. **Makes 6 servings.**

SALT PORK PRIMER

■ Many people confuse salt pork with bacon and fatback. Bacon is cut from the side of a pig. Fatback is cut from the pig's back and is not salted or smoked. Salt pork is cut from the pig's belly and sides (thus it is fattier than bacon), and is salt-cured but not smoked. Its saltiness varies; to reduce the saltiness, parboil the pork before using it. If tightly wrapped, salt pork will keep for up to a month in the refrigerator.

Seafood Chowder

Make lots. This is as good—and maybe better—the second day.

1 piece salt pork (2 inches), diced

2 medium onions, chopped

4 medium potatoes, peeled and diced

1 pound skinned fish fillets, cut into 1-inch cubes

½ pound sea scallops, cut into bite-size pieces, or bay scallops

¼ pound small cooked shrimp (not canned), peeled

1 cup heavy cream

4 cups milk, or to taste

freshly ground black pepper, to taste

Fry the salt pork over low heat in a stockpot until the fat is rendered and the salt pork is crispy. Remove it from pot, set it aside, and drain off and discard all but about 3 tablespoons of the fat. Sauté the onions in the fat until they are soft but not brown. Arrange the potatoes over the onions and add water to cover. Cover the pot and bring to a near boil. Simmer for about 10 to 15 minutes, or until the potatoes are tender. Place the fish and scallops on top of the potatoes, cover the pot, and steam until the fish is done (check after 5 minutes; do not overcook). Add the shrimp, then gently stir in the cream and milk (use enough milk to give desired consistency; add more if necessary). Heat through, but do not boil. Garnish individual portions with pepper and salt pork bits. **Makes 6 servings.**

Quick Fisherman's Stew

1 tablespoon vegetable oil

1 cup chopped onion

2 cloves garlic, minced

1 can (8 ounces) tomato sauce

1 can (28 ounces) tomatoes, undrained, mashed

1 bay leaf

1 teaspoon dried basil

1 teaspoon dried thyme

1 teaspoon dried marjoram

¼ teaspoon freshly ground black pepper

½ cup dry white wine

1 pound skinless cod, haddock, or other firm white fish fillets, cut into 1-inch cubes

½ pound sea scallops

3 tablespoons chopped fresh parsley

Heat the oil in a large Dutch oven and sauté the onion and garlic for 3 minutes. Add the tomato sauce, tomatoes, spices, and wine. Simmer uncovered for 25 minutes. Add the fish and scallops and continue cooking for 10 more minutes, or until the fish flakes easily with a fork and the scallops are opaque and tender. Remove the bay leaf and discard. Stir in the parsley. **Makes 4 servings.**

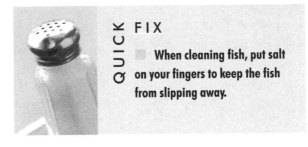

QUICK FIX

When cleaning fish, put salt on your fingers to keep the fish from slipping away.

Brunswick Stew

5 tablespoons butter, divided

3 medium onions, sliced

¼ cup all-purpose flour

2 teaspoons dried rosemary

1 teaspoon salt

1½ pounds chicken pieces (thighs, legs, wings)

2 cups chicken stock

2 tomatoes, peeled, seeded, and chopped

1 cup cooked, cut sweet corn, fresh, frozen, or canned

Heat 2 tablespoons of butter in a Dutch oven. Add the onions and sauté until tender. Using a slotted spoon, remove and reserve the onions. Combine the flour, rosemary, and salt in a bowl or plastic bag and dredge, or coat, the chicken in the mixture. Melt the remaining 3 tablespoons of butter in the Dutch oven and brown the chicken over moderate heat. Stir in the stock and bring to a boil. Reduce the heat, cover, and simmer for 30 minutes. Add the sautéed onions, tomatoes, and corn. Cover and simmer for 10 to 15 minutes. **Makes 4 servings.**

Roast Turkey Stew

3 pounds turkey thighs

salt and pepper

½ cup chopped onion

2 cloves garlic, chopped

½ teaspoon dried basil

¼ teaspoon dried thyme

1 can (14 ounces) turkey or chicken broth

3 potatoes, peeled and quartered

6 carrots, peeled and sliced into rounds

1 tablespoon cornstarch

Preheat the oven to 425°F. Rinse the turkey thighs and pat dry. Place the thighs skin side up in a Dutch oven and season with salt and pepper. Bake for 25 minutes, or until the skin is crisp. Drain and discard the skin and fat. Reduce the oven temperature to 375°F. Return the thighs to the Dutch oven and add the onion, garlic, basil, thyme, and broth. Cover the Dutch oven and bake for 1 hour. Add the potatoes and carrots and cover and cook for 20 to 25 minutes, or until the vegetables are tender. Transfer the turkey and vegetables to a large platter or serving bowl and keep warm. Skim the fat from the pan juices. Discard the fat. Over medium heat, simmer the pan juices in the Dutch oven. In a small bowl, whisk the cornstarch with ¼ cup of cold water and stir the mixture into the juices. Cook and stir constantly, until the juices have thickened. Return the turkey and vegetables to the pot. **Makes 6 servings.**

Caledonian Beef Stew

A classic beef stew thickened with oatmeal, not flour.

3 tablespoons butter, divided

1 pound chuck or stew beef, cut into 1-inch cubes

1 onion, finely chopped

2 carrots, peeled and diced

1 small turnip (optional), pared and sliced

4 tablespoons old-fashioned rolled oats

2 teaspoons, or 2 cubes, beef bouillon

⅛ teaspoon freshly ground black pepper

3 potatoes, peeled and diced

1½ cups frozen peas

½ teaspoon gravy browning and seasoning sauce (such as Kitchen Bouquet)

Preheat the oven to 350°F. In a Dutch oven, melt 2 tablespoons of butter and brown the meat on all sides. Using a slotted spoon, transfer the meat to a 2-quart casserole. Add the remaining butter to the Dutch oven and sauté the onion, carrots, and turnip, if desired, until the onion is golden; transfer all to the casserole. Add the oats, bouillon, 2½ cups of water, and pepper, and bake for 3 hours. Remove from the oven long enough to add the potatoes, peas, and browning sauce. Check the water level; add more to cover if necessary, and continue baking for 1 more hour. Refrigerate overnight. Reheat at 350°F for 20 to 25 minutes or until bubbling. **Makes 4 to 6 servings.**

Pioneer Beef Stew

Complete this meal with mashed potatoes and biscuits.

½ cup dried lima beans, picked over and
   rinsed

½ cup all-purpose flour

1 teaspoon salt

½ teaspoon freshly ground black pepper

1½ pounds stew beef, cut into 1-inch cubes

2 tablespoons vegetable oil

2 medium onions, chopped, divided

1 green bell pepper, seeded and chopped

½ cup beef stock

1 can (14.5 ounces) tomatoes, chopped and
   undrained

1 teaspoon salt

1 bay leaf

4 carrots, peeled and sliced

3 stalks celery, sliced

chopped fresh parsley, for garnish

Place the lima beans in a large pot. Add water to cover plus 2 inches and soak overnight. Drain and rinse. Combine the flour, salt, and pepper in a bowl or plastic bag and dredge, or coat, the beef in the mixture. Heat the oil in a Dutch oven and brown the beef over low heat on all sides. Stir in one onion and the green pepper, stock, tomatoes, salt, and bay leaf. Cover and simmer for 1 hour. Add the drained beans, carrots, celery, and remaining onion. Cover and simmer for 30 minutes. Remove the bay leaf and discard. Garnish individual portions with parsley. **Makes 4 servings.**

QUICK FIX

   To clean a pot with black lines or marks from cooking, fill it with water, add some cream of tartar, and bring to a boil.

Lobster Stew

As many New Englanders will tell you, the simpler a lobster stew is, the better it tastes.

3 tablespoons butter

1 medium onion, chopped

2 cups milk

2 cups heavy cream

1 cup cooked lobster meat chunks

2 tablespoons cooking sherry, or to taste

salt and pepper, to taste

paprika, for garnish

Melt the butter in a Dutch oven and sauté the onion until tender. Slowly add the milk, cream, and lobster meat. Heat but do not boil. Remove the stew from the heat and stir in the sherry. Season with salt and pepper. Garnish individual portions with paprika. **Makes 4 servings.**

To learn how to cook a lobster, see page 173.

Wild Mushroom Bisque

Dried, plain, white mushrooms can be substituted for any portion of the mushrooms in this wonderful cream-based soup.

1 tablespoon dried porcini mushrooms

1 tablespoon dried shiitake mushrooms

1 tablespoon dried morel mushrooms

1 tablespoon dried chanterelle mushrooms

3 cups chicken broth

¼ cup butter

¼ cup chopped shallots

½ teaspoon dried tarragon

4 tablespoons flour

3 cups half-and-half

¼ teaspoon cayenne pepper

Place dried mushrooms in a food processor or blender and chop until very fine. In a medium saucepan, bring the chicken broth to a boil. Add the mushrooms, remove from heat, and let stand, covered, for 10 minutes. Melt the butter in a soup pot or Dutch oven. Sauté the shallots and tarragon until the shallots are cooked, about 5 minutes. Stir in the flour until well combined. Slowly add the chicken broth–mushroom mixture. Continue heating and stirring until the soup is thick and smooth. Whisk in the half-and-half and cayenne pepper. Heat until the soup is warmed through. **Makes 6 servings.**

Salads and Dressings

Asian Wild Rice and Chicken Salad

DRESSING:

¼ cup olive oil

3 tablespoons roasted sesame oil

3 tablespoons lemon juice

3 tablespoons soy sauce

1 tablespoon sugar

1 teaspoon ginger juice or 1 teaspoon
    peeled and grated fresh ginger or
    ½ teaspoon ground ginger

SALAD:

1½ cups cooked wild rice, cooled to room
    temperature

1½ cups cooked, chopped chicken or turkey

1½ cups fresh snow pea pods, lightly steamed

1 can (5 ounces) sliced water chestnuts, drained

½ cup coarsely chopped onion

2 stalks celery with tops, chopped

1 cup crisp Chinese noodles, for topping

lemon slices, for garnish

For dressing: Whisk the dressing ingredients in a small bowl until the sugar is dissolved. Let stand at room temperature for 15 to 20 minutes to allow the flavors to blend.

For salad: Place the wild rice and the next five ingredients in a large salad bowl and toss gently. Pour the dressing over the salad and toss until well coated. Refrigerate for 1 to 2 hours. Just before serving, toss once more and top with Chinese noodles. Garnish with lemon slices. **Makes 4 to 6 servings.**

–Ron Glassburn, Tenino, Washington

SALADS AND DRESSINGS

Poppy Seed Potato Salad

DRESSING:

¼ cup olive oil

6 tablespoons frozen apple juice
　　concentrate, thawed

1 tablespoon cider vinegar

1 large clove garlic, pressed

1 tablespoon currants

1 tablespoon diced red onion

2 teaspoons poppy seeds

½ teaspoon grated lemon peel

½ teaspoon ground cinnamon

½ teaspoon coarsely ground black pepper

SALAD:

3 bunches watercress, coarse stems removed, torn into bite-size pieces

1 head radicchio, torn into bite-size pieces

⅓ cup chopped fresh parsley

6 medium red potatoes, cooked, each cut into 6 wedges

2 red apples, cored and sliced

3 slices bacon, cooked crisp and crumbled, for topping

¼ cup sliced almonds, for topping

lemon twists, for garnish (optional)

For dressing: Combine all of the dressing ingredients in a jar with a tight-fitting lid and shake well.

For salad: Combine the watercress, radicchio, and parsley with half of the dressing. Arrange the greens on six salad plates. In a large bowl, toss the potatoes and apples with the rest of the dressing. Mound a portion of the potato mixture on the greens, and top with the bacon and almonds. Garnish with lemon twists, if desired. **Makes 6 servings.**

–Roxanne E. Chan, Albany, California

THIRD PRIZE

1996 Old Farmer's Almanac *Recipe Contest: "Salads"*

Indonesian Red Lentil Salad

DRESSING:

¾ cup vegetable oil

½ cup red-wine vinegar

2 tablespoons sugar

2 teaspoons salt

2 teaspoons pepper

1 teaspoon ground cumin

1 teaspoon ground mustard

½ teaspoon turmeric

½ teaspoon ground mace

½ teaspoon ground coriander

½ teaspoon ground cardamom

¼ teaspoon ground cayenne pepper

¼ teaspoon ground cloves

¼ teaspoon ground nutmeg

¼ teaspoon ground cinnamon

SALAD:

1 pound dried red lentils, picked over and rinsed

1 cup currants

⅓ cup capers, drained

1½ cups finely chopped onion

For dressing: Combine all of the dressing ingredients in a jar with a tight-fitting lid and shake well.

For salad: In a saucepan, bring 3 cups of water to a boil. Add the lentils. Boil for 3 minutes, then reduce the heat to a simmer. Cook the lentils for 20 minutes. Rinse and drain. In a large bowl, combine the lentils with the dressing; cover and refrigerate overnight. Two hours before serving, add the currants, capers, and onion. This keeps in the refrigerator for 1 month. **Makes 6 to 8 servings.**

–Ginger Harrison, Idaho Falls, Idaho

Roasted Red Pepper and Spinach Salad

DRESSING:

¾ cup olive oil

¼ cup lemon juice

¼ cup red-wine vinegar

1 clove garlic, minced

1 teaspoon salt

1 teaspoon sugar

¼ teaspoon crushed red pepper flakes

SALAD:

3 red bell peppers, roasted
(see below)

1 pound fresh spinach, washed and
trimmed

1 medium zucchini, thinly sliced

½ cup sliced scallions (white part only)

For dressing: Combine all of the dressing ingredients in a jar with a tight-fitting lid and shake well.

For salad: Slice the roasted red bell peppers into thin strips. Dry the spinach thoroughly and tear into bite-size pieces. In a large salad bowl, combine the roasted red peppers, spinach, zucchini, and scallions. Before serving, toss with the dressing. **Makes 6 servings.**

HOW TO ROAST PEPPERS

■ Preheat the broiler. Cut the peppers in half and remove the core and seeds. Lay the peppers on a broiler rack or sheet pan, cut side down, and place under the heat until the skin is blackened. Transfer the peppers to a brown paper bag, close the top tightly, and let the peppers steam for 10 minutes. Remove and peel off the charred skin. Use the peppers according to the recipe directions. Store the leftovers in the refrigerator.

Spinach and Citrus Salad

Use baby spinach, if possible. Sliced avocado is a nice addition to this salad.

DRESSING:

½ cup sesame or olive oil

2 tablespoons rice or other vinegar

SALAD:

2 bunches, or packages, fresh spinach

1 large, sweet grapefruit, peeled and
    sectioned, with pith and membranes
    removed

1 large, sweet red onion, thinly sliced

For dressing: In a small bowl, whisk together the oil and vinegar.

For salad: Pick over the spinach, discard the stems, and rinse the leaves. Spin or towel dry. Stack the leaves and cut them into broad strips, and place them into a large salad bowl. Pour half of the dressing onto the spinach strips and toss to coat. Top with the grapefruit sections and thin-sliced onion. Drizzle with the rest of the dressing. **Makes 6 servings.**

A CITRUS SHORTCUT

■ If peeling a grapefruit seems a chore, try this: Slice the grapefruit in half across its equator. Using a paring knife, separate the fruit from the membrane between the sections. Then, draw the straight blade—or better, a curved one—around the pith. Spoon out the segments of each half (a grapefruit spoon with a partially serrated edge works best for this).

Three Bean Salad

Tasty and easy to make, this classic has a fresh crunch.

DRESSING:

¼ cup white vinegar

½ cup olive oil

¼ teaspoon ground mustard

salt and pepper, to taste

SALAD:

½ pound fresh green beans, cut into pieces

½ pound fresh wax beans, cut into pieces

1 can (15 ounces) red kidney beans,
    drained and rinsed

1 small red onion, diced

1 large red or green bell pepper, cored and diced

¼ cup chopped fresh parsley

For dressing: In a large mixing bowl, whisk together the vinegar, oil, mustard, salt, and pepper.

For salad: In a saucepan, cook the fresh beans in a small amount of salted water for 5 minutes, just until crisp-tender, and drain. Add the hot beans, kidney beans, onion, bell pepper, and parsley to the bowl and toss with the dressing to coat evenly. Taste and add salt, if necessary. Cover and chill in the refrigerator to let the flavors combine. **Makes 6 servings.**

Coleslaw

Coleslaw has many variations. To some of us, the addition of celery seed is essential for the taste of true coleslaw, but if you like pickles, peppers, or pineapple, go right ahead.

DRESSING:

½ cup mayonnaise

½ cup plain yogurt or sour cream

SLAW:

6 cups shredded cabbage (1 small to medium
    green cabbage or part red cabbage)

1 to 2 carrots, peeled and shredded

¼ cup sweet onion, minced or grated

½ teaspoon celery seed

salt and ground cayenne pepper, to taste

For dressing: In a small bowl, blend the mayonnaise and yogurt.

For slaw: In a large salad bowl, toss together the shredded cabbage, carrots, onion, celery seed, and seasonings. Stir in just enough dressing to moisten the salad. **Makes 6 to 8 servings.**

Golden Raisin and Carrot Salad With Peanuts

SALAD:

½ cup golden raisins

8 medium carrots, peeled and coarsely shredded

3 tablespoons finely chopped fresh parsley

¾ teaspoon salt

DRESSING:

3 tablespoons safflower oil

1 tablespoon whole yellow mustard seeds

3 tablespoons sesame seeds

2 tablespoons freshly squeezed lemon juice

2 teaspoons freshly grated lemon peel

⅛ teaspoon freshly ground black pepper

½ cup peanuts, coarsely chopped for topping

For salad: Place the raisins in a small bowl and cover with hot water. Let stand for 1 hour, then drain. In a large salad bowl, combine the raisins, carrots, parsley, and salt.

For dressing: Heat the oil in a skillet over medium heat, and add the mustard seeds. In a few seconds, they will begin to pop. As soon as popping starts, add the sesame seeds and cook until these start to pop or turn a golden brown. Pour the oil and toasted seeds over the carrot mixture. Add the lemon juice, lemon peel, and pepper. Toss gently until well blended. Sprinkle with the peanuts immediately before serving. **Makes 8 servings.**

American-Style Potato Salad

2 pounds potatoes, cooked

¼ cup cider vinegar, divided

½ cup olive or vegetable oil

¼ cup sweet pickles, chopped

½ cup mayonnaise

½ cup chopped fresh parsley

3 hard-boiled eggs, diced

½ cup chopped green onion

2 stalks celery, chopped

salt and pepper, to taste

Slice the potatoes while they're still warm, sprinkle with half of the vinegar, and set them aside. In a small bowl, start the dressing by whisking together the remaining vinegar with the oil, pickles, and mayonnaise. Mix the remaining ingredients and the dressing with the potatoes. Gently toss to coat evenly. Refrigerate until ready to serve. **Makes 4 to 6 servings.**

A TASTY SUBSTITUTE

■ Consider using leftover juice from your pickle jar in place of plain vinegar when making salad dressing. Not only is it economical, but it tastes better, too.

ONE POTATO, TWO POTATO . . .

■ The best potatoes to use in salads are new, red-skinned, white round, and purple.

■ Potatoes will retain more flavor and vitamins if boiled or baked with their skins on. Once they have cooled, peel or not, as desired, to use in your salad.

■ To enhance the flavor of potatoes, sprinkle them with half of the dressing's vinegar while they are still warm and before adding the other ingredients.

German-Style Potato Salad

2 pounds potatoes, cooked
½ cup cider vinegar
1 medium red onion, chopped
5 slices bacon, cooked crisp and crumbled, drippings reserved
½ cup chopped fresh parsley
salt and pepper, to taste

Slice the potatoes while they're still warm and place in a large bowl. Sprinkle the potatoes with the vinegar and set aside. Cook the onion in the skillet of bacon drippings (or oil) until soft. Toss the cooked onion with the potatoes. Add the bacon and parsley, and season with salt and pepper. Serve warm or at room temperature. **Makes 4 to 6 servings.**

Pesto Potato Salad

DRESSING:

1 cup mayonnaise

½ cup pesto (recipe below)

2 tablespoons prepared mustard

SALAD:

6 large potatoes, peeled, quartered, boiled,
    and drained

4 hard-boiled eggs, chopped

¾ cup chopped celery

⅓ cup black olives, pitted and chopped

salt and pepper, to taste

4 slices bacon, cooked crisp and crumbled, for topping

1 small red onion, thinly sliced into rings, for topping

For dressing: Mix together the mayonnaise, pesto, and mustard in a bowl.

For salad: Dice the potatoes and combine them with the eggs, celery, and olives in a large bowl. Pour the dressing over the mixture and toss gently until well blended. Season with salt and pepper. Arrange the bacon and onion rings on top. **Makes 6 to 8 servings.**

Pesto

There are lots of ways to enjoy pesto: Mix into a salad, toss with your favorite pasta, top a baked potato, spread on a sandwich or slice of toasted Italian bread, or enjoy as an accompaniment to grilled chicken or fish.

4 cloves garlic

2 cups fresh basil leaves

¼ cup pine nuts

½ teaspoon salt

¼ teaspoon pepper

3 ounces Parmesan cheese, freshly grated

¾ cup olive oil, divided

In a blender or food processor, combine the garlic, basil, nuts, salt, pepper, cheese, and half of the olive oil. Purée, slowly adding remaining oil. (Add more oil if necessary to make the desired consistency.) Pesto will keep in the refrigerator for one week. If not using within a week, freeze mixture in a zipper sealed bag, squeezing out any air. **Makes about 1½ cups.**

Macaroni Salad

Pasta salad lends itself to almost endless variation. Add cubed cold meats such as ham or roast beef, slices of salami, or tuna. Be sure to include peppers, some onion, and a green vegetable such as peas to make it colorful and tasty.

½ **pound macaroni or other pasta**

½ **cup olive oil**

1 **cup fresh peas, or sugar snap peas with pods**

2 **tablespoons red-wine vinegar (or a milder vinegar, such as rice)**

1 **cup chopped scallions**

1 **large red bell pepper, seeded and diced**

2 **cups ripe cherry tomatoes, cut in half**

½ **cup pitted black or green olives (optional)**

½ **cup chopped fresh herbs, such as parsley, basil, or cilantro**

½ **cup mayonnaise (optional)**

1 **cup cubed cheese, such as feta or sharp cheddar (optional)**

salt and cayenne pepper, to taste

Cook the macaroni according to the package directions. Drain, transfer to a large bowl, and then immediately add the oil to keep the macaroni from clumping. Blanch the peas (see "How to Blanch," below). Add the remaining ingredients, toss gently, and season to taste. Serve chilled. **Makes 4 to 6 servings.**

HOW TO BLANCH

■ **To blanch something, dip it in boiling water for 1 to 2 minutes, then plunge immediately into cold water and drain. This process sets the color and flavor, especially before freezing. It is also used to loosen the skin of fresh fruits and vegetables, such as peaches and tomatoes, before peeling.**

Black Beans and Rice Salad

DRESSING:

2 **teaspoons olive oil**

2 **tablespoons chicken stock**

1 **teaspoon prepared Dijon-style mustard**

1 **tablespoon lemon juice**

SALAD:

½ **cup long-grain white rice**

1 **can (15 ounces) black beans, drained**

¼ **cup chopped fresh parsley**

¼ **cup chopped red onion**

salt and pepper, to taste

For dressing: In a small bowl, whisk together the ingredients, or combine them in a jar with a tight-fitting lid and shake well.

For salad: Cook the rice in 1 cup of water, covered, for 20 minutes, or until tender but firm; rinse and drain. Into a large bowl, put the rice, beans, parsley, onion, salt, and pepper. Pour the dressing over salad. Toss well to coat. Serve cold (over greens, if desired). **Makes 4 servings.**

Italian-Style Pasta Salad

A variation on a theme, this pasta salad uses vermicelli instead of shells or twists.

DRESSING:

2 tablespoons vegetable oil

2 tablespoons white-wine vinegar

¾ teaspoon ground mustard

½ teaspoon dried oregano

½ teaspoon dried basil

1 clove garlic, minced

SALAD:

4 ounces vermicelli or spaghetti

1 jar (6 ounces) marinated artichoke hearts, drained, with marinade reserved

1 very small zucchini, halved and thinly sliced

1 carrot, peeled and shredded

¼ pound thinly sliced and chopped cooked ham

1 cup shredded mozzarella

2 tablespoons grated Parmesan cheese

For dressing: In a small bowl or jar, combine the oil, vinegar, mustard, herbs, and reserved artichoke marinade; mix well.

For salad: Cook the pasta according to the package directions and drain well. While the pasta cooks, coarsely chop the artichokes. In a large bowl, combine the pasta, vegetables, ham, and cheeses. Pour the dressing over the pasta and toss gently to coat evenly. Refrigerate for several hours before serving. **Makes 4 to 6 servings.**

Rice Salad With Salmon and Peas

Long-grain rice makes the best salad, as the grains stay separate after cooking.

1 to 1½ pounds salmon fillet with skin

olive oil

salt and pepper, to taste

1½ cups long-grain or basmati rice

2 cups fresh peas, or sugar snap peas with pods

⅓ cup olive oil

juice of 1 fresh lemon

¼ cup chives, or finely chopped scallions

¼ cup chopped fresh dill

salt and pepper, to taste

Preheat the broiler. Brush both sides of the salmon with a little olive oil, and season with salt and pepper. Broil for 5 minutes on each side, or until fish flakes easily with a fork. (Poach or bake the salmon, if you prefer.) Cool, remove the skin, and then carefully break the fish into bite-size pieces. Cook the rice in 3 cups of water, covered, for 20 minutes, or until tender but firm. Blanch the peas (see "How to Blanch," page 73). In a large salad bowl, whisk together the ⅓ cup of olive oil and lemon juice. Add the cooked rice, salmon, peas, chives, and dill and gently toss to coat evenly. Season with salt and pepper. Serve at room temperature for the best flavor. **Makes 4 to 6 servings.**

Curried Chicken Salad

A perfect summer lunch!

DRESSING:

½ cup mayonnaise

½ cup sour cream

½ cup plain yogurt

1 teaspoon curry powder

1 teaspoon lime juice

1 teaspoon sugar

2 tablespoons chutney

½ teaspoon salt

⅛ teaspoon freshly ground black pepper

SALAD:

2 cups diced cooked chicken

¾ cup diced celery

½ cup seedless grapes, cut in half

¼ cup chopped peanuts

¼ cup shredded coconut

red leaf lettuce

For dressing: Combine the ingredients in a bowl and whisk well.

For salad: In a medium bowl, mix the chicken with the celery, grapes, peanuts, and coconut. Pour the dressing over the chicken mixture and gently toss to coat evenly. Arrange a bed of lettuce on each of four plates. Mound a portion of the salad on top of each bed. **Makes 4 servings.**

Tangy Turkey Salad

Serve on a bed of lettuce leaves with cantaloupe slices or between two slices of whole-grain bread.

½ cup sweetened dried cranberries

2 cups chopped cooked turkey

1 cup chopped celery

1 large apple, cored and chopped

½ cup chopped walnuts or pecans

½ cup mayonnaise

1 tablespoon Dijon-style mustard

¼ cup chopped fresh parsley or cilantro

Combine the cranberries, turkey, celery, apple, and nuts in a medium bowl. Blend the mayonnaise and mustard, and gently stir into the salad. Add the parsley and stir to blend. **Makes 4 servings.**

Dilled Seafood Salad

Prepare and refrigerate this salad up to 24 hours ahead of time. Add the dressing just before serving.

DRESSING:

⅓ cup sour cream

3 tablespoons mayonnaise

2 tablespoons buttermilk

1 teaspoon finely minced fresh parsley

¼ teaspoon finely minced onion

1 small clove garlic, crushed and minced

salt and pepper, to taste

SALAD:

2 cups (8 ounces) sugar snap peas

12 ounces crabmeat or lobster meat,
    cut into bite-size pieces

½ medium cucumber, scrubbed, cut in half lengthwise, seeded, and thinly sliced

½ cup thinly sliced celery

½ medium red bell pepper, cored and sliced into short, thin strips

1 small red onion, thinly sliced

2 tablespoons finely snipped fresh dill

lettuce leaves

For dressing: Combine all of the dressing ingredients in a jar with a tight-fitting lid. Shake vigorously and chill for several hours.

For salad: Blanch the sugar snap peas (see "How to Blanch," page 73). Blot away the excess moisture from the snap peas, cut them in half crosswise, and place them in a large bowl. Add the crabmeat, cucumber, celery, pepper, onion, and dill. Toss gently, cover, and chill.

Just before serving, make a bed of lettuce leaves on a serving platter. Pour the dressing over the salad and gently toss to coat evenly. Mound the salad on the lettuce bed. **Makes 4 servings.**

Pecan and Pork Salad

1 head Boston or oakleaf lettuce

⅓ cup pecan halves

1 tablespoon butter

¼ teaspoon paprika

1 cup (4 ounces) grilled pork tenderloin
    (or cooked turkey, steak, or chicken),
    cut into strips

⅛ teaspoon dried oregano

salt and pepper, to taste

vinaigrette of your choice (see "Dressings" beginning on page 78)

Rinse, dry, and tear the lettuce leaves and place them into a salad bowl. In a skillet, sauté the pecan halves in the butter and paprika for 2 to 3 minutes. Transfer the pecans to a small bowl and set aside. Heat the pork strips in the same skillet. Add the oregano, salt, and pepper. When it is just warm, add the seasoned pork to the salad bowl, then toss with the pecans and vinaigrette. **Makes 4 servings.**

Summer Tuna Salad

3 oranges, peeled and seeded
¼ cup olive oil
¼ cup vinegar
2 cloves garlic, minced
1 small red onion, sliced
1 can (9 ounces) water-packed tuna, drained
¼ cup chopped black olives
¼ cup chopped fresh parsley
salt and pepper, to taste
salad greens
½ cup toasted pine nuts, for garnish

With a sharp paring knife, cut away the membranes and pith from the oranges, saving the juice and pulp. (Alternatively, cut and pare the oranges as you would a grapefruit. See "A Citrus Shortcut," page 68.) In a large salad bowl, whisk together the oil, vinegar, and garlic. Add the orange (including the juice and pulp), onion, tuna, olives, and parsley. Toss well and season to taste. Divide the greens among four plates and top with tuna salad. Garnish with toasted pine nuts. **Makes 4 servings.**

HOW TO **HANDLE GREENS**

Don't cut salad greens—tear them. Metal from knives may cause oxidation and browning. (Tearing saves time with cleanup, too.)

Cranberry Waldorf Salad

This colorful salad could become a new Thanksgiving tradition, but why wait? It's a great complement to roast pork, too. For a fruit salad, omit the mayonnaise.

3 cups (12 ounces) fresh cranberries
2 cups sugar
4 medium tart green apples
½ cup red seedless grapes
⅓ cup chopped celery
½ cup chopped walnut pieces
⅓ cup mayonnaise (optional)

Wash and pick over the cranberries. Drain well. Coarsely chop the cranberries in a food mill or processor. Stir the sugar into the berries, cover, and chill for 4 hours. Place the cranberries in a sieve and allow to drain well (this takes 1 to 2 hours). When the cranberries are drained, core and chop the apples, and cut the grapes in half. Combine the apples, celery, grapes, walnuts, and mayonnaise, if desired. Gently fold in the cranberries. **Makes 8 servings.**

Dressings

Basic Vinaigrette

This dressing works on just about any combination of vegetables. Experiment with herbs to find flavors you like. Or, modify the recipe by using half lemon juice and half orange juice, or half lemon juice and half balsamic or flavored vinegar.

¾ cup olive oil

¼ cup fresh lemon juice

1 teaspoon Dijon-style mustard

garlic clove(s), crushed or finely chopped, to taste

fresh or dried herbs (basil, dill, rosemary, and/or tarragon), to taste

salt and pepper, to taste

Combine the olive oil, lemon juice, and mustard in a jar with a tight-fitting lid. Add as much or as little crushed or chopped garlic as you like. Same with the herbs: Add as much or as little as you prefer. Season with salt and pepper. Shake well. **Makes 1 cup.**

Tomato Basil Vinaigrette

Drizzle this simple dressing over mixed salad greens, endive leaves, chopped romaine, or hearts of iceberg lettuce.

1 cup chopped ripe tomatoes

¼ cup chopped fresh basil leaves

1 small clove garlic, minced

½ teaspoon salt, or to taste

¼ cup olive oil

1 teaspoon red-wine vinegar

freshly ground black pepper, to taste

Combine the tomatoes, basil, garlic, and salt in a food processor. With the blade whirling slowly, add the oil until the mixture is blended. Add the vinegar and pepper and pulse-process to combine. **Makes 1¼ cups.**

Vinaigrette for Pasta Salad

Use this dressing with any combination of cooked or chilled pasta and chopped fresh vegetables (such as zucchini, broccoli, cauliflower, red and/or green bell peppers), and with pitted Kalamata or other black olives. Double or triple to suit your needs.

¼ cup olive oil

2 tablespoons lemon juice

2 tablespoons balsamic vinegar

1 tablespoon dried basil

1 teaspoon dried oregano

salt and pepper, to taste

Combine all of the ingredients in a jar with a tight-fitting lid and shake well. Shake again and toss with salad before serving. **Makes ½ cup.**

SALADS AND DRESSINGS

Garlicky Yogurt Dressing

Yogurt adapts to many different herbs and flavors. Add chopped fresh basil, chives, cilantro, dill, or tarragon, or fresh lemon juice.

2 cups plain yogurt

2 tablespoons minced garlic

1 tablespoon chopped fresh parsley

2 tablespoons Dijon-style mustard

¼ teaspoon freshly ground black pepper

2 tablespoons chopped fresh herbs (see above) or lemon juice

Combine all of the ingredients in a jar with a tight-fitting lid and shake well. **Makes 2 cups.**

Buttermilk Ranch Dressing

¾ cup mayonnaise

½ cup buttermilk

1 teaspoon dried parsley flakes

½ teaspoon dried minced onion

1 clove garlic, crushed

½ teaspoon salt

dash ground cayenne pepper, or to taste

Combine all of the ingredients in a jar with a tight-fitting lid. Shake well and chill for several hours. **Makes 1¼ cups.**

Horseradish Dressing

A hearty dressing for a cabbage salad, or as a sauce for hot or cold cooked vegetables.

2 cloves garlic, crushed

½ teaspoon celery seed

1 teaspoon prepared hot mustard or
     ground mustard

¼ cup prepared horseradish

½ cup olive oil

¼ cup wine vinegar

⅔ cup cottage cheese

salt, to taste

Put all of the ingredients into a blender and process until smooth. Thin to desired consistency with a little water. **Makes 1½ cups.**

TOO GOOD TO LEAVE OUT

Festive Cranberry and Mandarin Orange Salad

Busy holiday chefs will love the simplicity, color, and taste of this salad.

DRESSING:

2 tablespoons maple syrup

2 tablespoons cider vinegar

1 teaspoon Dijon-style mustard

⅛ teaspoon salt

1 teaspoon poppy seeds

¼ cup orange juice

½ cup canola oil

SALAD:

2 heads Boston or Bibb lettuce

2 cans (15 ounces each) mandarin orange segments, drained

freshly ground black pepper, to taste

1 package (6 ounces) sweetened dried cranberries

For dressing: Combine all of the dressing ingredients in a jar with a tight-fitting lid. Shake well and refrigerate until ready to serve.

For salad: Wash and dry the lettuce, then tear it into bite-size pieces. Add the orange sections and the dressing, and toss gently. Season with pepper. Sprinkle the cranberries on top. **Makes 8 servings.**

SALADS AND DRESSINGS

CHAPTER

Vegetables and Side Dishes

The 1990 Old Farmer's Almanac *Recipe Contest: "Best Dried Beans and Peas"*

Curried Cassoulet

**3 cups dried white beans, picked over
and rinsed**

½ pound ham, cubed

½ pound salt pork, scored to rind

2 pounds lean lamb, cubed

2 large onions, chopped

1 cup chopped celery

¼ cup olive oil

pinch of dried thyme

salt and pepper, to taste

2 tablespoons curry powder, or to taste

Soak the beans to prepare for cooking. (See "When You Don't Know Beans About Beans," below, for suggestions.) Place the soaked beans in a large Dutch oven and add enough water so that the level reaches 1 inch above them. Add the ham and salt pork, and bring to a boil. Simmer, with the lid on, for 1½ hours, or until the beans are almost tender. Continue to add water as it cooks down. In a large skillet, brown the lamb, onions, and celery in olive oil. Pour off the excess fat, and add 1 cup of the bean soup. Stir, and bring the mixture to a simmer. Add the seasonings and transfer the lamb mixture to the Dutch oven with the beans. Continue to simmer. When the beans are tender, remove the salt pork and season with curry powder to taste. Serve with rice. (This can be prepared in advance and reheated.) **Makes 8 to 10 servings.**

–*Helen M. Marty, Phoenix, Arizona*

To make your own curry powder, see the recipe on page 323.

WHEN YOU DON'T KNOW BEANS ABOUT BEANS

■ **There are two common ways to soak dried beans (or split peas) to prepare them for cooking:**

The TRADITIONAL METHOD is to soak dried beans overnight in cold water, allowing about 2½ to 3 cups of water for each cup of beans and making sure that the water completely covers them.

The QUICK-SOAK METHOD is to put the dried beans into a pot, cover them with 2 to 3 inches of water, and bring them to a boil. Cook them for 5 minutes, remove them from the heat, and let them soak for 1 to 2 hours. Drain and rinse. (To quick-soak split peas, boil them for 2 minutes and soak them for 1 hour. Drain and rinse.)

■ **Season the initial cooking water with onions or herbs, but parboil beans before adding salt, fat, or meat. They will become tender faster.**

VEGETABLES AND SIDE DISHES

Spinach Greens and Northern Beans

1 pound Great Northern beans, picked
    over and rinsed

2 cloves garlic, minced

2 scallions, chopped

1 teaspoon paprika

5 tablespoons olive oil

1 package (10 ounces) fresh spinach,
    washed and chopped

½ teaspoon hot sauce

¼ teaspoon ground cayenne pepper

salt, to taste

1 cup chopped smoked ham (optional)

½ cup chopped green olives (optional)

Soak the beans to prepare for cooking. (See "When You Don't Know Beans About Beans," below, for suggestions.) Place the soaked beans in a large Dutch oven and add enough water so that the level reaches 1 inch above them. Bring the contents to a boil; reduce the heat and simmer, covered, for 1 to 2 hours, or until the beans are tender. In a large skillet, sauté the garlic, scallions, and paprika in olive oil until the garlic is light brown. Reduce the heat and stir in the spinach. Add one-half of the liquid from the beans and stir until the spinach is cooked (about 5 minutes). Transfer the cooked spinach to the Dutch oven and stir in the hot sauce, cayenne, and salt. Add the optional ingredients, if desired. Serve with or over crusty Italian bread. **Makes 6 servings.**

–Andrea Moriniti, DeWitt, New York

■ When cooking beans during stovetop simmering or oven baking, make sure that they have at least 1 inch of water above them.

■ Dried beans swell up when soaked. Keep these equivalents in mind as you plan a meal:

    1 cup dried beans = 2 to 3 cups cooked beans

    1 cup dried beans = 4 servings

    2 cups dried beans = 1 pound

■ When using canned beans, be sure to rinse them thoroughly before adding them to the recipe.

VEGETABLES AND SIDE DISHES

Butter Bean Spread

½ cup dried lima or butter beans, picked over and rinsed

1 clove garlic, minced

4 ounces cream cheese

4 ounces smoked ham, finely chopped

3 to 4 drops hot sauce

salt and pepper, to taste

Place the beans in a saucepan with 2 cups of water and bring to a boil. Reduce the heat and simmer, covered, until the beans are very soft, adding water as necessary. Drain. Place the beans, garlic, and cream cheese in a food processor or blender and mix until smooth. Add the ham and hot sauce. Season to taste. Chill, and serve with crackers. **Makes 1½ to 2 cups.**

–Ann L. Combs, New Hampton, New Hampshire

Boston Baked Beans

2 pounds dried navy or pea beans, picked over and rinsed

¼ to ½ pound salt pork, scored to rind

½ to 1 cup maple syrup

1 teaspoon ground mustard

salt and pepper, to taste

Soak the beans to prepare for cooking. (See "When You Don't Know Beans About Beans," page 82, for suggestions.) Place the soaked beans in a large Dutch oven and add enough water so that the level reaches 1 inch above them. Bring to a boil, reduce the heat, and simmer, covered, for 1½ to 2 hours, or until the beans are tender. Preheat the oven to 250°F. Put the beans into a large, deep casserole or bean pot, place the salt pork in the center, and add the syrup, mustard, salt and pepper, and enough boiling water to cover, plus 1 inch over the contents. Bake for 8 hours. **Makes 12 to 14 servings.**

VEGETABLES AND SIDE DISHES

Southern Baked Beans

1 pound dried Great Northern or navy
    beans, picked over and rinsed

2 cloves garlic, minced

2 small onions, sliced

1 dried red chile

1 bay leaf

3 tablespoons molasses

¼ cup ketchup

1 teaspoon ground mustard

½ teaspoon ground ginger

½ teaspoon salt

8 ounces smoked bacon, diced

¼ cup brown sugar

Soak the beans to prepare for cooking. (See "When You Don't Know Beans About Beans," page 82, for suggestions.) Place the soaked beans in a large Dutch oven and add enough water so that the level reaches 1 inch above them. Stir in the garlic, onions, chile, and bay leaf. Bring to a boil; reduce the heat and simmer, covered, for 1 to 2 hours, or until the beans are tender. Drain, reserving 2½ cups of the liquid. Preheat the oven to 275°F. Stir the molasses, ketchup, mustard, ginger, and salt into the bean liquid. Place the beans in a large casserole or bean pot, stir in the bacon, add the liquid mixture, and sprinkle with brown sugar. Bake for 4 hours. **Makes 6 to 8 servings.**

Roman-Style Green Beans

1 pound fresh green beans

3 tablespoons olive oil

1 medium yellow onion, sliced into thin
    rounds

½ green bell pepper, cored and sliced into
    thin strips

1 clove garlic, minced

1 cup peeled, chopped Roma tomatoes,
    fresh or canned with juices

1 bay leaf

1 teaspoon salt

¼ teaspoon freshly ground black pepper

1 tablespoon chopped fresh chervil (or 1 teaspoon dried)

Wash the beans and snap off the ends; set them aside. In a large skillet or saucepan, heat the oil and sauté the onion until translucent. Add the green pepper, garlic, tomatoes, and bay leaf. Simmer, uncovered, for 20 minutes, or until the sauce thickens. Add the salt, pepper, chervil, ⅓ cup of water, and the green beans. Cover and cook for 20 minutes, or until the beans are tender. (Add more water if necessary.) **Makes 6 servings.**

ADVICE

    If a recipe calls for half an onion, use the top half. The root will help preserve the lower half for use later.

    To keep the remainder of a raw onion fresh when you've used only part of it, seal it in a glass jar in the refrigerator. (Use it within a day or two.) The glass will prevent the onion odor from permeating other foods.

    After peeling onions, rub salt on your wet hands to get rid of the onion smell.

Easy Corn Creole

2 slices bacon

2 tablespoons vegetable oil

½ cup chopped green bell pepper

1 large onion, chopped

2 cups canned tomatoes, drained

1 teaspoon sugar

½ teaspoon salt

⅛ teaspoon pepper

⅛ teaspoon cayenne pepper

2 cups corn kernels, fresh or frozen

1½ cups shredded cheddar cheese

Cook the bacon until it is crisp; drain on a paper towel and crumble; set aside. Discard the bacon drippings. In a large skillet, heat the vegetable oil and sauté the green pepper and onion for 5 minutes, or until soft. Add the tomatoes and sugar, and cook for 10 minutes, stirring occasionally. Add the salt, peppers, and corn. Cook for 5 minutes, or until tender. Turn off the heat, and sprinkle the cheese and bacon over the corn. Cover the dish only long enough to melt the cheese. **Makes 8 servings.**

IN SEARCH OF "UN-CANNY" TASTE (OR, HOW TO PEEL TOMATOES)

■ Instead of reaching for a can, use fresh, ripe tomatoes when time permits. They are unrivaled in flavor. Here's how to remove the skins.

Bring a large, nonreactive saucepan two-thirds full of water to a boil. Fill a large bowl halfway with cold water. (Add a few ice cubes to keep the water cold.) With a large slotted spoon, lower one or two whole tomatoes at a time into the boiling water for about 10 seconds. (Too long will cook the flesh, making it mushy.)

Remove the tomatoes and immediately plunge them into the cold water for about 10 seconds. Score the skin with a paring knife and peel off the skin. Core, if desired. To seed, cut crosswise and remove the seeds with the blunt end of a spoon.

Red Cabbage With Apples and Chestnuts

Serve hot with pork or game.

2 tablespoons butter

4 cups shredded red cabbage

⅓ cup lemon juice

¼ cup firmly packed light brown sugar

2 medium apples, cored and thinly sliced

1 tablespoon caraway seeds

½ teaspoon salt

½ cup coarsely chopped cooked chestnuts

Melt the butter in a large saucepan and add the cabbage, ¼ cup of water, lemon juice, and brown sugar. Cover the pan and simmer for 15 minutes. When the cabbage is soft, stir in the apples, caraway seeds, and salt. Cook another 5 minutes, or until the apples are tender. Stir in the chestnuts. **Makes 6 servings.**

Creamy Mushroom Bake

6 tablespoons (¾ stick) butter

1 pound small white mushrooms, cleaned
   and sliced

¼ teaspoon grated nutmeg

¼ teaspoon salt

⅛ teaspoon freshly ground black pepper

¼ cup heavy cream

8 slices (1-inch thick) French bread

½ cup shredded Gruyère or Swiss cheese

Preheat the oven to 400°F. In a large skillet, melt the butter and sauté the mushrooms for 5 minutes. Reduce the heat and add the nutmeg, salt, and pepper. Stir in the cream. Arrange the bread slices in a greased, shallow casserole or baking dish. Spoon the creamed mushrooms over the bread and sprinkle with cheese. Bake for 10 minutes, or until golden brown. **Makes 8 servings.**

HOW TO USE CARROTS

■ Grate peeled carrots and toss with lemon juice and black pepper, as is done in France. Serve alone or with diced, pickled beets as an appetizer.

■ Thinly slice garden carrots and steam for 4 to 5 minutes, or until cooked through. Serve plain or toss with herbs (such as sweet marjoram), with equal parts lime juice and honey, or with butter and sugar.

■ Cut carrots into thin matchsticks and use to garnish soups. Or peel paper-thin strips of carrots, roll them up, and let them sit in ice water to crisp for carrot curls.

■ Place finely grated carrots into commercial tomato sauce before heating to freshen its taste and reduce its acidity.

■ Grate carrots, blanch them in boiling water for 1 to 2 minutes, drain, and add to mashed potatoes.

■ Purée leftover cooked carrots and use to thicken soups.

■ Chop leftover cooked carrots and add to hamburger meat or use to extend meat loaves or meatballs.

Eggplant Tomato Casserole

This dish goes well with chicken or lamb.

1 medium eggplant, sliced

salt

8 tablespoons olive oil, divided

2 cloves garlic, minced

4 large ripe tomatoes, peeled and
    chopped

¼ teaspoon salt

⅛ teaspoon black pepper

1 teaspoon sugar

½ cup bread crumbs

½ cup shredded cheddar cheese

Sprinkle both sides of the eggplant slices generously with salt. Place the slices on paper towels and let stand 30 minutes. Heat 3 tablespoons of olive oil in a skillet and sauté the garlic for 1 to 2 minutes. Add the chopped tomatoes, ¼ teaspoon of salt, and pepper, and simmer for 20 minutes.

Preheat the oven to 350°F. Mix the sugar, bread crumbs, and cheese in a bowl. Rinse the eggplant slices in cold water and pat them dry. Dredge each slice in the crumb mixture. In a large skillet, heat the remaining olive oil and sauté the eggplant slices until tender; drain on paper towels. Place a layer of eggplant in a greased 2-quart casserole. Cover the eggplant with a layer of tomatoes, then the remaining crumb mixture. Repeat the layers until the vegetables are gone, finishing with a topping of crumb-cheese mixture. Bake for 30 minutes, or until the top is browned. **Makes 6 servings.**

Baked Fresh Spinach and Cheddar

1 package (10 ounces) fresh spinach,
    washed and trimmed

1 cup fresh bread crumbs

2 tablespoons minced onion

1 cup milk

1 large egg, beaten

1 tablespoon minced fresh parsley

¼ teaspoon ground nutmeg

½ teaspoon salt

⅛ teaspoon pepper

½ cup shredded cheddar cheese

⅛ teaspoon paprika

Preheat the oven to 350°F. Grease a 2-quart casserole. Chop the spinach into 2-inch pieces and place them in a medium bowl with the bread crumbs and onion. In another bowl, whisk together the milk and egg. Add the parsley, nutmeg, salt, and pepper; stir, then pour the liquid over the spinach mixture. Toss until evenly coated. Spoon the spinach into the casserole and sprinkle with the cheese and paprika. Place the casserole in an ovenproof pan and add enough hot water to reach halfway up the side of the casserole. Bake for 35 minutes, or until set. **Makes 6 servings.**

Stuffed Red Peppers

4 red bell peppers

2 tablespoons olive oil

1 medium onion, chopped

2 cloves garlic, minced

½ cup chopped fresh mushrooms

2 sprigs fresh parsley, chopped

2 fresh basil leaves, chopped

2 sprigs fresh oregano, chopped

2 sprigs fresh thyme, chopped

1 tablespoon peeled and grated fresh
    ginger

2 cups peeled, chopped tomatoes

1½ cups cooked brown rice

½ teaspoon ground cumin

1 teaspoon red-wine vinegar

1 tablespoon tamari

½ cup golden raisins

¾ cup shredded cheddar cheese, divided

salt and pepper, to taste

water or broth

Cut the stem end from the peppers and scoop out the seeds and membranes. Steam the peppers over boiling water for 2 minutes, or until just soft.

Preheat the oven to 375°F. Heat the oil in a large skillet over medium-high heat. Add the onion, garlic, mushrooms, herbs, and ginger, and sauté for 5 minutes, or until the onion is soft and the herbs are wilted. Reduce the heat to medium-low, add the tomatoes, and cook for 5 minutes. Stir in the rice, cumin, vinegar, tamari, raisins, and ¼ cup of the cheese. Season with salt and pepper. Stuff the mixture into the peppers. Place the peppers in an 8-inch square baking dish and sprinkle the tops of the peppers with the remaining ½ cup of cheese. Pour ¼ inch of water or broth into the bottom of the baking dish and cover the dish with foil. Bake for 30 minutes, or until the rice is heated through. **Makes 4 servings.**

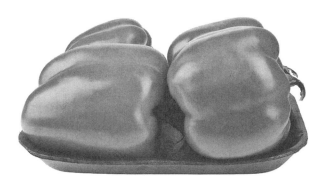

Stuffed Acorn Squash

3 acorn squashes, halved, seeded, and
    stemmed
8 tablespoons (1 stick) butter, divided
1 medium onion, chopped
1 cup minced celery
½ teaspoon dried sage
½ teaspoon dried thyme
½ teaspoon dried oregano
3 tablespoons chopped fresh parsley
salt and pepper, to taste
5 cups dry bread cubes or packaged
    stuffing

Preheat the oven to 350°F. Place the six squash halves in shallow baking pan(s), with the cut sides up. Pierce the halves with a fork and use 2 tablespoons of the butter, melted, to brush the insides. Add ½ inch of water to the pan(s) and cover tightly with foil. Bake for 30 minutes. In a skillet, sauté the onion and celery in the remaining 6 tablespoons of butter until tender; stir in the seasonings. In a large bowl, pour the sautéed onion mix over the bread cubes, mixing well to coat evenly. Remove the squash pan(s) from the oven and carefully lift off the foil. Fill each partially cooked squash half with the stuffing and return them to the oven, uncovered. Bake for another 15 minutes, or until the squashes are tender. **Makes 6 servings.**

Fried Green Tomatoes

3 medium green tomatoes
½ cup cornmeal
salt and pepper, to taste
⅓ cup vegetable oil, for frying
½ cup sour cream, for serving
2 scallions, chopped, for serving

Preheat the oven to 175°F. Wash, dry, and cut the tomatoes into ⅜-inch-thick slices. Place the cornmeal into a shallow bowl and season with salt and pepper. Dredge the tomato slices in the cornmeal mix. Heat the oil in a large, heavy skillet over medium heat. Add the tomato slices, without crowding. When the tomatoes start to sizzle, turn them over and brown the other side. They should be just tender—not mushy. As the slices become done, remove them to a baking sheet lined with paper towel. Keep the sheet in the oven with the door slightly open until all of the slices are cooked. Serve them warm, with a dollop of sour cream and sprinkling of scallions. **Makes 4 servings.**

TO ZUCCHINI

■ When zucchinis are plentiful, grate 1- or 2-cup portions and freeze to use in soups, stews, and nut breads throughout the winter.

Zucchini With Dill Sauce

2 pounds zucchini, peeled and cut into thin
   strips
½ teaspoon salt
2 tablespoons butter
2 tablespoons all-purpose flour
1 cup sour cream
1 teaspoon sugar
2 teaspoons white vinegar
1 tablespoon fresh dill, finely chopped,
   or 1½ teaspoons dried
freshly ground black pepper, to taste

Place the zucchini in a bowl, and sprinkle with salt. Transfer it to a colander and let stand for 30 minutes. Shake off the excess moisture and pat it dry with paper towels. In a large saucepan over medium-high heat, melt the butter and add the zucchini, stirring well to coat evenly. Cover and cook for 5 to 7 minutes, or until the zucchini is crisp-tender. Blend the flour into the sour cream, pour it over the zucchini, and stir gently. Reduce the heat and simmer gently for 2 to 3 minutes, or until the sauce is smooth and thick. Stir in the sugar, vinegar, dill, and pepper. **Makes 4 to 6 servings.**

Corn-Stuffed Zucchini

3 or 4 medium zucchinis
¼ cup chopped onion
1 tablespoon butter
2 large eggs, lightly beaten
1 can (12 ounces) whole-kernel corn,
    drained
½ cup coarsely crumbled saltines
¼ cup grated Parmesan cheese
½ teaspoon salt
dash of garlic powder
dash of dried thyme
salt and pepper, to taste
grated Parmesan cheese, for topping

Preheat the oven to 350°F. Trim the ends off the zucchinis. In a large pot of boiling water, cook the whole zucchinis for 5 to 8 minutes, and drain. Halve each zucchini lengthwise and carefully scoop out the squash pulp, leaving the shells intact. Set the shells aside. Chop the squash pulp and sauté it in a skillet with the onion and butter until tender. In a large bowl, combine the eggs, corn, saltines, and the ¼ cup of cheese. Stir in the chopped squash and add seasonings. Fill each squash shell with the corn stuffing. Place the squash in a lightly greased 13x9-inch baking dish. Bake for 30 minutes. Top with Parmesan cheese. **Makes 6 to 8 servings.**

Zucchini Pizza

3 to 4 cups coarsely grated zucchini
1 teaspoon salt
2 large eggs, beaten
⅓ cup all-purpose flour
½ cup shredded mozzarella or cheddar
    cheese
½ cup grated Parmesan or Romano
    cheese
2 tablespoons chopped fresh basil,
    or 1 teaspoon dried
salt and pepper, to taste
½ cup tomato sauce, for topping
½ to 1 cup shredded cheese, for topping

Preheat the oven to 350°F. Sprinkle the grated zucchini with salt, then toss and let stand in a colander for 30 minutes. Squeeze out the excess moisture with your hands or wring, wrapping with cheesecloth or a paper towel, until the zucchini is very dry. Combine the zucchini, eggs, flour, mozzarella, Parmesan, and basil; season with salt and pepper. Spread the mixture evenly into a lightly greased 10-inch round or 13x9-inch baking pan. Bake for 20 to 25 minutes, or until the surface is dry and begins to brown. Broil for 5 minutes, or until the top is firm and lightly browned. Remove from the oven and spread with tomato sauce. Sprinkle with shredded cheese. Bake another 10 to 15 minutes, until cheese is melted. **Makes 6 to 8 servings.**

Oven-Roasted Ratatouille

Double this recipe if you want leftovers; feel free to vary it with seasonal vegetables.

2 or 3 medium fresh tomatoes

1 eggplant

1 red bell pepper, cored and seeded

1 medium onion

2 summer squashes or zucchinis

1 seeded jalapeño or ½ teaspoon crushed
    red pepper flakes

8 whole cloves garlic, peeled

2 tablespoons olive oil

4 cloves garlic, chopped

1 tablespoon chopped fresh rosemary

1 tablespoon chopped fresh parsley

1 tablespoon chopped fresh basil, plus
    additional for garnish

salt, to taste

Preheat the oven to 400°F. Chop the tomatoes, eggplant, bell pepper, onion, squashes, and jalapeño. Place them and the eight whole garlic cloves in a large, flat, greased roasting pan. Toss the vegetables with the olive oil, chopped garlic, and herbs. Roast for 45 minutes to an hour, or until everything is tender, turning the vegetables occasionally so they don't stick. Season with salt, to taste, and garnish with additional fresh basil. **Makes 6 to 8 servings.**

SALT LAST

When roasting onions, turnips, or other root vegetables, don't add salt until after the vegetables have browned. Salt slows the browning process.

HANG ON TO THE HARVEST

■ To keep your leafy vegetables fresher longer, put a layer of newspaper and then a layer of paper toweling in refrigerator bins to soak up moisture that can rot the food prematurely.

Curried Cauliflower and Potatoes With Peas

If you prefer, add 2 cups of cooked chickpeas or a pound of fresh, chopped spinach in place of the peas.

¼ cup vegetable oil

2 medium onions, finely chopped

1 head cauliflower, cored and coarsely chopped

1 pound potatoes, peeled and diced

½ teaspoon ground turmeric

½ teaspoon chili powder, or to taste

1 teaspoon ground cumin

1 teaspoon salt

2 medium tomatoes, peeled and chopped

1 cup peas, fresh or frozen

½ teaspoon garam masala (recipe below; also available in health food and specialty stores)

Heat the oil in a large skillet over medium-high heat and sauté the onions until soft and golden. Stir in the cauliflower and potatoes. Add the turmeric, chili powder, cumin, salt, and tomatoes, stirring and cooking for 3 to 4 minutes. Reduce the heat to medium-low, and cover and simmer for 15 minutes, or until the potatoes and cauliflower are almost tender. Stir occasionally to keep the vegetables from sticking. Add the peas and cook, covered, 5 to 7 minutes. Sprinkle with garam masala just before serving and stir gently to mix. **Makes 4 to 6 servings.**

GARAM MASALA

A traditional spice blend used in northern Indian cooking, it also serves as a condiment that can be added to a dish just before serving. The mixture may also include fennel, coriander, saffron, pepper, chiles, and caraway.

2 tablespoons cumin seeds

2 tablespoons coriander seeds

2 tablespoons cardamom seeds

2 tablespoons black peppercorns

1 stick cinnamon (3 inches), broken up

1 teaspoon whole cloves

Preheat the oven to 350°F. Combine the spices in a baking pan. Roast for 10 to 15 minutes, or until the seeds become several shades darker and give off a sweet, smoky aroma, stirring often. Transfer the mixture to a spice mill or food processor, and grind to a fine powder. Allow to cool completely and store in an airtight container. **Makes ⅓ cup.**

VEGETABLES AND SIDE DISHES

Winter Vegetable Curry

3 tablespoons vegetable oil

3 cloves garlic, finely chopped

1 tablespoon peeled and grated fresh ginger

1 large onion, finely chopped

1 teaspoon ground cumin

1 teaspoon chili powder

1 teaspoon ground cayenne pepper, or
    to taste

½ teaspoon ground cardamom

1 green bell pepper, cored and finely chopped

2 large carrots, peeled and finely chopped

2 large parsnips, peeled and finely chopped

1 cup orange juice

1 large tart apple, peeled, cored, and chopped

2 tablespoons raisins

salt and pepper, to taste

Heat the oil in a large skillet, and add the garlic, ginger, onion, and spices. Cook over low heat, stirring, until the onion is soft. Add the remaining vegetables, orange juice, apple, and raisins. Stir and cook for 15 minutes over medium heat, or until the vegetables are tender. Season with salt and pepper. **Makes 6 servings.**

TOO GOOD TO LEAVE OUT

Corn Fritters

2 large eggs

2 cups cooked corn kernels

¼ teaspoon salt

3 to 4 tablespoons all-purpose flour

1 teaspoon sugar

1 tablespoon butter, melted

¼ cup vegetable oil, for frying (more, if
    needed)

maple syrup

Beat the eggs in a large bowl. Mix in the corn, salt, flour, sugar, and butter. Heat the oil in a large, heavy skillet over medium heat. Drop the batter (1 heaping tablespoon per fritter) into the hot oil, without crowding. Fry for 3 to 4 minutes on each side, or until golden brown. Serve warm with maple syrup. **Makes 18 small fritters.**

Strata

(see page 13)

Clam-Stuffed Mushrooms
(see page 32)

Mexican Chicken and Bean Soup
(see page 49)

Dilled Seafood Salad
(see page 76)

Stuffed Red Peppers
(see page 90)

Grilled Star-Spangled Chicken
With Fireworks Salsa
(see page 100)

French Farmer's Baked Beef and Barley

(see page 136)

Baked Stuffed Salmon With Garlic Dill Sauce

(see page 166)

CHAPTER

6

Poultry

TIMES AND TEMPERATURES

■ For a complete chart of cooking times based on internal temperatures for meat and poultry, turn to page 314.

FIRST PRIZE
The 1998 Old Farmer's Almanac *Recipe Contest: "Chicken"*

Mediterranean Chicken

6 boneless, skinless, chicken breast halves
¼ cup ranch dressing
3 ounces sun-dried tomatoes
8 ounces cream cheese, softened
⅓ cup grated fresh Parmesan cheese
¼ cup pitted, sliced ripe olives
1 clove garlic, minced
6 fresh basil leaves
1 cup ground pistachio nuts
½ cup Italian-style bread crumbs
lemon slices and additional fresh basil leaves, for garnish

Rinse the chicken and pat it dry. Arrange the chicken between two sheets of waxed paper and flatten to a ¼-inch thickness with a meat mallet. Place the chicken in a shallow dish and pour ranch dressing over the pieces, turning to coat. Marinate for 1 hour in the refrigerator. In a small bowl, rehydrate the dried tomatoes by pouring enough boiling water to cover. Let stand for 15 minutes until tomatoes are softened. Drain and squeeze out the excess water from the tomatoes, then coarsely chop. Place the cream cheese, tomatoes, Parmesan cheese, olives, garlic, and basil into a food processor and process until smooth. Chill the filling for 30 minutes.

Preheat the oven to 375°F. Remove the chicken from the marinade. Put 1½ tablespoons of cream cheese filling in the center of each breast. Roll up and secure with toothpicks or bind with cooking twine. In a shallow bowl, mix the pistachio nuts and breadcrumbs. Dredge each stuffed breast in the nut mixture. Place chicken, seam side down, in an ungreased 13x9-inch baking dish. Bake for 45 minutes. **Makes 6 servings.**

–Liz Barclay, Annapolis, Maryland

POULTRY

Cheesy Chicken Crunch Casserole

3 cups cubed cooked chicken (or turkey)

2 cups diced celery

½ cup shredded American cheese

¼ cup shredded Swiss cheese

⅓ cup slivered almonds

¾ cup mayonnaise

½ teaspoon salt

2 teaspoons finely minced onion

2 teaspoons lemon juice

2 cups crushed potato chips, for topping

Preheat the oven to 400°F. Grease a 13x9-inch baking dish or 2-quart casserole. In a large bowl, combine all of the ingredients except the potato chips. Spread the chicken mixture evenly in the baking dish and top with the potato chips. Bake for 15 to 20 minutes. **Makes 6 to 8 servings.**

–Marcia Puri, Rockford, Illinois

POULTRY

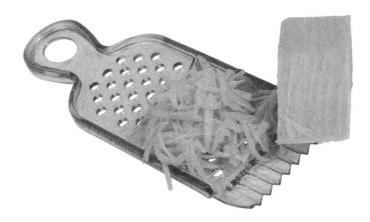

Grilled Star-Spangled Chicken With Fireworks Salsa

SALSA:

1 red bell pepper

1 yellow bell pepper

1 green bell pepper

1 can (20 ounces) pineapple tidbits, well
   drained

1½ teaspoons chipotle chile purée or
   powder, to taste

½ small red onion, diced

1 tablespoon fresh lime juice

1 tablespoon melted jalapeño jelly, or to
   taste

1 to 2 teaspoons finely minced fresh
   cilantro leaves

CHICKEN:

6 boneless, skinless, chicken breast halves

2 tablespoons apricot jam

2 tablespoons mango chutney

1 cup mayonnaise

2 teaspoons Worcestershire sauce

1 tablespoon stone-ground mustard

2 tablespoons fresh lime or lemon juice

For salsa: Halve the peppers and remove the stems, seeds, and large ribs. Set aside half of each color. Dice the remaining pepper halves and place them in a nonreactive bowl with the remaining salsa ingredients. Stir well. Allow the salsa to meld at room temperature for at least 1 hour before serving. Taste and adjust seasonings, as desired.

Cut the remaining pepper halves into julienne strips and small star shapes for garnish; dice the trimmings and add to the salsa.

For chicken: Rinse the chicken and pat it dry. Place the chicken breasts in a large resealable plastic bag. Whisk together the remaining ingredients in a small bowl to make a marinade and pour it over the chicken. Seal the bag and refrigerate it for several hours or overnight, turning occasionally.

Preheat the grill. Remove the chicken from the marinade and pour the marinade into a small bowl. Coat the grill rack with vegetable cooking spray and place it 4 to 6 inches from medium-hot coals or flame. Arrange the chicken on the grill and cook for 6 to 8 minutes per side, basting with the marinade and turning occasionally. The chicken is cooked through when the juices are no longer pink and the internal temperature reads 180°F on a meat thermometer.

Place a dollop of salsa on each serving plate and put a chicken breast half in the center. Garnish with the pepper stars and stripes. **Makes 6 servings.**

–Diane Halferty, Tucson, Arizona

Forgotten Chicken and Baby Limas

1 pound dried baby lima beans, picked
over and rinsed

4½ to 5 pounds chicken pieces

6 slices bacon, diced

1 cup all-purpose flour

2 teaspoons poultry seasoning

4 sweet onions, sliced

2 cloves garlic, minced

1½ teaspoons dried thyme

4 cups chicken broth, boiling hot

2 teaspoons salt

½ teaspoon freshly ground black pepper

Place the beans in a Dutch oven and add water to cover by several inches. Soak for at least 1 hour. Rinse the chicken and pat it dry. Drain the beans in a colander and set aside. Preheat the oven to 275°F. Cook the bacon in the dry Dutch oven until it curls (not crisp), remove, and set aside, leaving the bacon drippings. Combine the flour with the poultry seasoning in a large, resealable plastic bag. Shake to mix. Put the chicken into the bag and seal. Shake the bag until all of the pieces are lightly coated. Heat the bacon drippings to medium-hot and add the chicken pieces.

Cook the chicken until browned, remove, and set aside. In the remaining drippings, cook the onions and garlic until translucent (not brown). Transfer them to a large bowl. Pour off any excess bacon drippings, leaving just enough to grease the Dutch oven, and add the chicken. Combine the beans, bacon, and thyme in the large bowl with the onions and garlic and mix well. Spoon the mixture over the chicken. Add the hot broth and season with salt and pepper. Bake uncovered, for 5½ hours, or until the beans are tender and the liquid is absorbed. This should be moist but not soupy. **Makes 6 to 8 servings.**

–Jamie Parchman, Ogden, Utah

POULTRY

Moroccan-Style Chicken Breasts With Spiced Couscous

CHICKEN:

6 boneless, skinless, chicken breast halves

**2 cans (16 ounces each) Italian-style
stewed tomatoes with juice**

1 cup chopped onion

2 tablespoons chopped garlic

**1½ cups chopped, unpeeled, seeded
zucchini**

½ teaspoon salt

½ teaspoon coarsely ground black pepper

1 tablespoon ground cinnamon

1 teaspoon ground ginger

¼ cup honey

COUSCOUS:

2¼ cups chicken broth

1 teaspoon ground turmeric

½ cup chopped roasted red bell pepper

1 package (10 ounces) couscous

toasted sesame seeds, for garnish (optional)

For chicken: Rinse the chicken and pat it dry; set aside. In a large Dutch oven, mix all of the ingredients except the chicken; stir to blend, and add the chicken. Turn to coat. Cover and cook for 45 minutes over medium-low heat, until the chicken is tender.

For couscous: In a medium saucepan, about 15 minutes before serving, combine the broth, turmeric, and roasted red pepper. Cover and bring to a boil. Remove the pan from the heat, stir in the couscous, and let stand for 5 minutes.

To serve, spoon the couscous onto a serving platter, arrange the chicken on top, and pour the sauce from the Dutch oven over the chicken. Sprinkle with sesame seeds, if desired. **Makes 6 servings.**

–Marilou Robinson, Portland, Oregon

For tips on roasting your own peppers, turn to page 67.

POULTRY

Grilled Chicken in Chocolate Sauce Piquante

SAUCE:

½ teaspoon whole peppercorns

1 dried chile

3 whole cloves

1 tablespoon butter or margarine

1 clove garlic, finely chopped

1 1-inch piece fresh ginger, peeled and
    finely chopped

1 small onion, finely chopped

1 cup chicken stock

½ cup brewed coffee

1 tablespoon molasses

1 tablespoon tomato paste

1 tablespoon brown sugar

4 ounces semisweet baking chocolate

1 teaspoon cornstarch dissolved in
    4 teaspoons cold water

CHICKEN:

1 broiler-fryer chicken (3 pounds),
    quartered

1 tablespoon butter or margarine,
    softened

1 teaspoon all-purpose flour

½ teaspoon freshly ground black pepper

1 lemon wedge

For sauce: Grind the peppercorns, chile, and cloves together in a small mill or with a mortar and pestle. In a medium saucepan, heat the butter. Add the chopped garlic, ginger, and onion; stir, cover, and cook on low for 3 minutes. Mix in the ground spices, cover, and cook on low for 3 minutes. Add the chicken stock and coffee. Cover and simmer for 20 minutes. Strain the sauce, discarding solids and reserving the liquid. Bring the liquid to a simmer and add the molasses, tomato paste, and brown sugar. Add the chocolate, 1 ounce at a time, stirring constantly until dissolved. Add the dissolved cornstarch and continue stirring, letting the mixture simmer for 2 minutes or until it thickens.

For chicken: Rinse the chicken and pat it dry. Place the chicken in a stockpot, cover with water, and bring to a boil. Simmer with the lid on for 20 minutes. Remove the chicken, rinse with cold water, drain, cool, and pat dry. Rub the chicken with the butter, sprinkle with flour and pepper, and drizzle with juice from the lemon wedge. Preheat the grill.

Grill the chicken quarters for 10 to 15 minutes, turning frequently until browned and the internal temperature reads 180°F on a meat thermometer. Arrange the grilled chicken quarters on a plate. Spoon the sauce over the chicken and serve hot. **Makes 6 servings.**

–Alain Lefevre, Arundel, Quebec

POULTRY

Louisiana-Fried Chicken

This recipe, adapted from the National Broiler Council, uses a traditional buttermilk marinade.

2½ **pounds chicken pieces**

1 **cup buttermilk**

¾ **cup all-purpose flour**

¼ **cup cornmeal**

½ **teaspoon salt**

½ **teaspoon celery salt**

½ **teaspoon freshly ground black pepper**

½ **teaspoon ground cayenne pepper**

1½ **teaspoons paprika**

4 **cups vegetable oil, for frying**

Rinse the chicken and pat it dry. Place the chicken in a large glass bowl and pour the buttermilk over it. Cover and refrigerate for 30 minutes. In a medium bowl, mix the flour, cornmeal, salts, peppers, and paprika. Dredge the chicken pieces in the flour mixture, turning to coat all sides thoroughly. Rest the dredged chicken for 20 to 30 minutes, to allow the buttermilk to absorb the batter. In a large cast-iron skillet, add the oil to a depth of three-quarters of an inch. Over medium-high heat, warm the oil to 350°F, using a kitchen thermometer to test the temperature. Carefully put the chicken (a couple of pieces at a time), skin side down, into the oil. Reduce the heat to medium and cook for 15 minutes, or until nicely browned. Turn the chicken and cook for an additional 10 minutes, or until the internal temperature registers 180°F on a meat thermometer. Remove the chicken and drain it on paper towels. **Makes 4 to 6 servings.**

BOARDS OF SAFETY

To avoid cross-contamination, use separate cutting boards for fruits and vegetables and raw meats. Try color-coding them—for example: green for produce, red for meats.

Speedy Stir-Fried Chicken

4 boneless, skinless, chicken breast halves

¼ cup peanut oil

½ cup diced red bell pepper

½ cup sliced green onions, including some of the green tops

2 cloves garlic, crushed

1 cup sliced fresh mushrooms

½ cup maple syrup

¼ cup reduced-sodium soy sauce

¼ cup sherry

2 tablespoons cornstarch

½ teaspoon ground ginger

dash of ground cayenne pepper

½ cup cashew halves

Rinse the chicken and pat it dry. Cut the chicken into 2-inch pieces. Heat the oil in a large skillet and cook the chicken over medium heat for 8 minutes, or until it is opaque. Add the bell pepper, green onions, garlic, and mushrooms. Stir-fry for 3 to 4 minutes. In a small bowl, whisk together the maple syrup, soy sauce, sherry, cornstarch, ginger, and cayenne until the cornstarch dissolves. Pour over the chicken and vegetables and cook for 3 minutes, stirring until sauce thickens and develops a glaze. Stir in the cashews and heat for 1 minute more. Serve over rice. **Makes 4 servings.**

POULTRY

Chicken Fricassee

4 pounds chicken pieces

2 tablespoons butter

2 tablespoons vegetable oil

1 medium onion, chopped

2 cups chicken stock

½ pound fresh mushrooms, sliced

3 carrots, peeled and sliced

1 cup heavy cream

2 large egg yolks

Rinse the chicken and pat it dry. Heat the butter and oil in a Dutch oven and brown the chicken pieces over low heat. Add the onion and stock, cover, and simmer for 15 minutes. Add the mushrooms and carrots, cover, and simmer for 15 minutes more. Beat the cream and egg yolks together and temper by adding a bit of hot stock to the cream, stirring until smooth. Pour the cream sauce over the chicken. Heat slowly without boiling, about 5 minutes. **Makes 6 to 8 servings.**

Chicken Curry

Yogurt's natural acidity tenderizes meat and poultry when it's used as a marinade. Complement this dish by serving it with rice and chutney. (For a simple, homemade curry powder, see the recipe on page 323. For garam masala, see page 95.)

1 broiler-fryer chicken (3 pounds), cut up,
    or 4 chicken breast halves
1 teaspoon ground cayenne pepper
1 cup plain yogurt
2 onions, finely chopped
2 cloves garlic
1½-inch piece fresh ginger, peeled and
    grated (optional)
¼ cup vegetable oil
1 tablespoon curry powder or garam
    masala

Rinse the chicken and pat it dry. Season the chicken with cayenne, and rub with yogurt, using your hands. Place the chicken in a bowl and marinate for at least 1 hour in the refrigerator. In a cast-iron skillet with a lid, or a heavy casserole, sauté the onions, garlic, and ginger in oil until light brown. Add the curry powder, stir, and cook for 1 minute. Drain the chicken for a few minutes to allow any excess yogurt to drip off and add the chicken to the pot. Cook uncovered on medium heat for 5 minutes. Turn the chicken over, cover, and reduce heat to low. Cook for 25 minutes, or until the chicken is tender, stirring often. Add ¼ cup of water, if necessary to prevent sticking. **Makes 4 servings.**

Chicken Potpie With Vegetables

1 broiler-fryer chicken (3 pounds)

1 bay leaf

1 teaspoon salt

1½ cups peeled, chopped carrots

5 small onions, quartered

1 cup fresh or frozen peas

1 cup chopped fresh mushrooms

½ teaspoon poultry seasoning

salt and pepper, to taste

⅓ cup all-purpose flour

½ cup milk

pastry for a single-crust 9-inch pie

1 egg yolk, beaten with 1 tablespoon water, for egg wash

Rinse the chicken and pat it dry. Place the chicken, bay leaf, salt, and 2 cups of water in a 4-quart Dutch oven. Bring to a boil, then reduce the heat to low. Cover and simmer for 1 hour, or until the chicken is tender. Remove the chicken and set aside until it is cool to the touch. Strain the broth, discard the bay leaf, and return the liquid to the Dutch oven. Add the carrots and onions and cook, covered, for 15 minutes.

Meanwhile, remove the skin and debone the chicken. Discard the skin and bones. Cut the meat into large chunks and set aside. When the carrots and onions are tender, drain them, reserving the broth. Leave the vegetables in the Dutch oven and set aside. Add enough water to the broth to measure a total of 2½ cups of liquid and return it to the Dutch oven. Stir in the peas, mushrooms, seasonings, and chicken. Combine the flour and milk in a small bowl and mix until smooth. Stir the flour mixture into the broth and cook over medium heat, stirring constantly, until it boils and thickens. Pour the hot mixture into a 2-quart casserole.

Preheat the oven to 400°F. Roll out the pastry to fit the top of the casserole. Place the crust over the chicken mixture and trim the edge, leaving enough to form a ridge. Flute the edge and brush with egg wash. Make slits in the top to vent. Bake for 30 to 35 minutes, or until the crust is golden and the filling is bubbly. **Makes 6 servings.**

POULTRY

HOW TO MAKE A GOLDEN CRUST

To glaze the crust of a chicken potpie, combine 1 teaspoon molasses, one egg yolk, and 1 teaspoon water. Mix well and brush it over the crust before baking.

Sautéed Chicken Breasts With Lemon and Thyme

Simple and delicious, this dish makes a wonderful summer supper when accompanied by rice pilaf and asparagus.

4 boneless, skinless, chicken breast halves

3 tablespoons all-purpose flour

½ teaspoon salt

¼ teaspoon white pepper

2 tablespoons olive oil, divided

1 tablespoon butter

1 medium onion, chopped

1 cup chicken broth

3 tablespoons fresh lemon juice, divided

½ teaspoon dried thyme

lemon wedges and chopped parsley, for garnish

Rinse the chicken and pat it dry. Combine the flour, salt, and pepper in a large resealable plastic bag. Shake to mix. Add each chicken piece to the bag separately, seal, shake to coat, and then set aside. Save the excess seasoned flour. Heat 1 tablespoon of oil in a large skillet and add the chicken pieces. Brown on one side; add the remaining tablespoon of oil and brown the chicken on the other side. Transfer the chicken to a plate. Add the butter and onion to the skillet and sauté until soft. Sprinkle the reserved seasoned flour over the onion and cook over low heat, stirring constantly until the flour is completely incorporated. Stir in the broth, 2 tablespoons of lemon juice, and thyme. Bring the mixture to a boil, stirring constantly. Return the chicken to the skillet. Reduce the heat, cover, and cook for 5 minutes, or until the chicken is tender and opaque throughout. Before serving, stir the remaining tablespoon of lemon juice into the sauce in the skillet. Garnish with lemon wedges and parsley. **Makes 4 servings.**

Jamaican Pineapple Orange Chicken

1 broiler-fryer chicken (3 pounds), cut up
½ cup all-purpose flour
1 teaspoon salt
1 teaspoon chili powder
3 tablespoons vegetable oil
¾ cup orange juice
½ cup golden raisins
¼ cup rum, preferably dark
¼ teaspoon ground cinnamon
⅛ teaspoon ground cloves
1 can (8 ounces) crushed pineapple,
   undrained

Preheat the oven to 350°F. Rinse the chicken and pat it dry. Combine the flour, salt, and chili powder in a large, resealable plastic bag. Shake to mix. Add the chicken to the bag, seal, and shake until the chicken is thoroughly coated. Heat the oil in a large skillet and brown the chicken on all sides. Place the chicken in a lightly greased, shallow baking dish. In a bowl, mix together the orange juice, raisins, rum, cinnamon, cloves, and pineapple (with juice). Pour the mixture over the chicken. Bake uncovered for 50 minutes, or until the chicken is tender, occasionally basting with juices. **Makes 6 servings.**

Easy Cranberry Chicken

6 boneless, skinless, chicken breast halves
½ cup all-purpose flour
½ teaspoon salt
¼ teaspoon freshly ground black pepper
¼ cup (½ stick) butter
1 can (15 ounces) whole-berry cranberry
   sauce
dash ground nutmeg

Rinse the chicken and pat it dry. Combine the flour, salt, and pepper in a large, resealable plastic bag. Shake to mix. Place the chicken in the bag, seal, and shake until the chicken is evenly coated. Melt the butter in a large skillet over medium heat and brown the chicken. Remove the chicken and set aside. Add the cranberries, ½ cup of water, and nutmeg to the skillet, stir, and bring to boil. Reduce the heat, and return the chicken to the skillet. Cover and simmer for 20 minutes, or until the chicken is tender. Baste with the sauce and serve. **Makes 6 servings.**

This is one of the most popular recipes at Almanac.com/food. Reviewer comments at the site include: "I am constantly asked for the recipe . . . a good, old-fashioned dish."

Mother's Old-Fashioned Chicken and Dumplings

CHICKEN:

1 whole fryer chicken or hen

4 to 5 bay leaves

salt and pepper, to taste

4 to 6 tablespoons butter

DUMPLINGS:

1 teaspoon salt

½ cup vegetable oil

2 small eggs

3 cups all-purpose flour

For chicken: Rinse the chicken well and place it in a large Dutch oven. Add enough water to cover and add bay leaves. Season with salt and pepper and add the butter (the more butter, the richer the dish). Bring to a boil over medium-high heat, and cook uncovered for 1 hour, or until the chicken is well done. Remove the chicken and set aside until it is cool to the touch. Discard the bay leaves and skim off the fat. Separate the chicken and discard the skin and bones. Return the deboned chicken to the broth. About one-half to three-quarters of a pot of broth should remain; if necessary, add water to bring to that level.

For dumplings: In a large bowl, mix together the salt, oil, ¾ cup of water, and eggs. Slowly add the flour, blending it constantly with a fork. Stir only long enough to mix the dough. Divide the dough into two portions. Turn out half onto a floured surface and roll to a ¼-inch thickness using a rolling pin. Slice the dough into ½-inch-wide strips, then crosswise into pieces 4 to 8 inches long, for ease in handling. Repeat with the other half portion.

Bring the broth and chicken back to a boil, and season again with pepper, to taste. Drop the dumpling strips into the boiling stock. Boil uncovered for 20 minutes, or until the dumplings are done (they'll be puffy), stirring occasionally to prevent sticking. Most of the broth will be absorbed. **Makes 8 to 10 servings.**

Harvest Chicken Rolls

CHICKEN:

6 boneless, skinless, chicken breast
    halves

2 tablespoons butter

1 cup peeled, cored, chopped apple

⅓ cup chopped onion

½ teaspoon grated orange peel

¼ teaspoon ground cinnamon

6 slices bacon

SAUCE:

1½ cups apple juice

2 tablespoons apple brandy

1 tablespoon cornstarch

¼ teaspoon cinnamon

cored apple slices, for garnish (optional)

For chicken: Preheat the oven to 350°F. Rinse the chicken and pat it dry. Using a meat mallet, pound each breast to a ¼-inch thickness. In a medium skillet, melt the butter and add the apple and onion. Sauté until tender, then stir in the orange peel and cinnamon. Spoon 2 tablespoons of the apple mixture onto the center of each breast. Roll the chicken up around the stuffing. Wrap a slice of bacon around each chicken roll and secure with toothpicks or bind with cooking twine. Arrange the chicken rolls on a lightly greased broiler pan. Bake for 25 minutes, and then broil 3 inches from heat for 2 to 3 minutes, or until the bacon is browned on top.

For sauce: While the chicken is baking, whisk the sauce ingredients together in a saucepan until the cornstarch dissolves. Cook the sauce over medium heat until the mixture thickens and boils, stirring constantly. Transfer the cooked chicken rolls to a heated serving platter and cover with sauce. Garnish with apple slices, if desired. **Makes 6 servings.**

POULTRY

Stuffed Chicken Breasts

4 boneless, skinless, chicken breasts
4 tablespoons (½ stick) butter, divided
4 cups stuffing (see "Stuff It!," page 114)
2 tablespoons melted butter, for basting

Preheat the oven to 350°F. Rinse the chicken and pat it dry. Spread open 1 whole chicken breast to lie flat. In a large skillet, melt 1 tablespoon of butter. Sauté the chicken on both sides, until it is no longer pink, then set aside on a flat work surface. Repeat for each chicken breast. When the chicken has cooled enough to be handled, place 1 cup of stuffing in the center of each breast, and roll the chicken up around the stuffing. Secure with skewers or bind with cooking twine. Place on a rack in a roasting pan. Brush with one-third of the melted butter and bake for 15 minutes. Turn, brush with another third of the butter, and bake for 15 minutes more. Baste occasionally with the remaining butter. **Makes 4 generous servings.**

Stuffed Cornish Hens

Cornish hens, which are lower in fat than large roasting chickens, are an easy and elegant dish for company.

4 Cornish hens (1¼ pounds each)

salt and pepper

STUFFING:

½ cup golden raisins

¼ cup sherry, warmed

¼ cup (½ stick) butter

½ medium onion, finely chopped

½ cup finely chopped celery

½ teaspoon dried sage

⅛ teaspoon ground nutmeg

½ teaspoon salt

1½ cups cooked rice (white, brown, or wild)

¼ cup pine nuts

Preheat the oven to 450°F. Rinse the hens inside and out and pat them dry. Remove all visible fat from the cavity and season the inside with salt and pepper.

For stuffing: Soak the raisins in warm sherry for 10 minutes. In a large skillet, melt the butter and add the onion, celery, and sage. Sauté until tender, then add the nutmeg, salt, rice, and pine nuts. Toss lightly and add the raisins with the sherry. (The stuffing should hold together; if not, add a little water or wine.)

Loosely stuff each hen with the rice dressing, and secure the cavity with a skewer or tie the legs together with cooking twine. (Extra dressing may be warmed in a greased casserole for 20 to 25 minutes before serving.) Place the hens breast side up in a greased, shallow roasting pan and put it into the oven. Immediately reduce the heat to 350°F. Roast uncovered for 1 hour, or until the hens are well browned and the juices run clear when a thigh is pierced with a fork. To serve, cut the hens in half lengthwise and place each half stuffing side down. **Makes 4 generous servings.**

POULTRY

QUICK FIX

Always use soap and water to wash your hands, the utensils, the sink, and anything else that comes in contact with raw poultry and its juices.

Stuff It!

The following recipes will complement any poultry or game bird. Use them as shown or as a guide, and increase, decrease, add, or subtract ingredients to taste.

HOW MUCH IS ENOUGH?

APPROXIMATE STUFFING PER POUND OF POULTRY OR GAME BIRD

Capon	1 cup
Chicken	¾ cup
Cornish game hen	½ cup
Duck	⅔ cup
Game birds	½ cup
Goose	¾ cup
Turkey	1 cup

Old-Fashioned Bread Stuffing

2 loaves slightly stale white bread, crusts removed

2 teaspoons salt

1 teaspoon freshly ground black pepper

1 teaspoon dried sage

1 medium onion, chopped

⅔ cup milk or water

⅔ cup butter

2 large eggs

Break the bread into small bits and place into a large bowl. Season with salt, pepper, and sage. Add the onion, mix well, and set aside. In a saucepan, heat the milk and butter until the butter is melted. Let cool slightly, then beat in the eggs. Pour the liquid over the bread mixture and toss until well blended. **Makes 8 to 10 cups.**

POULTRY

Pecan and Corn Bread Stuffing

¼ cup (½ stick) butter

1 medium onion, diced

2 stalks celery, diced

3 cups crumbled corn bread

1 cup chopped pecans

½ teaspoon dried thyme

Melt the butter in a skillet, add the onion and celery, and sauté until soft. Combine the corn bread and pecans in a large bowl, and toss in the sautéed vegetables and butter. Sprinkle with thyme and toss again. **Makes 4½ cups.**

Chestnut Stuffing

3 cups shelled chestnuts

¼ cup (½ stick) butter, melted

½ teaspoon salt

¼ teaspoon freshly ground black pepper

¼ cup heavy cream

2 to 3 cups bread crumbs

½ cup chicken stock

Place the chestnuts in a saucepan of boiling, salted water and cook until tender. Drain and mash. Stir in the butter, salt, pepper, cream, bread crumbs, and chicken stock. Mix until well blended. **Makes 3 to 4 cups.**

Mushroom Stuffing

¼ cup (½ stick) butter

4 medium onions, chopped

4 stalks celery, diced

1 green or red bell pepper, cored and diced

2 cups diced fresh mushrooms

2 cups mashed potatoes

salt and pepper, to taste

Melt the butter in a large skillet. Add the onions, celery, bell pepper, and mushrooms, and sauté until soft. Stir in the mashed potatoes and season with salt and pepper. **Makes 6 cups.**

Apple and Sweet Potato Stuffing

2 tablespoons butter

4 tart apples, unpeeled, cored, and diced

2 medium onions, diced

2 cups mashed sweet potatoes

2 tablespoons sugar

¼ cup dry white wine

Melt the butter in a skillet, add the apples and onion, and sauté until soft. Mix in the sweet potatoes, sprinkle with sugar, and moisten with wine. Stir gently until blended. **Makes 4 cups.**

Cranberry Raisin Stuffing

½ cup (1 stick) butter

10 cups bread bits

1 cup chopped cranberries

1 cup raisins

2 tablespoons sugar

1 teaspoon salt

1 teaspoon ground cinnamon

Melt the butter in a large skillet, add the bread bits, and gently toss to coat. Stir in the cranberries and raisins. Sprinkle with sugar, salt, and cinnamon, and toss until well blended. **Makes 12 cups.**

Fruit Stuffing

2 tablespoons butter

2 onions, chopped

2 pears, peeled, cored, and chopped

1 apple, peeled, cored, and chopped

1 pound partially cooked ground sausage

1 cup prunes, cooked, pitted, and chopped

2 cups mashed potatoes

¼ cup white wine

Melt the butter in a skillet and sauté the onions until they are soft. In a large bowl, combine the onions, pears, apple, sausage, prunes, and mashed potatoes. Add the wine and stir until well blended. **Makes 6 cups.**

Rice and Apricot Stuffing

2 cups chicken stock

1 cup uncooked rice

1 cup diced dried apricots

¼ teaspoon ground cinnamon

Combine the chicken stock and rice in a saucepan. Cover and simmer for 20 minutes, over low heat. Stir in the apricots and cinnamon. **Makes 4 cups.**

Oyster Stuffing

¼ cup (½ stick) butter

3 medium onions, chopped

2 stalks celery, chopped

2 cups (1 pint) shucked oysters, whole
    or chopped, with liquid

5 cups stale bread crumbs

2 tablespoons lemon juice

¼ to ½ cup chicken stock

salt and pepper, to taste

Melt the butter in a skillet, add the onions and celery, and sauté until soft. Combine the oysters and bread crumbs in a large bowl. Add the sautéed vegetables, lemon juice, and enough chicken stock to achieve the desired consistency. Season with salt and pepper. **Makes 8 cups.**

POULTRY

Sausage Stuffing

1 pound pitted prunes

1 slice lemon

1 pound ground sausage

8 small onions, chopped

8 tart apples, peeled, cored, and
    chopped

½ cup chicken stock

1 teaspoon dried thyme

1 teaspoon dried sage

1 cup bread crumbs

salt and pepper, to taste

Place the prunes and lemon slice in a saucepan, cover with cold water, and bring to a boil. Reduce the heat, and simmer uncovered for 30 minutes. Drain, discard the lemon, and chop the prunes. Place the prunes in a large mixing bowl and set aside. In a heavy skillet, brown the sausage. Transfer the sausage to the large bowl, using a slotted spoon. In the remaining pan drippings, sauté the onions and apples for 5 minutes over medium heat. Stir in the stock and herbs, and simmer over low heat until the onions and apples are soft. Add the skillet mixture and bread crumbs to the prunes and sausage, and toss until well blended. Season with salt and pepper. **Makes 10 cups.**

TALKIN' TURKEY

■ Allow 1 pound of turkey per person.

■ Buy a fresh turkey only 1 to 2 days before you plan to cook it, and store it in the refrigerator. Place it on a tray or pan to catch any juices that may leak.

■ Avoid prestuffed fresh turkeys. Harmful bacteria may be in the stuffing.

■ There are three ways to safely defrost a frozen turkey: In the refrigerator, in cold water, and in a microwave oven.

IN THE REFRIGERATOR, allow approximately 24 hours for every 4 to 5 pounds. Keep the turkey in its original wrapper. A thawed turkey can remain in the refrigerator for 1 to 2 days.

IN COLD WATER, allow about 30 minutes per pound. Wrap the turkey securely, making sure that water will not leak through the wrapping. Submerge in cold water, and change the water every 30 minutes. Cook immediately after it is thawed. Do not refreeze.

IN A MICROWAVE, check your owner's manual for the size turkey that will fit, the minutes of defrosting per pound, and the proper level to use for thawing. Remove all outside wrapping, place the turkey on a microwave-safe dish to catch all of the juices, and cook the turkey immediately after thawing. Do not refrigerate or refreeze.

How to Roast a Perfect Turkey

Arrange the racks in the oven so that the turkey will sit in the lower third. Preheat the oven to 325°F (use an oven thermometer to make sure that the temperature is correct). This low roasting temperature leads to a juicy bird, and the drippings will be less likely to burn—which is important if you're making gravy.

Remove the neck and giblets from the body cavity and drain any juices. Rinse the bird under cold water, then blot dry. Let it reach room temperature.

After stuffing a turkey, truss it by taking a 4- to 6-foot piece of cooking twine and tying the legs together at the ankles. Run the twine around the thighs and under the wings. Pull tightly and make a knot around the excess flesh where the turkey's neck used to be. Cut off any excess twine. Trussing a whole turkey into a compact shape helps to ensure that it cooks evenly and makes it easier to carve as well.

Place the turkey on a rack in a pan deep enough to collect any juices that may run off during cooking. Lightly brush the bird with vegetable oil or butter, and lightly season with salt.

APPROXIMATE ROASTING TIMES

(with oven temperature of 325°F)

SIZE	ROASTING TIME

Unstuffed Turkey

8 to 12 pounds	2¾ to 3 hours
12 to 14 pounds	3 to 3¾ hours
14 to 18 pounds	3¾ to 4¼ hours
18 to 20 pounds	4¼ to 4½ hours
20 to 24 pounds	4½ to 5 hours

Stuffed Turkey

8 to 12 pounds	3 to 3½ hours
12 to 14 pounds	3½ to 4 hours
14 to 18 pounds	4 to 4¼ hours
18 to 20 pounds	4¼ to 4¾ hours
20 to 24 pounds	4¾ to 5¼ hours

HOW TO MAKE IT MOIST

If your roast turkey (or chicken) is very dry or to refresh leftovers, slice the meat and place on a platter. Pour equal portions of melted butter and chicken broth, combined, over the meat and let it stand for 10 minutes in a 250°F oven to soak up the juices.

Roast the turkey, basting every 40 to 60 minutes with the pan drippings. When the skin is golden brown (after approximately 1 to 2 hours), shield the breast with a tent of aluminum foil, shiny side out (the foil will reflect heat away from the breast, lowering temperatures).

One-half hour before the approximate roasting time is reached, begin taking the turkey's temperature with an instant-read meat thermometer in both the thigh and breast areas. (Do not leave the thermometer in the oven.) Continue doing this every 15 minutes. Make sure that the thermometer is in the thickest part of the meat and not in contact with any bone, fat, or gristle. (Take several readings in each area if you're not sure.) When the thermometer reads at least 180°F in both areas, remove the bird from the oven.

Cover the turkey with aluminum foil and let it sit for ½ hour. Resting the bird prior to carving allows the juices to retreat back into the meat, resulting in a more succulent turkey that's also easier to carve.

Turkey Potpie

½ **pound potatoes, peeled and cubed**

2 **teaspoons butter**

1 **small onion, chopped**

4 **stalks celery, chopped**

¼ **cup all-purpose flour**

4 **cups chopped cooked turkey**

2 **carrots, peeled and chopped**

1½ **cups chicken or turkey broth**

¼ **cup chopped fresh parsley**

1 **package (9 ounces) plain biscuit dough**

Preheat the oven to 400°F. Cook the potatoes in boiling, salted water until tender. Drain and set aside. In a skillet, melt the butter, add the onion and celery, and sauté until soft. Sprinkle with the flour and continue cooking and stirring for 1 minute. Add the turkey, carrots, and broth. Cook, stirring constantly, until thickened. Add the potatoes and parsley. Spoon into a deep-dish pie plate or casserole. Split the unbaked biscuits in half and arrange them on top in a single layer. Bake for 15 minutes. **Makes 6 servings.**

For a recipe for fluffy, homemade biscuits, turn to page 214.

POULTRY

Turkey Tetrazzini

This recipe can be prepared ahead and baked right before mealtime.

½ **pound vermicelli**

2 **tablespoons butter**

2½ **cups sliced fresh mushrooms**

2 **tablespoons all-purpose flour**

2 **cups milk, warmed**

2 **tablespoons sherry**

¼ **cup chopped fresh parsley**

½ **cup grated Parmesan cheese, divided**

¼ **teaspoon ground nutmeg**

⅛ **teaspoon freshly ground black pepper**

2 **cups cooked turkey, cut into chunks**

½ **cup blanched slivered almonds, for topping**

In a large pot of boiling water, cook the vermicelli (al dente) according to the package directions. Drain and set aside.

Preheat the oven to 350°F. Grease a 2-quart casserole. In a large saucepan, melt the butter, add the mushrooms, and sauté until just tender. Stir in the flour and cook for another 2 minutes, or until the flour is no longer visible. Gradually add the milk, stirring constantly, and simmer until the sauce thickens. Add the sherry, parsley, ¼ cup of the Parmesan cheese, nutmeg, and pepper. Combine the turkey and the vermicelli with the sauce. Spoon the mixture into the casserole and top with the remaining ¼ cup of cheese and almonds. Bake uncovered for 20 minutes, or until heated through. **Makes 6 servings.**

Turkey Cranberry Casserole

2 tablespoons butter

3 tablespoons flour

¾ cup chicken broth

½ cup milk

1½ cups cubed cooked turkey

2 cups sliced fresh mushrooms

1 cup chopped celery

½ cup fresh cranberries, chopped

3 tablespoons sherry

2 cups bread bits, for topping

Preheat the oven to 350°F. Grease a 2-quart casserole. In a medium saucepan, melt the butter and stir in the flour to make a paste. Gradually add the chicken broth and milk, and cook, stirring constantly until the sauce thickens. Combine the turkey, mushrooms, celery, cranberries, and sherry with the sauce. Spoon the mixture into the casserole and top with the bread bits. Bake uncovered for 30 minutes. **Makes 5 servings.**

Turkey Burritos

1 ripe avocado, peeled and pitted

juice of 1 lime

hot sauce, to taste

1½ cups peeled, seeded, diced tomatoes

½ cup chopped sweet onions

salt and pepper, to taste

4 to 6 flour tortillas

½ cup canned kidney beans, rinsed, or
 ½ cup canned refried beans

1 cup shredded cooked turkey

lettuce leaves

¼ cup shredded Monterey Jack or cheddar cheese

Mash the avocado, mix in the lime juice and a dash of hot sauce, and set aside. Combine the tomatoes and sweet onions, season with salt and pepper, and set aside. Make the burritos (one at a time): Place a tortilla on a plate, spread the avocado mixture over it, and top with beans, the tomato mixture, and the turkey. Cover with lettuce leaves and cheese. Roll the tortilla to enclose the filling. **Makes 4 to 6 servings.**

Turkey Noodle Casserole

1 tablespoon butter

1 medium onion, chopped

1 clove garlic, minced

1 tablespoon all-purpose flour

2 cups chicken or turkey stock

¼ cup dry white wine

1 pound noodles, cooked and drained

2 cups coarsely chopped, cooked turkey

2 carrots, peeled, chopped, and boiled
   until barely tender

¼ cup shredded cheese, for topping

Preheat the oven to 325°F. Grease a 2-quart casserole. In a skillet, melt the butter, add the onion and garlic, and sauté until tender. Sprinkle with flour and stir over low heat until the mixture is smooth. Add the stock and wine and bring to a boil, stirring constantly, until mixture begins to thicken. Simmer for 5 minutes. Place the noodles, turkey, and carrots in the casserole. Pour the sauce over the noodle mixture and sprinkle the top with cheese. Bake for 20 to 30 minutes, or until bubbly. **Makes 4 to 6 servings.**

Wild Rice and Turkey Casserole

1 cup wild rice

¼ cup (½ stick) butter

1 pound fresh mushrooms, sliced

½ cup chopped onion

1¼ cups heavy cream

3 cups diced cooked turkey

½ cup blanched sliced almonds

3 cups chicken broth

salt and pepper, to taste

Rinse the rice thoroughly. Place in a large saucepan and add enough water to cover by several inches. Bring to a boil, then remove from heat. Cover and set aside for 1 hour. Drain.

Preheat the oven to 350°F. Grease a 2-quart casserole. In a large skillet, melt the butter, add the mushrooms and onion, and sauté for 8 minutes, or until browned. Add the rice and remaining ingredients to the skillet and mix well. Spoon the mixture into the casserole and bake for 1 hour, or until the rice is tender. **Makes 6 to 8 servings.**

CHAPTER

7

Meats

Apple and Pork Burger Delights

BURGERS:

1 pound ground pork

1 Granny Smith apple, peeled, cored,
    and shredded

1 Golden Delicious apple, peeled, cored,
    and shredded

⅛ teaspoon ground cloves

⅛ teaspoon ground cinnamon

⅛ teaspoon ground cumin

3 cloves garlic, minced

½ tablespoon chopped fresh cilantro

½ bunch green onions, chopped

1 tablespoon balsamic vinegar

½ to 1 cup soft bread crumbs

½ cup olive oil

TOPPING:

1 Granny Smith apple, peeled, cored, and shredded

1 Golden Delicious apple, peeled, cored, and shredded

½ tablespoon chopped fresh cilantro

½ bunch green onions, chopped

1 tablespoon balsamic vinegar

drizzle of olive oil

salt and pepper, to taste

For burgers: In a medium bowl, mix the first ten ingredients and ½ cup of the bread crumbs. (Add more crumbs if too wet; slightly moist is better. Otherwise, the burgers will be tough and dry.) Using your hands, mix thoroughly and form into four to six patties. Refrigerate for 30 minutes.

For topping: In a small bowl, mix the apples, cilantro, onions, and vinegar. Drizzle with olive oil and season with salt and pepper. Set aside.

Place the ½ cup of olive oil, then the burgers, in a large skillet over medium heat. Cook for 20 to 25 minutes, turning once. When the burgers are done, serve them with the slaw topping. **Makes 4 to 6 servings.**

–*Ginger Moreno, Rancho Palos Verdes, California*

MEATS

Spicy Sausage and Red Cabbage

1 pound spicy ground pork sausage

1 large onion, chopped

5 cups shredded red cabbage

3 cups cored, unpeeled, cubed apple

⅓ cup brown sugar

⅓ cup vinegar

1 teaspoon caraway seed (optional)

Brown the sausage and onion in a large heavy skillet over medium heat, and drain the fat. Mix in the cabbage and apple. In a small bowl, combine the brown sugar, vinegar, and caraway seed; pour it over the cabbage mixture. Cover the skillet tightly and cook over low heat, stirring occasionally, for 15 to 20 minutes or until the cabbage and apples are tender. **Makes 8 servings.**

–Gloria Kirchman, Eden Prairie, Minnesota

Ham and Pineapple Casserole

¼ cup (½ stick) margarine, softened

½ cup sugar

5 large eggs

1½ cups cubed cooked ham

1 can (20 ounces) cubed pineapple, drained

2 tablespoons fresh lemon juice

8 to 10 slices slightly stale white bread, crust removed and cubed

Preheat the oven to 325°F. Coat a 13x9-inch casserole with vegetable cooking spray. In a large bowl, cream together the margarine and sugar. Beat in the eggs, one at a time, until well blended. Stir in the ham, pineapple, and lemon juice, and fold in the bread cubes. Pour the mixture into the prepared casserole and smooth the top. Bake, uncovered, for 30 to 35 minutes, or until the custard is set and the top is golden. **Makes 6 to 8 servings.**

–Marilou Robinson, Portland, Oregon

MEATS

ROASTING RULES

■ For success in making your roast as tender and juicy as possible, remember this:

1. Remove the meat from the refrigerator far enough ahead of roasting time that it will be able to warm to room temperature and cook evenly.

2. Preheat the oven.

3. Do not salt the exterior flesh of the roast, as salt draws the juices to the surface. Instead, salt the meat when you serve it.

4. Bones conduct heat, so bone-in and partially boned roasts require slightly less time to cook than boneless cuts.

5. Allow about 1 pound of meat per person if a roast contains a bone, and ½ pound per person if it is boneless.

6. Always use a meat thermometer—preferably the instant-read type—inserted into the thickest part of the flesh, away from bone, fat, and gristle.

7. Let the roast stand for at least 20 minutes before you carve it to allow the flesh to reabsorb the juices.

For a complete chart of cooking times based on internal temperatures for meat and poultry, turn to page 314.

'TIS THE SEASONINGS

■ Rubbing the surface of a roast with black pepper or a mixture of spices adds to its flavor. Consider these:

Combine equal parts paprika, onion powder, garlic powder, and ground cayenne pepper in a jar or small bowl. Rub it on the raw meat.

A light rub of Dijon-style mustard improves lamb and pork.

■ Commercial spice blends may contain sugar, which burns at high temperatures.

Rib Roast With Potatoes and Yorkshire Pudding

Rib roast is one of the easiest holiday meats you can fix. Sear the exterior at a high temperature, lower the heat, and remove it when it's done for a perfectly cooked roast beef every time. The onion gives flavor to the pan drippings.

1 standing rib roast, 5 to 6 pounds

freshly ground black pepper

1 sweet onion, peeled and cut into narrow wedges

4 to 6 russet potatoes, washed and quartered

Yorkshire Pudding (see below)

Preheat the oven to 500°F. Rub the roast with black pepper. Place it in a roasting pan (don't use a rack) fat side up and surround it with the onion pieces. Cook for 20 minutes, then reduce the oven temperature to 350°F and remove the roast from the oven. Carefully transfer the meat to a plate. To the pan, add the potatoes and coat them with the drippings. Then, push the potatoes to the side, return the meat to the pan, and put it all into the oven for 50 minutes, or until a meat thermometer inserted into the roast's thickest part reads 155°F. Remove the roast from the oven and let stand for 20 minutes before carving. (As a roast stands, its internal temperature goes up about five degrees, bringing it to around 160°F, or medium; for well-done meat, remove it from the oven at about 165°F.) **Makes 6 to 8 servings.**

YORKSHIRE PUDDING

This popover-like accompaniment is traditional fare in England. Some recipes recommend cooking the batter on top of all the drippings in the roasting pan, but the result can be greasy. Instead, use only 3 tablespoons of drippings. For thick slices of pudding, use a pan that is smaller than the roasting pan. Allowing the batter to stand while the roast cooks results in a more tender texture.

3 large eggs

1⅓ cups milk

¼ teaspoon ground mustard

pinch of salt

1¼ cups plus 2 tablespoons all-purpose flour

3 tablespoons beef pan drippings

Combine the eggs, milk, mustard, and salt in a mixing bowl and beat until fluffy. Add the flour, and blend just until thoroughly combined. Let stand while the roast cooks. After the roast is removed from the oven, use 3 tablespoons of the pan drippings to coat the bottom of an 8- or 9-inch square pan. Increase the oven temperature to 450°F. Place the baking pan in the oven until the pan and drippings are hot, about 5 minutes. Immediately pour the pudding mixture into the pan and bake for 15 minutes. Reduce the heat to 350°F and bake for 15 minutes more, or until the mixture is puffy and lightly browned. Cut into squares and serve immediately, as the pudding collapses quickly. **Makes 6 to 8 servings.**

Old-Fashioned Pot Roast

1 boneless chuck roast (3 pounds)

1 clove garlic, halved

¼ cup all-purpose flour

1 teaspoon paprika

¼ teaspoon salt

⅛ teaspoon coarsely ground black pepper

2 tablespoons vegetable oil

1 cup chopped onion

½ teaspoon dried thyme

1 bay leaf

1 can (14.5 ounces) tomatoes, undrained

1 tablespoon all-purpose flour mixed
   with ¼ cup cold water, for thickening
   (optional)

Rub the meat with the garlic clove. Mix the flour, paprika, salt, and pepper in a shallow dish. Dredge the meat in the seasoned flour. In a Dutch oven or large heavy pan with a lid, heat the oil. Add the meat and brown well on all sides. Pour off the excess fat and add the onion and thyme. Stir until the onion begins to brown, then add the bay leaf and tomatoes. Cover tightly and simmer for 3 hours, or until tender. During cooking, turn the meat several times; if necessary, add water, stock, or red wine.

When the meat is tender, transfer to a heated platter. Remove the bay leaf from the pan sauce. If desired, bring the sauce to a boil over medium heat and add flour mixture, stirring constantly, until the sauce becomes a thick gravy. Serve the meat with boiled potatoes, carrots, and gravy. **Makes 6 servings.**

HOW TO MAKE GRAVY STARTERS

■ A SLURRY is made by mixing cornstarch and cold water. It can be added directly to simmering pan drippings to thicken. Slurry gravy will be more transparent than that prepared with a roux.

■ A ROUX is made by blending equal portions of flour and melted fat (butter, meat or poultry fats, margarine, or vegetable oil), and tends to be a more flavorful thickener than a slurry. A roux should be lightly cooked and stirred over low heat to a smooth consistency before being combined with pan drippings to make the gravy.

MEATS

This is one of the most popular recipes at Almanac.com/food. Reviewer comments at the site include: "A wonderful meal for a cold day!"

New England Boiled Dinner

An entire meal from one pot, with beets on the side.

1 corned beef brisket (4 pounds)

15 peppercorns

8 whole cloves

1 bay leaf

8 small beets

2 turnips, cut into pieces

16 small new potatoes, peeled

16 baby carrots

8 small white onions

1 head cabbage, cut into 8 wedges

Place the beef in a large stockpot and add enough cold water to just cover. Cover the pot and simmer for 10 minutes. Skim off and discard the residue that forms on top of the water. Add the peppercorns, cloves, and bay leaf. Cover and simmer for 3 hours, or until the meat is tender. Put the beets into a separate pan with a little water. Bring to a boil, then reduce the heat and simmer until tender, about 30 minutes. Peel before serving. Add the turnips, potatoes, carrots, and onions to the stockpot with the meat. Simmer, covered, 15 minutes more. Add the cabbage and cook, covered, 15 minutes more. Transfer the meat to a carving board and slice into serving pieces. Place on a platter surrounded by the well-drained vegetables. **Makes 8 servings.**

MEATS

Apple-Glazed Corned Beef Brisket

BRISKET:

1 corned beef brisket (4 pounds)

1 large onion, peeled and halved

1 large clove garlic, halved

8 whole cloves

GLAZE:

1 cup apple jelly

4 tablespoons Dijon-style mustard

4 tablespoons brown sugar

2 tablespoons apple brandy

APPLE GARNISH:

6 cooking apples

8 tablespoons butter, divided

½ cup brown sugar

⅔ cup apple brandy

⅛ teaspoon grated nutmeg

For brisket and glaze: Preheat the oven to 350°F. Place the beef brisket in a large pot and cover with boiling water. Add the onion, garlic, and cloves. Bring to a full boil, then lower the heat. Simmer slowly, partially covered, for about 3 hours, or until very tender when tested with a fork. Meanwhile, mix the glaze ingredients together and set aside. When the meat is done, remove it from the pot and drain. Place the meat in an ovenproof serving dish and pour the glaze over the top to coat thoroughly. Bake for 30 minutes, or until the glaze is nicely browned.

For apple garnish: Peel and core the apples. Slice crosswise into ¼-inch rings. Melt 2 tablespoons of the butter in a large skillet and add a single layer of apple slices; sauté until browned, about 5 minutes. With a slotted spoon, transfer the apples to a bowl. Repeat until all the apples are cooked, adding butter as needed. Add the brown sugar to the butter remaining in the skillet and stir until it dissolves. Add the apple brandy and nutmeg, and bring to a boil. Boil for 5 minutes, stirring constantly. Return the apples to the skillet, reduce heat, and simmer for another 5 minutes, or until the apples are heated through. Keep warm. Remove the meat from the oven and place on a heated platter. Garnish with apple rings and sauce. **Makes 10 servings.**

Basic American Meat Loaf

1½ pounds ground meat

1 large egg

1 cup liquid (such as milk or tomato juice)

½ cup dry ingredients (such as bread
crumbs)

¼ cup chopped onion

salt and pepper, to taste

Preheat the oven to 350°F. Combine all of the ingredients in a large bowl. Using your hands, mix together until thoroughly blended. Pat the mixture into a 9x5-inch loaf pan and bake for 1 hour. **Makes 6 to 8 servings.**

MEAT LOAF MAKEOVERS

■ For the liquid ingredient, use beer, ketchup, canned tomato or mushroom soup, sour cream, applesauce, chicken stock, tomato sauce, or vegetable juice.

■ Instead of bread crumbs, use oatmeal, dry cereal, slices of bread softened in the liquid, crushed crackers, stuffing mixes, bulgur, or cooked rice.

■ In addition to onion, add chopped green or red bell peppers, grated carrots, dried onion soup mix, sun-dried tomatoes, chopped parsley, canned corn, minced or pressed garlic, cooked bacon, chopped spinach, sliced artichoke hearts, or grated cheeses (from Parmesan to Monterey Jack).

■ Along with salt and pepper, try horseradish, mustard, anchovy paste, hot sauce, basil, cayenne, celery flakes, curry powder, dill, ginger, nutmeg, sage, savory, or thyme for seasonings.

■ Top with ketchup or tomato sauce before baking. Or, for a classic meat loaf glaze, combine ¼ cup ketchup with ¾ cup water, 2 tablespoons vinegar, 2 tablespoons Dijon-style mustard, and 2 tablespoons brown sugar; pour some of this mixture over the meat loaf before cooking and use the rest to baste the loaf occasionally as it cooks.

Apple Meat Loaf

1 large onion, finely chopped
1 tablespoon butter
2½ pounds ground beef
2 cups peeled, cored, and chopped apples
1½ cups dry bread crumbs
3 large eggs, beaten
¼ cup ketchup
1 tablespoon prepared mustard
1 tablespoon chopped fresh parsley
1 teaspoon salt
½ teaspoon freshly ground black pepper
¼ teaspoon ground allspice

Preheat the oven to 350°F. Grease a 14x10-inch baking pan. In a skillet, sauté the onion in butter until soft. Combine the remaining ingredients in a large bowl and add the cooked onion. Using your hands, mix together until thoroughly blended. Press the mixture into the prepared pan and bake for 1 hour. Let stand 15 minutes before serving. **Makes 8 servings.**

Italian-Style Meatballs

1 pound lean ground beef
warm water
4 or 5 slices dry bread
1 large egg, slightly beaten
1 clove garlic, finely minced
1 small onion, finely chopped
salt and pepper, to taste
⅓ to ½ cup grated Parmesan cheese
¼ cup olive oil

Break up the meat in a large mixing bowl. In another bowl, soak the bread in warm water, then remove it and squeeze out excess moisture. Break up the soaked bread into small bits and add it to the meat. Add the egg, garlic, and onion, and season with salt and pepper. Knead by hand until well mixed, adding enough Parmesan cheese to stiffen the mixture. Divide the mixture into quarters, then shape five equal-size meatballs from each quarter. Heat the olive oil in a large skillet, add the meatballs, cover, and cook thoroughly over medium heat. Turn as they cook to brown evenly on all sides. Add the meatballs to your favorite spaghetti sauce and simmer slowly, stirring occasionally. **Makes 20 large meatballs.**

Swedish Meatballs

MEATBALLS:

3 slices bread

2 cups warm water

2 teaspoons vegetable oil

1 medium onion, minced

2 pounds ground beef

2 medium potatoes, peeled, boiled, and mashed

1 tablespoon salt

⅛ teaspoon freshly ground black pepper

2 large eggs

2 to 3 tablespoons vegetable oil, for frying

GRAVY:

3 to 4 tablespoons butter

½ cup all-purpose flour

3 cups beef stock

1 cup heavy cream

salt and pepper, to taste

For meatballs: Soak the bread in the warm water and set aside. Heat the 2 teaspoons of oil in a small skillet, sauté the minced onion until soft, and set aside. Squeeze the liquid out of the bread. Tear the bread into small bits, dropping them into a large bowl. Add the beef, onion, potatoes, salt, pepper, and eggs. Using your hands, mix together until thoroughly blended. Use a teaspoon to scoop out enough meat mixture to form 1½-inch balls and shape each spoonful in the palms of your hands. Place a large heavy skillet over medium heat, add enough oil to coat the bottom, and cook the meatballs, turning them frequently, until evenly browned. (You can instead brown the meatballs in a large, ungreased baking pan in a 400°F oven. Cook for 20 minutes or until lightly browned, turning occasionally.) Use a slotted spoon to transfer the meatballs from the skillet to a large saucepan.

For gravy: Drain the excess oil from the skillet after all of the meatballs are browned. Over medium heat, melt the butter and add the flour, stirring constantly until a paste is formed. Gradually add the beef stock, stirring briskly to avoid lumps. Stir in the cream and season with salt and pepper. Pour the mixture over the meatballs in the saucepan, cover, and cook on low heat for 40 to 60 minutes, stirring occasionally. **Makes 50 to 60 meatballs.**

QUICK FIX

■ **Add a few grains of rice to the salt shaker to keep salt flowing freely.**

MEATS

Mexican Chili

1 pound dry pinto beans
2 tablespoons vegetable oil
1 medium onion, chopped
2 pounds lean ground beef
2 tablespoons all-purpose flour
1 can (14.5 ounces) tomatoes
2 cloves garlic, crushed
2 tablespoons chili powder
1 tablespoon salt
1 teaspoon dried oregano
¼ teaspoon ground cumin

Place the beans into a large Dutch oven. Add enough water to cover several inches above the beans and soak overnight. Drain and rinse. Return the beans to the Dutch oven and add enough water to cover 1 inch above the beans. Bring to a boil, then reduce the heat and simmer, covered, for 1½ hours. Drain and set aside the beans. Wash and dry the Dutch oven. Heat the oil in the Dutch oven and sauté the onion until soft. Add the meat, cook until brown, and stir in the flour. Add the tomatoes, seasonings, and beans. Add enough water to achieve a broth of desired consistency. Simmer uncovered for 30 minutes, stirring occasionally. **Makes 8 servings.**

IN A HURRY?

Instead of cooking the dry pinto beans, substitute two 15.5-ounce cans of pinto beans, drained and rinsed.

To make your own spicy-hot chili mixes,
see the variations on page 319.

MEATS

HOW TO CLEAN A CUTTING BOARD

To clean a wooden cutting board after preparing raw meat, scrub the board with soapy hot water. Rinse. (Never submerge the entire board in the sink.) Once the board has dried, coat it with a thin layer of mineral oil. Wait a few hours, then wipe off any excess oil. Occasionally oiling the board will help to protect it against the absorption of bacteria.

Texas Tamale Pie

FILLING:

1 tablespoon butter

1 medium onion, chopped

1 green bell pepper, cored and diced

¾ pound lean ground beef

1 can (15 ounces) tomato sauce

1 can (12 ounces) whole-kernel corn,
    drained, or 1 package (10 ounces)
    frozen whole-kernel corn

½ cup pitted ripe olives, chopped

1 clove garlic, minced

1 tablespoon sugar

1½ teaspoons chili powder

1 teaspoon salt

½ teaspoon pepper

1 cup shredded Monterey Jack cheese

TOPPING:

¾ cup cornmeal

½ teaspoon salt

2 cups cold water

1 tablespoon butter

For filling: Grease an 8x8-inch or 10x6-inch baking dish. In a large skillet, melt the butter, add the onion and green pepper, and sauté until tender. Add the meat and brown. Stir in the tomato sauce, corn, olives, garlic, sugar, chili powder, salt, and pepper. Simmer for 20 minutes. Add the cheese and stir until melted. Pour the mixture into the prepared dish and set aside.

For topping: Preheat the oven to 375°F. In a medium saucepan, stir the cornmeal and salt into the cold water. Cook over medium heat, stirring until thickened. Stir in the butter.

Spoon the cornmeal mixture over the meat filling in strips. Bake for 40 minutes. **Makes 6 to 8 servings.**

French Farmer's Baked Beef and Barley

1½ pounds stew beef

3 tablespoons vegetable oil

1 medium onion, chopped

5 cups beef stock

½ teaspoon dried thyme

½ teaspoon dried marjoram

¼ teaspoon dried rosemary

1 cup pearl barley

1 tablespoon finely chopped fresh parsley,
  for garnish

Preheat the oven to 350°F. Trim all of the fat from the beef and cut into ½-inch cubes. Heat the oil in a large skillet and sauté the onion. Add the beef cubes and brown them on all sides. Transfer the onion and beef to a 3-quart ungreased casserole and set aside. Combine the stock, herbs, and barley in the skillet and bring to a boil. Pour the stock mixture over the sautéed onion and beef, cover, and bake for 1 hour. Garnish with parsley and serve in shallow soup bowls with French bread. **Makes 4 servings.**

Oriental Beef Stir-Fry

1 pound beef flank steak

2 tablespoons soy sauce

4 teaspoons dark roasted sesame oil,
  divided

1½ teaspoons sugar

1 teaspoon cornstarch

2 cloves garlic, chopped

1 tablespoon peeled and minced fresh
  ginger

¼ teaspoon crushed red pepper flakes

2 scallions, thinly sliced

1 small red bell pepper, cored and
  julienned

1 package (8 ounces) frozen baby corn, thawed

4 ounces snow pea pods, cut into thin strips

Cut the flank steak lengthwise into two pieces and slice it across the grain into ⅛-inch-thick strips. In a small bowl, whisk the soy sauce, 2 teaspoons of sesame oil, sugar, and cornstarch until dissolved, and pour this over the steak strips. Heat the remaining 2 teaspoons of sesame oil in a large skillet or wok over medium-high heat. Stir-fry the garlic, ginger, red pepper flakes, and scallions for 30 seconds. Add the bell pepper and corn and stir-fry for 2 minutes. Add the pea pods and stir-fry for 30 seconds. Remove the vegetables from the skillet and set them aside. Stir-fry the beef strips in two batches for 2 minutes on each side. Return the vegetables to the skillet and heat through. Serve over rice. **Makes 4 servings.**

MEATS

Beef With Red Peppers and Mushrooms

2 teaspoons butter

½ cup chopped onions

¾ cup thinly sliced red bell peppers

1 to 1½ cups sliced fresh mushrooms

¼ cup chopped fresh parsley

1½ to 2 cups thinly sliced leftover beef,
    cut into ½-inch-wide strips

1 to 1½ cups leftover pan sauce or gravy

salt and pepper, to taste

1 to 2 teaspoons soy sauce, or ¼ to
    ⅓ cup sour cream

In a large skillet, melt the butter, add the onions and red peppers, and cook over moderate heat, stirring frequently, for 2 minutes. Stir in the mushrooms and parsley. Cook, stirring frequently, for 3 minutes more. Stir in the beef and sauce. Reduce the heat and simmer for 3 minutes, or until the beef is heated through. Taste and season with salt and pepper. Add the soy sauce and serve. **Makes 4 servings.**

SLICE ADVICE

When slicing meat into paper-thin strips to stir-fry, partially freeze the meat until it is firm but not solid. It will be easier to cut.

Easy Swiss Steak

6 veal round steaks (2 pounds), cut
    ½-inch thick

1 clove garlic, halved

¼ cup all-purpose flour

½ teaspoon salt

⅛ teaspoon coarsely ground black pepper

3 tablespoons olive oil

⅓ cup finely chopped onion

⅓ cup finely chopped celery

⅓ cup peeled, finely chopped carrots

⅓ cup dry red wine

1¼ cups stewed tomatoes

Arrange the veal on a flat work surface and rub each steak, front and back, with the garlic clove. Season the flour with the salt and pepper and, using a meat mallet, pound flour into both sides of each veal steak—as much flour as it will hold. Steaks should be ¼- to ⅛-inch thick before cooking. Heat the oil in a large skillet and sear the steaks on one side until brown. Turn them over. Add the vegetables, red wine, and tomatoes. Cover and simmer gently for 1½ to 2 hours, or until the meat is tender. **Makes 6 servings.**

Super Steak Sandwich

Serve with a fresh green salad for a perfect summer supper.

MARINADE:

⅓ cup vegetable oil

1 cup beer

4 cloves garlic, chopped

½ teaspoon freshly ground black pepper

1 teaspoon salt

2 tablespoons Dijon-style mustard

2 beef flank steaks (1 pound each)

3 tablespoons butter

2 cups onions, sliced into thin rings

2 cups sliced mushrooms

½ teaspoon paprika

1 large loaf French bread

For marinade: In a medium bowl, combine the oil, beer, garlic, pepper, salt, and mustard. Marinate the steaks overnight in the refrigerator.

In a large skillet, melt the butter and sauté the onions and mushrooms with the paprika until tender and lightly browned; keep warm while cooking the steaks. Remove the steaks from the marinade and broil or grill for about 4 to 5 minutes per side, or to desired doneness. Slice the meat diagonally into ¼-inch pieces. Cut the French bread into four equal pieces, then cut each piece in half horizontally. Divide the onion-mushroom mixture evenly among four pieces of the bread, top with meat, and cover with the remaining bread. **Makes 4 servings.**

Lemon Veal Cutlets

4 veal cutlets

¼ cup all-purpose flour

¼ teaspoon salt

⅛ teaspoon freshly ground black pepper

1 tablespoon butter

1 tablespoon olive oil

2 tablespoons fresh lemon juice

2 tablespoons chopped fresh parsley

2 tablespoons chopped fresh basil

½ cup seeded, diced fresh tomatoes

lemon half, thinly sliced, for garnish

Arrange the cutlets between two sheets of wax paper and, using a meat mallet, pound them to a ¼-inch thickness. In a shallow bowl, combine the flour, salt, and pepper. Dredge the cutlets in the seasoned flour. Heat the butter and olive oil in a large skillet over medium-high heat. Add the cutlets (do not crowd them, or you will get a steamed effect and the delicate veal will become leathery) and cook until lightly browned on each side. The total cooking time should be under 5 minutes. Transfer the browned veal to a warmed platter. Reduce the heat and add the lemon juice, scraping the pan to loosen the browned bits. Add the parsley, basil, and tomatoes and continue cooking for 5 minutes. Return the veal to the skillet and increase the heat just long enough to warm the cutlets and sauce together. Serve immediately, garnished with lemon slices. **Makes 4 servings.**

Veal Chops Braised in Cider

6 veal loin chops, 1-inch thick

1 teaspoon dried savory

1 teaspoon dried thyme

1 teaspoon paprika

salt and pepper, to taste

4 tablespoons (½ stick) butter, divided

1 large onion, finely chopped

1 cup apple cider

2 tablespoons cornstarch

1 apple, cored, sliced in thin rounds, and dipped in lemon juice, for garnish

Preheat the oven to 400°F. Select a baking pan that is just large enough to hold the veal chops. In a small bowl, mix the savory, thyme, paprika, salt, and pepper. Sprinkle this over the chops. Melt 2 tablespoons of butter in the baking pan. Sprinkle the onion over the bottom of the pan, and arrange the chops on top in a single layer. Melt the remaining butter in a small saucepan, and stir in the apple cider. Pour this over the chops. Cover with foil and bake for 45 minutes, or until tender, basting occasionally. Remove the chops to a serving platter. Transfer the pan juices to a saucepan and bring to a boil. Dissolve the cornstarch in a little cold water and add to the pan juices. Cook, stirring constantly, until thickened. Pour this over the chops. Garnish with apple slices. **Makes 6 servings.**

Veal Parmesan

4 large veal cutlets
1 large egg
1 cup dry bread crumbs
½ cup grated Parmesan cheese, divided
2 to 3 tablespoons olive oil
3 cups tomato sauce, divided
4 slices mozzarella cheese

Preheat the oven to 350°F. Arrange cutlets between two sheets of wax paper, and, using a meat mallet, pound the veal cutlets to a ⅛-inch thickness. In a shallow dish, beat the egg. In a separate shallow dish, combine the bread crumbs with ¼ cup of grated Parmesan. Dip each cutlet into the beaten egg, coating both sides, then dredge in the bread crumb mixture. In a large skillet over medium heat, sauté the cutlets in olive oil, two at a time, until browned on both sides, turning once. Transfer the veal to a lightly greased 13x9-inch baking dish, arranging in a single layer. Cover with 2 cups of tomato sauce. Place the cheese slices evenly over the top. Spoon on the remaining sauce and sprinkle with the remaining ¼ cup of grated Parmesan. Bake for 30 minutes. **Makes 4 servings.**

Quick Tomato Pork Stew

Although pork tenderloin is an expensive cut of meat, it cooks quickly and has great flavor.

1 pork tenderloin (8 ounces)
¼ cup all-purpose flour
salt and pepper, to taste
2 tablespoons olive oil
1 medium onion, chopped
1 clove garlic, minced
1 medium green bell pepper, cored and
    chopped
1 teaspoon ground cumin
1 teaspoon dried oregano
1 teaspoon dried rosemary
2 cups chicken stock
½ pound new potatoes, cut in chunks
1 can (14.5 ounces) whole tomatoes, drained
    and coarsely chopped
salt and pepper, to taste

Cut the pork into cubes. In a small bowl, combine the flour with the salt and pepper. Dredge the pork in the seasoned flour. In a Dutch oven or large heavy skillet, heat the oil, add the pork, and sauté until browned. Transfer the pork to a plate and set aside. Add the onion, garlic, and bell pepper to the pan and sauté until soft but not brown. Mix in the spices and continue cooking for 1 minute more, then add the stock. Bring to a boil, add the potatoes, and reduce the heat to a simmer. Continue cooking, uncovered, until the potatoes are barely tender, then add the coarsely chopped tomatoes and reserved pork. Continue cooking for 1 to 2 minutes to warm the pork and tomatoes. Adjust the seasonings to taste. **Makes 4 servings.**

MEATS

Pork in Pastry Pockets

Take these sumptuous pockets, served warm or at room temperature, to a potluck supper or a picnic.

1½ pounds pork tenderloin (approximately 2 tenderloins)

14 fresh sage leaves

4 tablespoons (½ stick) unsalted butter, divided

2 large cloves garlic, thinly sliced

1 large yellow onion, thinly sliced

1 large shallot, thinly sliced

4 large fresh white mushrooms, thinly sliced

1 package frozen puff pastry sheets

1 large golden Bartlett pear, cored, peeled, and cut into ⅛-inch slices

1 cup shredded Monterey Jack cheese

2 egg yolks beaten with 2 teaspoons of water, for egg wash

Preheat the oven to 375°F. Make slits in the meat and insert the sage leaves. In a large skillet, melt 2 tablespoons of butter. Remove the skillet from heat and roll the tenderloins in the butter to coat. Place the pork in a roasting pan and cover with foil. Cook for 25 to 30 minutes, or until the internal temperature reads 140°F on a meat thermometer. (Pork should be thoroughly cooked to a full 160°F for safe eating, but these medallions will finish cooking inside the pockets.) Let the pork stand for 1 minute, then slice each piece into ¼-inch medallions. Melt the remaining 2 tablespoons of butter in the skillet and sauté the garlic, onion, shallot, and mushrooms until golden.

Remove two pastry sheets from the package and spread them to form a 10x12-inch rectangle. Divide each sheet in thirds (10 inches by 4 inches) and, with a sharp knife, cut the corners to make long ovals. Arrange several pork medallions on one side of each pastry oval, ¼ inch from the edge. Place a spoonful of the onion mixture, a slice of pear, and a portion of the cheese on the pork in each oval. Brush the edges of each pastry oval with water to hold the seal. Fold the pastry flap over the filling, turning up the edges to enclose, and press the edges with a fork to seal. Brush each pocket with egg wash. Bake on greased baking sheets for 25 to 30 minutes, or until the pastry is golden. **Makes 6 large pockets.**

Roast Pork

Use a boneless pork loin, not a tenderloin, and allow about ½ pound of meat per person.

1 boneless pork loin roast (3 to 4 pounds)
1 to 2 cloves garlic, slivered
freshly ground black pepper

Preheat the oven to 500°F. Make slits in the pork and insert the garlic slivers. Season with pepper and place the pork loin, fat side up, on a rack. Roast for 45 to 50 minutes, or until a meat thermometer inserted into the middle of the roast reads between 155° and 160°F. Remove from the oven and let stand for 20 minutes before serving. **Makes 6 to 8 servings.**

Roast Pork With Carrots, Turnips, and Apples

1 boneless pork loin roast (2 pounds)
⅓ cup cider vinegar
4½ teaspoons dried parsley, divided
4½ teaspoons dried sage, divided
¼ teaspoon salt
**3 cups carrots, peeled, cut into ½-inch
    slices**
**1 pound turnips, peeled and cut into
    ½-inch chunks**
**2 medium Granny Smith apples, peeled,
    cored, and sliced**
2 tablespoons vegetable oil

Preheat the oven to 375°F. Place the roast in a shallow dish and pour the vinegar over it, turning to soak all sides. Sprinkle with 1½ teaspoons each of the parsley and sage, season with salt, and set aside. Put the carrots, turnips, and apples into a large roasting pan and drizzle with oil. Sprinkle with the remaining parsley and sage, and mix well. Place the roast, fat side up, on top of the vegetables and drizzle the remaining vinegar from the dish over the meat. Roast for 1¼ hours, or until the internal temperature of the meat reads 160°F on a meat thermometer and the vegetables are tender. Remove from the oven, cover the meat with aluminum foil, and let stand for 15 minutes before carving. **Makes 5 to 6 servings.**

Pork Chop and Sweet Potato Bake

2 tablespoons vegetable oil

½ cup chopped onion

4 lean pork chops

4 sweet potatoes, peeled and thinly sliced

2 tablespoons cornstarch

1½ cups chicken stock, divided

¼ teaspoon dried thyme

⅛ teaspoon freshly ground black pepper

Preheat the oven to 350°F. Grease a 3-quart casserole. Heat the oil in a large skillet, add the onion, and sauté until golden. Add the pork chops and brown on both sides. Arrange the sweet potato slices in the bottom of the casserole and top with the onions and pork chops. Dissolve the cornstarch in ½ cup of chicken stock. Heat the remaining 1 cup of chicken stock in the skillet with the thyme and pepper. Add the cornstarch mixture to the hot stock, stirring constantly until thick. Pour the sauce over the pork chops, cover, and bake for 1 hour, or until the pork chops and sweet potatoes are tender. **Makes 4 servings.**

Brandied Cranberry Chops

PORK CHOPS:

1 cup fresh or frozen cranberries

4 tablespoons brandy, divided

¼ cup fresh orange juice

3 tablespoons sugar

6 tablespoons butter (¾ stick), divided

¼ cup chopped scallions

¼ cup chopped celery

1 tablespoon chopped fresh parsley

4 cups dry bread cubes

½ teaspoon poultry seasoning

½ teaspoon salt

4 loin pork chops, cut 1½ inches thick

1 teaspoon freshly ground black pepper

BRANDY SAUCE:

1 tablespoon flour

1 tablespoon brandy

1 tablespoon fresh orange juice

For pork chops: Mix the cranberries, 2 tablespoons of the brandy, orange juice, and sugar in a small saucepan. Bring to a boil, lower heat, and simmer for 10 minutes, stirring occasionally.

Preheat the oven to 350°F. In a large skillet, heat 4 tablespoons of the butter and sauté the scallions, celery, and parsley. Add the bread cubes, poultry seasoning, salt, and cranberry mixture and mix well. Cut a pocket into each pork chop. Sprinkle the inside of the pocket with pepper and fill with bread stuffing. Secure with small skewers or toothpicks. Melt the remaining 2 tablespoons of butter with the remaining 2 tablespoons of brandy and brush both sides of the chops with half of this mixture. Place the chops on a rack in a metal baking pan and bake for 35 minutes. Brush both sides of the chops again with the butter-brandy mixture and return to the oven for an additional 35 to 45 minutes, or until the chops are done. Remove the chops from the oven, place on a heated platter, and remove the skewers.

For sauce: Place the metal pan with meat drippings on a stovetop burner and heat. Stir in the flour, scraping the pan until the flour is browned. Stir in ½ cup of water, brandy, and orange juice. Cook, stirring constantly, until thickened. Strain before serving. Pour the sauce over the chops and serve immediately. **Makes 4 servings.**

Easy Roasted Pork Strips

1½ pounds pork tenderloin
¼ cup lime juice
2 tablespoons brown sugar
¼ cup soy sauce
¼ cup dry sherry
2 cloves garlic, minced
¼ teaspoon ground mustard
¼ teaspoon freshly ground black
    pepper

Cut the pork into strips about 5 inches long. Combine the lime juice, brown sugar, soy sauce, sherry, garlic, mustard, and pepper in a large, resealable plastic bag, seal it, and shake well. Add the pork to the bag of marinade, reseal it, and refrigerate for 3 hours, turning the bag occasionally.

Preheat the oven to 425°F. Remove the pork from the marinade and place it on a rack in a roasting pan. Discard the marinade. Roast the pork for 5 minutes. Turn the meat over, baste with pan juices, and continue cooking for 5 minutes, or until the internal temperature reads 160°F on a meat thermometer. Let the pork stand for 5 minutes before slicing at an angle. Serve with fried rice. **Makes 4 servings.**

Dartmoor Fidget Pie

This particular Cornish pasty (pronounced "pass-tee")—perhaps because it is from Devon—is made in a pie plate with only a top crust, rather than the traditional turnover style.

½ pound smoked lean bacon
3 or 4 medium potatoes, peeled, and
    thinly sliced
3 medium yellow onions, chopped
    coarsely
salt and pepper, to taste
3 Granny Smith apples, peeled, cored,
    and sliced
2 to 3 tablespoons light-brown sugar
pastry for 1 crust
1 egg white, slightly beaten

Preheat the oven to 400°F. Grease the bottom of a deep pie plate with a bit of the uncooked bacon. Cut the bacon strips into ½-inch pieces. Layer the sliced potatoes and the chopped onion in the dish; add salt and pepper, to taste. Mix the bacon bits in with the potatoes and onion. Top with the apple slices, and sprinkle with brown sugar.

Roll out the pastry and cover the pie, making sure that the edges are tucked in securely. Make a dime-size hole in the center for the steam to escape. Brush with egg white. Bake for 10 minutes, then reduce the heat to 350°F and bake for another 20 minutes. Test with a long skewer through the center hole to make sure that the vegetables are soft. Place on a wire rack to cool. **Makes about 6 servings.**

Pork and Beef Pie

PASTRY:

2 cups all-purpose flour

¾ teaspoon salt

¾ cup shortening

2 tablespoons (¼ stick) butter

1 egg

3 tablespoons cold water

FILLING:

1 pound ground pork

1 pound ground beef

2 medium onions, chopped

2 cloves garlic, minced

1 tablespoon minced fresh parsley

2 teaspoons salt, or to taste

¼ teaspoon freshly ground black pepper

½ teaspoon ground cloves

½ teaspoon ground cinnamon

1 egg white, slightly beaten

For pastry: Sift together the flour and salt. Cut in the shortening and butter with a pastry blender. Beat the egg with the cold water and add to the pastry. Divide and shape the dough into two balls and chill for at least 30 minutes. With a rolling pin on a lightly floured surface, roll each pastry ball into a circle 11 inches wide and ⅛-inch thick. Place one pastry circle in the bottom of a 9-inch pie plate, and set the other aside.

For filling: Preheat the oven to 400°F. Cook the meat with the onions and garlic in a large skillet until slightly browned. Drain the fat, then add the parsley, salt, pepper, cloves, cinnamon, and ½ cup of water. Simmer for 3 minutes. Fill the crust-lined pie pan with the meat mixture. Cover with the top pastry. Turn under the edges and crimp. Brush with egg white. Using a fork, poke holes into the pastry crust to vent the steam. Bake for 10 minutes at 400°F. Reduce the heat to 350°F and bake for 40 minutes more, or until the crust is golden. **Makes 6 to 8 servings.**

Sweet Sausage and Spinach Frittata

½ **pound ground sweet sausage**

½ **cup chopped onion**

1 **10-ounce package frozen chopped spinach, thawed and drained**

8 **slices sweet bread, cubed, crusts removed**

2 **cups Gruyère cheese, shredded**

6 **large eggs**

¾ **cup milk**

¾ **cup heavy cream**

1 **cup sour cream**

1 **tablespoon fresh oregano, finely chopped**

1 **teaspoon ground mustard**

¼ **cup chopped green bell pepper**

¼ **cup chopped red bell pepper**

salt and pepper, to taste

In a large skillet, cook the sausage and onion until browned and cooked through, about 10 to 12 minutes. Drain on paper towels. In a large bowl, combine the sausage mixture and spinach. Stir to blend, and set aside. Lightly spray a 10-inch quiche pan with nonstick cooking spray. Spread the bread cubes evenly over the bottom of the pan. Spread the sausage mixture and cheese evenly over the bread.

In a large bowl, whisk together the eggs, milk, heavy cream, and sour cream. Add the oregano, mustard, green and red peppers, and salt and pepper. Slowly pour the egg mixture over the sausage and bread in the quiche pan. Cover and refrigerate for at least 4 hours, or overnight.

Preheat the oven to 350°F. Remove the quiche pan from the refrigerator, uncover, and bake until set and the top is a light golden brown, about 50 to 60 minutes. Remove the frittata from the oven and allow to set for 10 minutes before serving. **Makes 6 to 8 servings.**

HAVING HAM?

■ The precooked ham you buy at the supermarket will benefit from slow roasting, which firms the texture and removes most of the liquid that has been injected into the flesh. A glaze slightly sweetens the surface of the slices. As a variation, insert a fresh whole clove into each diamond before glazing. (Try using this tip for the Precooked Ham With Glaze and Country Ham With Glaze recipes that follow.)

A true country ham tastes best cold or at room temperature, and should be served in paper-thin slices.

For more on ham, see page 299.

Precooked Ham With Glaze

**1 precooked boneless ham half
(5 to 6 pounds)**

GLAZE:
¼ cup apricot jam
¼ teaspoon ground mustard
1 tablespoon brown sugar
**2 to 3 teaspoons freshly squeezed orange
or lemon juice**

Preheat the oven to 325°F. Remove any skin from the ham and trim off any fat. Place the ham into a baking pan and roast for 15 minutes per pound. Remove from the oven and score the outside of the meat in a diamond pattern.

For glaze: In a small bowl, mix together the jam, mustard, brown sugar, and juice. Spread the mixture over the surface of the ham, reserving about 1 tablespoon. Return the ham to the oven, and bake for another 30 to 40 minutes. Remove from the oven and immediately spread the remaining glaze over the ham. Serve warm or cool. **Makes 10 to 12 servings.**

Country Ham With Glaze

1 uncooked, bone-in country ham half
   (7 to 9 pounds)

GLAZE:
⅓ cup brown sugar
1 to 2 tablespoons orange juice
½ teaspoon ground mustard

Scrub the ham and soak it for several hours or overnight in water to cover. Drain, cover with water, and simmer on the top of the stove for 15 minutes per pound or until an instant-read thermometer reads 160°F.

Remove from the water bath, drain, and let cool. Trim off the skin and fat. Score the meat in a diamond pattern. Preheat the oven to 350°F.

For glaze: In a small bowl, mix together the brown sugar, orange juice, and mustard. Spread thinly on the surface of the ham. Place the ham in a baking pan and bake at 350°F for 20 to 30 minutes, or until the sugar mixture glazes the surface. Do not overcook or the glaze will burn and the meat will dry out. Cool before serving. **Makes 14 to 18 servings.**

Ham Pilaf

1 tablespoon butter
2 cups chicken stock
1 cup white rice (if using brown rice,
   add another ½ cup of stock and cook
   for 40 minutes)
¼ cup currants
1 cup diced cooked ham
¼ cup pine nuts
pineapple slices, for garnish

In a medium saucepan, combine the butter with the stock and bring to a boil. Add the rice, cover, and reduce the heat to low. Cook for 15 to 20 minutes, or until the liquid is almost completely absorbed. Add the currants, remove from the heat, and let stand for 5 minutes. Stir in the ham and pine nuts. Garnish with pineapple and serve. **Makes 4 servings.**

MEATS

Ham Loaf

LOAF:

1 pound ground ham

½ pound ground pork

1 egg, beaten

1 cup milk

1 cup lightly salted cracker crumbs

1 small green bell pepper, chopped

2 tablespoons minced onion (optional)

GLAZE:

¼ cup maple syrup

1 tablespoon ground mustard

MUSTARD SAUCE

1½ cups Dijon-style mustard

4 teaspoons ground mustard

¾ cup sugar

½ cup white vinegar

1⅓ cups vegetable oil

1 cup chopped fresh dill

salt, to taste

For loaf: Preheat the oven to 350°F. In a large bowl, mix together the ham, pork, egg, milk, cracker crumbs, pepper, and onion, reserving a few pieces of green pepper. Place in a greased loaf pan and top with the reserved green pepper pieces. Bake for 1 hour and 10 minutes.

For glaze: In a small bowl, mix together the maple syrup and dry mustard. Baste the top of the loaf during the last 20 minutes of baking time. Serve with Mustard Sauce (recipe below). **Makes 4 to 6 servings.**

Mix together the mustards and sugar. Add the vinegar, then gradually whisk in the oil. Add the dill and salt. The sauce will thicken as the oil is added. Refrigerate until ready to use. Before serving, warm the sauce over low heat. **Makes about 3 cups.**

Roast Leg of Lamb With Potatoes and Rutabaga

Allow 1 pound per serving and add a little extra cooking time if the roast is boneless.

1 leg of lamb, bone-in (5 to 6 pounds)
2 or 3 cloves garlic, slivered
1 tablespoon prepared Dijon-style mustard
freshly ground black pepper
4 to 6 russet potatoes, peeled and quartered
1 large rutabaga, peeled and cut into wedges

Preheat the oven to 500°F. Make slits in the meat and insert the slivers of garlic. Rub the surface of the lamb with the mustard and season generously with pepper. Place the lamb into a roasting pan and cook for 20 minutes. Reduce the oven temperature to 350°F and remove the pan from the oven. Add the potatoes and rutabaga around the lamb, and coat the vegetables with pan drippings. Return the pan to the oven and roast for 50 to 70 minutes more (depending on the bone), or until a meat thermometer reads 145°F (medium rare), basting occasionally with the pan juices. **Makes 6 servings.**

Lamb Chops With Mint Pesto

PESTO:
1 cup fresh mint leaves, packed
½ cup virgin olive oil
⅓ cup grated Parmesan cheese
¼ cup fresh parsley
¼ cup pine nuts
3 cloves garlic
1 tablespoon fresh basil leaves
salt and pepper, to taste

CHOPS:
4 lamb chops (4 ounces each)
2 teaspoons virgin olive oil
salt and pepper, to taste

For pesto: Combine all of the ingredients in a blender or food processor, and pulse until well mixed. Set aside.

For chops: Trim the visible fat from the lamb chops. Heat the oil in a skillet and sauté the lamb over medium heat until just barely pink inside. Season with salt and pepper and top with pesto. **Makes 4 servings.**

Braised Lamb Shanks With Gremolata

SHANKS:

2 tablespoons olive oil

1 teaspoon chopped garlic

1 large onion, sliced

2 large carrots, peeled and julienned

2 lamb shanks (1¼ pounds each)

½ cup dry white wine

1 large fresh tomato, chopped

¼ cup chopped fresh parsley

few springs fresh rosemary, or ½ teaspoon
   dried

2 bay leaves

½ teaspoon dried thyme

½ teaspoon dried basil

¾ cup beef, chicken, or veal stock

GREMOLATA:

3 tablespoons chopped fresh parsley

1 tablespoon grated fresh lemon peel

1 teaspoon minced garlic

For shanks: Heat the oil in a large skillet over medium-high heat. Add the garlic, onion, and carrots, and cook for 5 minutes or until brown. Push the vegetables to one side, add the lamb shanks, and brown on all sides for another 5 minutes. Add the wine to the pan and stir continually, scraping up any browned-on bits, until the liquid is reduced to a few tablespoons. Add the tomato, seasonings, and stock. Cover tightly and simmer for 2 hours, turning a few times during cooking, or until the lamb is very tender and begins to fall from the bones.

For gremolata: Mix the parsley, lemon peel, and garlic and sprinkle over the lamb when ready to serve. **Makes 2 servings.**

Backyard Barbecues

FLAVOR SAVERS

- Let meat or fish stand at room temperature for 30 minutes before grilling it.

- Sprinkle dried tarragon, rosemary, oregano, or other herbs onto hot coals just before grilling to enhance the taste of grilled foods.

- After cooking meat and poultry on the grill, keep them hot until served, 140°F or warmer. Let cooked meat rest on a platter for five minutes before serving.

Best Barbecue Sauce

This goes well with poultry, beef, or lamb.

½ cup olive oil

4 cloves garlic, minced

1 cup chopped onions

1 cup chopped fresh tomatoes

¼ cup chopped ripe olives

2 tablespoons soy sauce

1 cup orange juice

¼ cup brown sugar

2 tablespoons apple cider vinegar

¼ cup chopped fresh parsley

Heat the olive oil in a large skillet, add the garlic and onions, and sauté until soft. Add the tomatoes and cook until reduced by half. Stir in the remaining ingredients and simmer for 20 minutes. Use as a marinade or grilling sauce, or serve as a sauce to accompany grilled meats. **Makes 2½ cups.**

STEAK TIPS

Avoid beef that is bright red; it is blood fresh. Choose steak that is a little darker; it has been in the meat case a few days and thus has oxidized. It is likely to have some age and be more tender and flavorful. Also, look for a steak that is well marbled, as these bands of fat lend flavor.

Always start with a hot fire, whether using an oven broiler, a gas or charcoal grill, or an iron skillet on the stovetop. High heat will allow easy searing of the steak. Then cook over reduced heat.

A thicker steak cooks best, no matter what the method. For example, a 1¼-inch-thick steak cooks to medium-rare in 7 to 10 minutes, depending on the heat source.

STEAK-O-METER

Remove a steak from the cooking source just before desired doneness. (The internal temperature continues to go up as the steak sits off the heat.)

DONENESS	INTERNAL STEAK TEMPERATURE
Rare	140°F
Medium rare	160°F
Well done	170°F

Pacific Rim Glazed Flank Steak

Utah cook Chris Freymuller won the grand prize in the 1997 National Beef Cook-Off with this marinated steak recipe.

MARINADE:

1 cup prepared teriyaki marinade

½ cup chopped onion

⅓ cup honey

⅓ cup fresh orange juice

1 tablespoon chopped fresh rosemary

1 tablespoon dark sesame oil

1 large clove garlic, crushed

freshly ground black pepper, to taste

STEAK:

1 beef flank steak (1½ to 2 pounds)

orange slices and rosemary sprigs,
    for garnish

For marinade: In a shallow dish, combine the marinade ingredients. Whisk until blended. Reserve ¾ of a cup in a small saucepan for basting.

For steak: With a sharp knife, lightly score both sides of the steak in a crisscross pattern. Place the steak in the remaining marinade, turning to coat. Cover and marinate in the refrigerator at least 30 minutes, turning once.

Remove the steak and discard the used marinade. Grill the steak, uncovered, over medium coals for 10 to 20 minutes, depending on preference, basting occasionally with the reserved marinade and turning once.

Place the remaining basting marinade on the hottest part of the grill and bring to a boil. Meanwhile, carve the steak into thin slices, cutting diagonally across the grain, and arrange on a platter. Spoon hot marinade over the meat and garnish with orange slices and rosemary sprigs. **Makes 4 to 6 servings.**

Hawaiian Spareribs

SPARERIBS:

4 to 5 pounds pork spareribs

MARINADE:

1 cup pineapple juice

2 tablespoons fresh lemon juice

2 tablespoons soy sauce

½ teaspoon cumin

½ teaspoon curry powder

For spareribs: In a large stockpot, parboil the spareribs for 20 minutes in salted water to cover.

For marinade: In a small bowl, combine the marinade ingredients. Drain the water from the spareribs, pour on the marinade, and refrigerate for 1 to 6 hours, turning to recoat once or twice. Barbecue (or oven broil) the spareribs 4 to 6 inches from the heat for a total of 30 minutes. **Makes 6 servings.**

- Soak wooden skewers in water for 30 minutes before using them so that they won't burn during cooking.

- If you prefer metal skewers, use the square or twisted types. They hold food better than round ones.

- Place food snugly on wooden skewers to keep the heat from burning the stick. Metal skewers can be loaded with small spaces left between the pieces.

- Thread food on two parallel skewers rather than a single one to keep it from slipping off during cooking and turning.

- When using foods with different cooking times, such as shrimp and beef, cook them on separate skewers. Because beef takes longer to cook, start it first.

Skewered Lamb With Vegetables

LAMB:

1½ pounds leg of lamb cut into 1-inch cubes

2 large, sweet, red onions, cut into quarters, layers pulled apart

2 or 3 bulbs fennel, cut into chunks

2 or 3 large red bell peppers, cored and cut into squares

MARINADE:

1 cup olive oil

juice of two lemons

3 or 4 large sprigs fresh rosemary

2 or 3 cloves garlic, crushed

salt and pepper, to taste

fresh mint and rosemary, as garnish

For lamb: Thread the meat onto metal or presoaked wooden skewers, alternating with onion, fennel, and red bell pepper, and arrange them in a shallow baking dish.

For marinade: In a small bowl, combine the olive oil, lemon juice, rosemary, garlic, and salt and pepper and pour the mixture over the skewers, turning to coat evenly. Refrigerate the skewers and marinade until ready to cook.

Prepare the grill. Arrange the skewers on an oiled rack and cook until well browned, turning occasionally and brushing with the remaining marinade. (Cooking time depends on the heat and the size of the meat cubes.) Garnish with the herbs. **Makes 4 to 6 servings.**

GRILLING VEGETABLES

For best results, cut vegetables into large pieces and brush with olive oil before cooking. Season with salt, pepper, garlic, and/or lemon juice. Salt lightly again before serving, if you wish.

To achieve a professional chef's finish (charred crosshatches on the vegetables), place the vegetables on the grill at a 45° angle, then change the angle and cook for a few minutes more before you turn them over. Repeat on the other side.

Clean the grill surface before using so that the vegetables won't stick.

Serve the vegetables hot with your favorite summer sauces or put them between slices of grilled bread. Save the leftovers for sandwich fillings.

VEGETABLE	HOW TO PREPARE	GRILLING TIME
Artichokes	Cut in half lengthwise, press down to spread the leaves open. Rub with olive oil and season with salt.	15 to 20 minutes per side, or until base is tender
Asparagus	Roll spears in olive oil and season with salt and pepper.	5 to 10 minutes; turn every few minutes until tender
Corn	Leave the stem and husk on. Pull back the husk, remove the silk, and soak for 15 minutes in cold water. Then carefully pull the husk back up, smoothing and twisting it so that it stays closed.	10 to 20 minutes; turn several times
Eggplant	Cut lengthwise, or crosswise into circles ¼-inch thick. Brush with olive oil.	4 to 5 minutes per side
Fennel	Remove the stalks and cut the bulb in half lengthwise or slice, keeping part of the root attached. Brush with olive oil and season with salt. (Lightly steam large bulbs before grilling.)	5 to 6 minutes per side
Leeks	Cut white portions in half lengthwise and wash well in warm water. Brush with olive oil. (Lightly steam large leeks before grilling.)	4 to 6 minutes per side
Mushrooms	Use large caps, such as portobello. Brush with olive oil and slice after grilling.	8 to 10 minutes per side
Onions	Cut into ½-inch slices. Brush with olive oil and season with salt.	8 to 10 minutes per side
Peppers	Cut bell peppers in half lengthwise, remove seeds, and brush with olive oil.	6 to 10 minutes skin side down, then 3 to 4 minutes on the other side
Summer Squash/ Zucchini	Cut into thirds or halves lengthwise. Brush with olive oil and season with salt.	5 to 8 minutes per side

Marinated Grilled Chicken With Cilantro and Scallions

MARINADE:

2 tablespoons honey

2 tablespoons soy sauce

1 tablespoon rice wine or dry sherry

1 tablespoon peeled and finely chopped
    fresh ginger

1 teaspoon finely chopped orange zest

1 teaspoon finely chopped garlic

CHICKEN:

4 chicken breast halves, bone-in

¼ cup finely chopped fresh cilantro

1 scallion, finely chopped

Preheat the grill.

For marinade: In a large glass pie plate, combine the honey, soy sauce, wine, ginger, zest, and garlic.

For chicken: Add the chicken to the marinade and turn to coat evenly. Grill, skin side down, for 8 minutes, or until well browned, brushing once with marinade. Turn and grill the other side, brushing with marinade, for about 8 minutes more.

In a small bowl, combine the cilantro and scallion, and sprinkle over the chicken before serving. **Makes 4 servings.**

Spicy Chicken Rub

RUB:

2 teaspoons chili powder

1 teaspoon ground oregano

1 teaspoon cilantro leaves, dried and
    crumbled

½ to 1 teaspoon ground cayenne pepper

1 teaspoon garlic powder

½ teaspoon freshly ground black pepper

½ teaspoon ground ginger

½ teaspoon ground cumin

CHICKEN:

4 boneless, skinless, chicken breast
    halves

fresh lemon juice

salt, to taste

For rub: Mix the spices and keep in an airtight jar in a cool place.

For chicken: When ready to use the rub, mix a small amount with water to form a paste. Rub the chicken pieces with some lemon juice and then the paste. Place the chicken in a covered bowl and refrigerate for a few hours. Season with salt. Grill over coals or flame, turning at least once, until the chicken is done, about 25 minutes. **Makes 4 servings.**

Spicy Barbecue Sauce for Fish

Use as a marinade or grilling sauce or serve as a sauce to accompany fish.

½ **cup vegetable oil**

¾ **cup chopped onion**

¾ **cup ketchup**

⅓ **cup fresh lemon juice**

2 **teaspoons salt**

3 **tablespoons sugar**

3 **tablespoons Worcestershire sauce**

2 **tablespoons prepared mustard**

½ **teaspoon freshly ground black pepper**

Heat the oil in a large skillet, add the onion, and sauté until tender but not brown. Add the remaining ingredients and mix well with ¾ cup of water. **Makes 2 cups.**

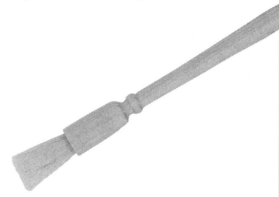

Grilled Salmon With Maple Mustard Glaze

GLAZE:

2 **tablespoons olive oil**

¼ **cup Dijon-style mustard**

2 **tablespoons maple syrup**

2 **teaspoons soy sauce**

juice of ½ **lemon**

1 **tablespoon peeled and chopped
   fresh ginger**

SALMON:

4 **salmon steaks, 1-inch thick**

salt and pepper, to taste

For glaze: In a small bowl, combine the oil, mustard, maple syrup, soy sauce, lemon juice, and ginger and whisk to blend. Pour half of the sauce into a small, nonreactive casserole.

For salmon: Blot the salmon with paper towels to remove surface moisture. Lightly salt and pepper both sides, and lay the salmon on the sauce in the casserole. Spoon the remaining sauce over and spread evenly. Cover with plastic wrap and refrigerate for 1 hour.

Prepare the grill. Cook the salmon over medium-hot coals for 5 to 6 minutes per side, turning once. **Makes 4 servings.**

Grilled Swordfish With Pineapple Salsa

For more flavor, lightly oil the grill grate, cook the pineapple slices for several minutes, cut, and add to the salsa.

SALSA:

3 or 4 slices pineapple (canned or fresh), cut into chunks (unless grilling)

1 orange, halved and sectioned

3 tablespoons chopped pickled jalapeños

2 scallions, thinly sliced

1 small ripe tomato, cored and diced

2 to 3 tablespoons chopped fresh parsley or cilantro

1 tablespoon brown sugar or honey

SWORDFISH:

4 swordfish steaks, 1-inch thick

vegetable oil

salt and pepper, to taste

For salsa: In a small bowl, combine the salsa ingredients and refrigerate for at least 1 hour. (If you grill the pineapple slices, add them later, cut into chunks.)

For swordfish: Prepare the grill. Rub a little oil onto both sides of the swordfish and season with salt and pepper. Cook over medium-hot coals for 5 to 6 minutes on each side, turning once. The fish should be opaque throughout when it's done. Serve with the salsa. **Makes 4 servings.**

CHAPTER

8

Fish and Seafood

Apple-Stuffed Baked Fish

STUFFING:

1 cup peeled, cored, and grated Golden
   Delicious apple

½ cup peeled, grated carrot

½ cup minced green onion

2 tablespoons fresh lemon juice

¼ teaspoon ground ginger

¼ teaspoon ground mustard

¼ teaspoon salt

¼ teaspoon freshly ground black pepper

⅛ teaspoon dried thyme

FISH:

4 white fish fillets (haddock, cod, sole, or other), 4 to 5 ounces each

½ cup chicken broth or water

Preheat the oven to 400°F. Lightly grease a small roasting pan.

For stuffing: Combine all of the ingredients in a medium bowl.

For fish: Rinse the fillets and pat dry with paper towels. Spread the stuffing mixture over the fillets and carefully roll up lengthwise. Place the stuffed fillets in the pan seam side down. Pour the broth over them and cover with aluminum foil. Bake for 10 to 15 minutes, or until the fish is opaque and barely flakes with a fork. **Makes 4 servings.**

–Art Sager, Agassiz, British Columbia

FISHERMAN'S MATTER

■ Fresh fish will have firm elastic flesh and no smell. Beware of these signs of spoilage: odor along the backbone, pinkish color, ability to float in water.

■ Refrigerate fish until ready to use. Fish that is cleaned and frozen immediately after being caught and is kept frozen until needed does not lose its flavor. Place frozen fish in the refrigerator overnight to thaw.

■ Crabs, lobsters, and other shellfish must be kept alive until cooked; it is best to cook them the day they are purchased. Clams, mussels, and oysters should be wrapped in wet towels or a wet paper bag and kept refrigerated. Stored this way, they can keep for 2 to 3 days.

FISH AND SEAFOOD

Baked Fish Fiesta

2 pounds cusk, cod, or other firm
　　fish fillets
¾ cup dry bread crumbs
4 tablespoons grated Parmesan cheese,
　　divided
2 tablespoons chopped fresh parsley
1 teaspoon salt
¼ teaspoon freshly ground black pepper
1 small clove garlic, minced
¼ cup vegetable oil
3 slices bacon, diced
1 can (8 ounces) stewed tomatoes, drained and chopped
2 hard-boiled eggs, sliced

Preheat the oven to 375°F. Rinse the fillets and pat dry with paper towels. Cut the fish into six equal portions. In a shallow dish, combine the bread crumbs, 2 tablespoons cheese, parsley, salt, pepper, and garlic. Dip each fish piece into the oil, drain, and dredge in the crumb mixture. Place the fillets in an ungreased baking dish. In a skillet, cook the bacon pieces until still soft, and drain. Top each fish portion with a portion of bacon, tomato pieces, and egg slices. Sprinkle with the remaining cheese. Bake for 20 minutes, or until the fish flakes easily with a fork. **Makes 6 servings.**

Savory Baked Haddock

1½ pounds haddock fillets
salt, to taste
½ teaspoon ground mustard
½ cup mayonnaise
1 teaspoon minced onion
1 teaspoon fresh lemon juice
½ teaspoon dried thyme leaves
dash freshly ground black pepper
paprika, for garnish

Preheat the oven to 350°F. Rinse the fillets and pat dry with paper towels. Season the fillets with salt, and arrange them in a greased baking dish. In a small bowl, stir the mustard with 2 teaspoons of water until dissolved. Add the mayonnaise, onion, lemon juice, thyme, and pepper. Spread the mixture on the fish and bake for 25 minutes, or until the top is brown and the fish flakes easily with a fork. Sprinkle with paprika. **Makes 6 servings.**

SQUEEZE

■ To get more juice from a cold lemon, microwave the uncut fruit for 20 seconds, then soften it by rolling it on the counter under the palm of your hand. Cut off one end and use a handheld wooden lemon reamer or a glass juicer.

Haddock Florentine

1½ pounds haddock fillets

2 packages (10 ounces each) frozen chopped spinach, thawed

¼ cup mayonnaise

¼ cup sour cream

¼ cup freshly grated Parmesan cheese, divided

2 tablespoons fresh lemon juice

½ teaspoon freshly ground black pepper

lemon wedges, for garnish

Preheat the oven to 350°F. Rinse the fillets and pat dry with paper towels. Squeeze the spinach to remove excess liquid. In a medium bowl, combine the spinach, mayonnaise, sour cream, and half of the Parmesan cheese. Spread the mixture evenly in an ungreased 13x9-inch baking dish. Arrange the fillets in a single layer on top of the spinach mixture. Sprinkle the fish with lemon juice and pepper. Bake uncovered for 20 to 25 minutes, or until the fish flakes easily with a fork. Sprinkle with the remaining Parmesan cheese. Garnish with lemon wedges. **Makes 4 servings.**

Mediterranean Broiled Fish

2 pounds haddock fillets, ½-inch thick

⅓ cup fresh lemon juice

1 teaspoon dried mint

2 teaspoons dried oregano

1¼ teaspoons salt

¼ teaspoon freshly ground black pepper

2 tablespoons melted butter or olive oil, divided

fresh parsley sprigs or lemon slices, for garnish

Preheat the broiler. Rinse the fillets and pat dry with paper towels. Cut the fish into six equal portions and arrange on a broiler rack. In a small bowl, combine the lemon juice, mint, oregano, salt, and pepper. Brush some of the seasonings onto the fish, and then brush the fish with 1 tablespoon of the melted butter. Place under a broiler 4 inches from the heat. Broil for 5 minutes, turn, brush with more seasonings and butter, and broil for 5 minutes more, or until brown. Remove from broiler and brush again with the seasonings. Garnish with parsley sprigs or lemon slices. **Makes 6 servings.**

Salmon With Winter Vegetables

1½ pounds small to medium red potatoes, washed and cut into halves or quarters (depending on size)

3 cups peeled carrots, cut into 1-inch slices

8 medium leeks (white part only), cut into 2-inch pieces and rinsed well

2 cups chicken broth

4 salmon steaks (6 to 8 ounces each)

¼ cup Dijon-style mustard

¼ cup (½ stick) butter

juice from 2 lemons

In a large saucepan, combine the potatoes, carrots, and leeks. Pour the chicken broth into the pan, bring to a slow boil over medium heat, then reduce heat and bring to a simmer. Cover the pan and steam the vegetables for 15 minutes or until almost soft. Place the salmon on top of the vegetables, and pour 1 cup of water over the fish. Bring the mixture back to a simmer, cover the pan, and steam for 10 to 12 minutes, or until the fish flakes easily with a fork. Transfer the vegetables and salmon to a platter, and cover to keep warm. To the liquid in the pan add the mustard, butter, and lemon juice. Cook uncovered over medium heat for 10 minutes, or until the sauce thickens, stirring occasionally. Pour the sauce over the vegetables and fish or serve separately. **Makes 4 servings.**

FISH AND SEAFOOD

Baked Stuffed Salmon With Garlic Dill Sauce

For best flavor, prepare the stuffing and sauce a day ahead. If a butterfly-filleted salmon is not available, use two skin-on fillets of similar size.

STUFFING:

1 pound white fish fillet

3 large eggs

1 small carrot, peeled and finely grated

1 small onion, grated

1 medium potato, peeled and finely
    grated

1 cup fine cracker crumbs

¼ cup half-and-half, or more as needed

½ teaspoon salt

⅛ teaspoon freshly ground black
    pepper

⅛ teaspoon paprika

SAUCE:

2 cups (1 pint) sour cream

3 tablespoons finely chopped fresh dill

1 large clove garlic, minced

½ teaspoon fresh lemon juice

2 teaspoons sugar

dash salt

SALMON:

1 fresh, butterfly-filleted salmon (2½ to 3 pounds)

salt and pepper, to taste

For stuffing: Steam the white fish until tender. Cool and purée in a food processor. Combine the fish purée with the eggs, carrot, onion, potato, cracker crumbs, and enough half-and-half to bind the mixture. Season with salt, pepper, and paprika. Cover and refrigerate.

For sauce: Combine all of the ingredients in a medium bowl. Cover and refrigerate.

For salmon: Preheat the oven to 425°F. Rinse the salmon and carefully pat dry. Place the butterflied fish, open with the skin side down, in a large roasting pan or on a heavy baking sheet and season lightly with salt and pepper. Spread the prepared stuffing along the length of one fillet flap. (Place any leftover stuffing in a small casserole and bake separately in a 350°F oven for 30 minutes.) Fold the other fillet flap over the stuffing and slide the closed stuffed fish to the center of the pan. Measure the fish at its thickest part and bake for 10 minutes per inch of thickness, or until the fish flakes easily with a fork. Remove from the oven and carefully peel away the top skin. Spread with the prepared sauce. **Makes 8 servings.**

Red Snapper Bake

1½ pounds red snapper fillets

1¼ teaspoons salt

⅛ teaspoon freshly ground black pepper

¼ cup fresh lime juice

2 tablespoons olive oil

¼ cup chopped fresh parsley

1 tablespoon dried oregano

1 teaspoon minced garlic

5 medium tomatoes (1½ pounds), cored
and sliced to ¼-inch thickness

Preheat the oven to 400°F. Rinse the fillets and pat dry with paper towels. Season the snapper with salt and pepper, and place skin side down in an ungreased 13x9-inch baking dish. In a small bowl, combine the lime juice, olive oil, parsley, oregano, and garlic. Pour the lime juice mixture over the fillets and marinate in the refrigerator for 15 minutes. Turn the fish skin side up and arrange tomato slices over the fillets. Bake for 12 to 15 minutes, or until the fish flakes easily with a fork. **Makes 4 servings.**

Fillet of Sole in Galliano Butter

2 pounds sole fillets

⅔ cup butter

⅔ cup whole or slivered blanched
almonds

¼ cup Liquore Galliano

¼ cup fresh lemon juice

¼ cup chopped fresh parsley

salt and pepper, to taste

Rinse the fillets and pat dry with paper towels. Cut into six portions and set aside. In a large skillet, melt the butter. Add the almonds and sauté until lightly toasted. Allow the butter to brown, then stir in the Galliano, lemon juice, parsley, salt, and pepper. Add the fillets. Cover and cook over medium heat for 7 to 10 minutes, or until the fish flakes easily, basting the fish with Galliano butter frequently. **Makes 6 servings.**

Savory Mustard Sole

6 sole fillets (about 4 ounces each)
¼ cup (½ stick) butter, melted
juice of 1 lemon
5 shallots, finely chopped
½ cup dry white wine
1 cup heavy cream
2 tablespoons Dijon-style mustard
¼ teaspoon salt
⅛ teaspoon freshly ground black pepper
6 scallions, sliced

Preheat the oven to 425°F. Rinse the fillets and pat dry with paper towels. Arrange the fillets full-length in an ungreased baking dish. Combine the melted butter with the lemon juice and pour it over the fish. Place the shallots and wine in a saucepan and simmer until the wine is evaporated. In a small bowl, mix together the cream, mustard, salt, and pepper and add to the shallots. Bring to a boil, remove from heat, and set aside to cool. Pour the mustard sauce over the fish and sprinkle with scallions. Bake for 10 minutes, or until the fish flakes easily with a fork. **Makes 6 servings.**

Crisp Batter-Fried Fish

1 to 2 pounds fresh white fish fillets
1 cup quick-cooking rolled oats
½ cup yellow cornmeal
1 cup milk
1 large egg
1 teaspoon baking powder
½ teaspoon salt
1 teaspoon finely chopped fresh dill
vegetable oil, for frying

Rinse the fillets and pat dry with paper towels. Cut into serving portions and set aside.

In a blender, grind the oats to the consistency of coarse flour. Make a batter in a shallow bowl by combining the ground oats, cornmeal, milk, egg, baking powder, salt, and dill. In a heavy skillet, preheat ½ inch of oil to 375°F. Dip the fish fillets into the batter, coating completely. Fry in hot oil for 2 minutes per side, or until golden brown and crisp, turning only once. Drain on paper towels. **Makes 4 to 6 servings.**

QUICK FIX

■ To rid the kitchen of odor after cooking fish, add whole cloves, cinnamon sticks, allspice, or lemon slices to a pan of water and simmer.

Fish Rolls With Lemon Parsley Sauce

FISH:
8 fresh fish fillets
juice of 1 large lemon
1½ cups cold water
1 bay leaf

SAUCE:
½ cup (1 stick) butter or margarine
1 tablespoon chopped fresh parsley
1 tablespoon grated fresh lemon rind

For fish: Rinse the fillets and pat dry with paper towels. Immerse the fish in lemon juice. Remove, reserving the juice. Roll up the fillets lengthwise and secure with toothpicks. Place the fillets into a shallow pan with the cold water and a bay leaf. Bring to a slow boil and cook for 30 seconds. Reduce the heat, cover, and simmer for 5 minutes, or until tender.

For sauce: While fillets are cooking, combine the reserved lemon juice, butter, parsley, and lemon rind in a saucepan. Heat until the butter is melted, stirring frequently. Place the cooked fillets on a hot platter. Remove the toothpicks and pour the lemon-parsley sauce over the fish. **Makes 8 servings.**

Creamed Fish

Serve over warm biscuits or toast or with corn bread.

¼ cup (½ stick) butter
3 tablespoons chopped onion
¼ cup all-purpose flour
2 cups milk
1½ cups flaked cooked fish (salmon, tuna, mackerel)
⅓ cup shredded cheddar cheese
salt and pepper, to taste

In a saucepan, melt the butter, add the onion, and sauté until soft. Add the flour and cook until bubbly, stirring constantly. Add the milk slowly and continue stirring until thickened. Add the fish and cheese, stirring until the cheese is melted and the sauce is smooth. Season to taste. **Makes 4 servings.**

This is one of the most downloaded recipes at Almanac.com/food. Reviewer comments: "Outstanding!" "Easy and elegant . . . great dinner party fare." "This was so good!"

Baked Scallops

2 pounds scallops
½ cup (1 stick) butter, melted
¼ cup grated Parmesan cheese
1 cup crushed Ritz crackers
1 tablespoon fresh lemon juice
¼ teaspoon freshly ground black pepper
¼ teaspoon garlic salt
1 tablespoon dry vermouth

Preheat the oven to 325°F. Rinse the scallops and pat dry with paper towels. Place the scallops in a greased 2-quart casserole or an 8-inch square baking dish. In a bowl, mix together the remaining ingredients and spoon on top. Cover the dish with a lid or aluminum foil and bake for 30 minutes. **Makes 6 servings.**

Scallops Portuguese

1 pound fresh sea scallops
¼ cup (½ stick) butter
1 clove garlic, minced
¼ teaspoon salt
dash of freshly ground black pepper
½ cup chopped fresh parsley

Cut the large scallops in half to make two disks and pat dry with paper towels. In a large heavy skillet, melt the butter, add the garlic and salt, and sauté until golden brown. Add the scallops and cook for 5 to 7 minutes, stirring often. Season with pepper. Add the parsley and cook for 1 minute longer. **Makes 4 servings.**

ABOUT SHRIMP

■ A pound of raw shrimp in the shell (called "green" shrimp) will yield about ½ pound of cooked shrimp without the shells and will serve about three people. Shrimp may be cooked with or without the shells (which add flavor); removing the shells before cooking makes it easier to eat the finished dish. Whether peeled or shell-on, shrimp should be deveined, using the tip of a knife or a pick, before cooking.

If you are using frozen shrimp, defrost them before cooking. Frozen shrimp can be defrosted by placing them in a colander under cold running water for about 5 minutes.

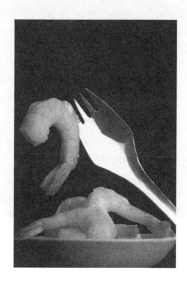

Shrimp With Herb Butter

2 pounds peeled and deveined fresh
    shrimp
2 cloves garlic, minced
½ cup (1 stick) butter, softened
2 tablespoons chopped fresh parsley
2 tablespoons chopped scallions (white
    part only)
1 teaspoon dried tarragon
1 teaspoon dried chervil
½ teaspoon salt
¼ teaspoon freshly ground black pepper
¾ cup dry bread crumbs
⅓ cup dry sherry

Grease a shallow baking dish or individual ramekins. Steam or boil the shrimp until just cooked. Drain them well and set aside. Preheat the oven to 450°F. In a medium bowl, blend the garlic into the butter with a fork. Gradually mash in the parsley, scallions, tarragon, chervil, salt, and pepper. Add the bread crumbs and sherry. Arrange the cooked shrimp in the dish(es), and top with the herb butter. Bake for 5 to 8 minutes, or until the topping is golden and shrimp is heated through. **Makes 4 servings.**

Five-Minute Shrimp

This one-bowl meal is a quick and easy dinner on a busy day, especially if the rice is ready. Vary the vegetables seasonally; broccoli substitutes nicely for snow pea pods.

4 cups chicken stock

1 tablespoon peeled and grated fresh ginger

3 cloves garlic, chopped

2 medium carrots, peeled and sliced

1 stalk celery, sliced

1 cup sliced fresh mushrooms

1 cup snow pea pods, trimmed, large ones cut in half

1½ pounds peeled and deveined fresh shrimp

3 cups warm, cooked rice

In the bottom of a vegetable steamer, combine the stock, ginger, and garlic. Heat to boiling. Put the carrots, celery, mushrooms, and snow pea pods into the steamer basket and cook over the boiling stock for 2 minutes. Add the shrimp and steam for 3 minutes more. Place a portion of cooked rice into a soup bowl, then add steamed vegetables, shrimp, and stock. **Makes 4 servings.**

Seafood Casserole

1½ pounds peeled and deveined fresh shrimp

1 pound fresh lump crabmeat, drained

1½ pounds scallops

2 tablespoons chopped fresh parsley

2 cloves garlic, minced

1 teaspoon salt

1 teaspoon freshly ground black pepper

½ cup (1 stick) butter, melted

4 cups shredded mozzarella or Monterey Jack cheese

Preheat the oven to 350°F. Grease a deep casserole and arrange the shrimp on the bottom. Spread the crabmeat in an even layer over the shrimp and then add the scallops. Sprinkle with the parsley, garlic, salt, and pepper. Drizzle with the melted butter, and top with cheese. Bake for 45 minutes. **Makes 8 servings.**

How to Cook a Lobster

■ In June 1979, *Yankee* Magazine published the story of Bertha Nunan, owner of the Lobster Hut in Cape Porpoise, Maine, and arguably America's most famous lobster cook. Inside the Hut's cramped kitchen, Nunan shared her secrets to cooking lobster. The lobster was great then, and it's great today. The Hut served its first lobster in 1953, and the pace there has never slowed. Although Bertha's sons have taken over the business, the Hut serves as much as 700 pounds of lobster on a typical summer night. It seems that a Nunan lobster is something no one's taste buds can forget. To make your own great-tasting lobster, here again are Nunan's tips.

"When you buy lobsters," she says, "you should know that from winter to summer the lobsters are hard-shelled. They're packed full of meat then, and you need fewer lobsters for a pound of meat if you're making stew. But I prefer them when they're soft-shelled. They're sweeter then.

"The secret to cooking lobsters is to not murder them. Give them a nice, slow, respectable way out. Don't put them in boiling water, and don't drown them in too much water.

"Boiling them in a lot of water just boils their flavor out, and too much water waterlogs them. I put in two inches of water, whether I'm cooking two lobsters or 14. I take a salt container and with the spout open I pour it three times around the pot, then I give a plop! at the end (about 3 teaspoons). Then I put in the lobsters, put the lid on, turn the heat on, and steam them for 20 minutes. Not a minute less or a minute more.

"When they're done, draw up your butter and serve the lobster with a dish of vinegar as well. Now, the next step is what a lot of people, and practically all restaurants, ignore. It's why people tell me our lobsters taste the best of any they ever had.

"I always wash the pot after each lobster cook. Lobsters are scavengers, and they can get pretty greasy from the bait. Look in the pot the next time you cook them and you'll see a sediment from the shell. So I always put in fresh salted water for every batch of lobsters.

"I'll never stop being surprised at what some people will do to a lobster. Some folks, to save time, precook their lobsters. When people arrive, they throw them in boiling water for a minute. That's the worst thing you can do. The lobster just fills with water. If you're eating lobster in a restaurant and when you crack it open water spurts everywhere, you can bet they just threw a precooked lobster in boiling water."

Lobster Newburg

3 tablespoons butter or margarine

3 tablespoons all-purpose flour

½ teaspoon salt

1½ cups milk

2 cups cooked, chopped lobster

1 cup sliced celery

2 tablespoons chili sauce

2 teaspoons fresh lemon juice

dash paprika

fresh parsley sprigs or olive slices, for garnish

In a saucepan, melt the butter and blend in the flour and salt. Remove from the heat. Gradually add the milk, stirring until the mixture is smooth. Return to the stove and cook over medium heat, stirring constantly, until the mixture boils and thickens. Reduce the heat and simmer for 1 minute. Add the lobster, celery, chili sauce, lemon juice, and paprika. Heat through and serve. Garnish with sprigs of parsley or olive slices. **Makes 4 servings.**

Hearty Lobster Stew

A good stew to serve as a main course. The "aging" in the refrigerator brings out the true and delicate flavor of the lobster.

¼ cup (½ stick) butter

2 cups boiled lobster meat, cut into pieces

1 quart scalded milk or half-and-half

salt and pepper, to taste

Melt the butter in a heavy kettle over low heat. Add the lobster meat and cook slowly until the rich pink of the lobster colors the butter. Stir constantly to prevent scorching. Remove from the heat, cool slightly, and slowly stir in the scalded milk. Add salt and pepper to taste. Refrigerate the stew for 5 to 6 hours; reheat before serving. **Makes 2 to 4 servings.**

Sauces

A tangy sauce will enhance the flavor of fish, whether it is fried, baked, or broiled. Pour the sauce on the fish just before serving or pass it for individual servings.

Butter Sauce

½ cup (1 stick) butter, melted
3 tablespoons fish broth
2 hard-boiled eggs, chopped,
    or ¼ cup chopped green onion
2 tablespoons capers, drained, or 2 tablespoons lemon juice

Mix all of the ingredients in a pan. Heat thoroughly. **Makes 1 cup.**

White Sauce

3 tablespoons butter or margarine
3 tablespoons all-purpose flour
1 cup milk
salt and white pepper, to taste

In a double boiler top or small heavy pan, melt the butter and stir in the flour. Blend over low heat and slowly stir in the milk. Bring to a boil, stirring constantly. Cook for 2 minutes. Remove from the heat and season with salt and pepper. **Makes 1 cup.**

Tartar Sauce

For variety, add a pinch of savory.

½ cup mayonnaise
2 tablespoons finely chopped sweet pickles
1 tablespoon minced fresh parsley
2 teaspoons finely grated onion
½ teaspoon Worcestershire sauce

Put the ingredients into a container or jar with a secure lid. Stir to blend thoroughly, cover tightly, and shake vigorously. Refrigerate to meld the flavors. **Makes ⅔ cup.**

Cheese Sauce

1 cup white sauce (recipe above)
¾ cup shredded cheddar cheese
2 tablespoons sherry

Combine all of the ingredients in a saucepan and heat until the cheese melts, stirring to blend. **Makes 2 cups.**

Cucumber Dill Sauce With Capers

1 cup diced, peeled, and seeded cucumber

2 tablespoons butter

2 tablespoons all-purpose flour

2 teaspoons fresh lemon juice

1 teaspoon grated lemon peel

1 teaspoon grated onion

½ teaspoon salt

freshly ground black pepper, to taste

1 tablespoon fresh chopped dill

1 tablespoon capers, drained

In a saucepan, cook the cucumber with ½ cup of water on medium heat until tender and clear, about 3 to 5 minutes. Drain, reserving the liquid, and set aside. Add enough water to the reserved liquid to equal 1 cup, and set aside. In the saucepan, melt the butter and blend in the flour over medium heat. Slowly add the reserved cooking water, stirring constantly, until the mixture is smooth and thickened. Add the lemon juice, lemon peel, onion, salt, pepper, dill, capers, and the cucumbers. Heat thoroughly and serve warm. **Makes 1¾ cups.**

Seafood Sauce

½ cup chili sauce

⅓ cup prepared horseradish

⅓ cup ketchup

¼ cup minced celery

2 tablespoons fresh lemon juice

1½ teaspoons Worcestershire sauce

¼ teaspoon salt

⅛ teaspoon freshly ground black pepper

Put the ingredients into a container or jar and stir until well blended. Cover and refrigerate to meld the flavors. **Makes about 1½ cups.**

Hollandaise Sauce

Serve this sauce with fish, eggs, or vegetables.

2 large egg yolks

⅛ teaspoon salt

1 tablespoon cold water

½ cup (1 stick) unsalted butter, melted

1 tablespoon fresh lemon juice

pinch cayenne pepper

In the top of a double boiler, whisk together the egg yolks, salt, and cold water. Stir over low heat until the mixture is warm. Slowly pour in half of the melted butter, stirring constantly. Continue adding the melted butter and stirring, until the sauce thickens. Whisk in the lemon juice and cayenne pepper and serve warm. **Makes about 1 cup.**

NOTE

If the sauce begins to separate, whisk in 1 or 2 tablespoons of cream until it's smooth again.

Stuffing

Whether cooked with fish or served on the side, stuffing adds body to a dish.

Basic Stuffing

3 tablespoons butter or margarine

¼ cup finely chopped onion

¼ cup finely chopped celery

1 cup soft bread cubes

¾ cup peeled, grated carrot

½ teaspoon salt

freshly ground black pepper, to taste

In a large skillet, melt the butter, add the onion and celery, and sauté until tender but not browned. Remove from the heat. Add the bread cubes, carrot, and seasonings. Mix thoroughly. **Makes 1¼ cups.**

Tomato Bread Stuffing

Enjoy this stuffing with cod, haddock, or other white fish.

¼ cup (½ stick) butter or margarine

¼ cup finely chopped onion

¼ cup finely chopped celery

2 cups soft bread cubes

¼ teaspoon salt

¼ teaspoon dried thyme, dried mint, or
**   poultry seasoning**

freshly ground black pepper, to taste

1 medium tomato, cored and chopped

In a large skillet, melt the butter, add the onion and celery, and sauté for 5 minutes, or until tender. Remove from the heat and combine with the bread cubes. Add the seasonings and tomato, and mix thoroughly. **Makes about 2⅓ cups.**

Rice Stuffing

¼ cup (½ stick) butter or margarine

¼ cup diced celery

¼ cup minced onion

¼ cup diced green bell pepper

½ cup sliced fresh mushrooms

1 teaspoon salt

⅛ teaspoon freshly ground black pepper

¼ teaspoon dried tarragon

¼ teaspoon dried marjoram

¼ to ½ cup fish stock or water

3 cups cooked brown rice

In a large skillet, melt the butter. Add the celery, onion, and bell pepper, and cook until tender. Add the mushrooms, seasonings, and stock. Combine with the rice and mix thoroughly. **Makes 4 cups, enough to stuff one large fish.**

JUST PLAIN STUFFED

■ Don't make stuffing ahead of time. It should be prepared just before you are ready to use it.

■ Don't compact your stuffing by pressing or pushing it down. Fluff it gently with a fork and spoon it lightly into place. Stuffing will expand as it cooks.

CHAPTER

9

Pasta, Potatoes, and Rice

Italian Potato Torte

3 pounds white potatoes, peeled and cut into pieces

1½ cups milk

¼ cup (½ stick) butter

3 tablespoons olive oil

3 cloves garlic, minced

2 teaspoons dried parsley, crumbled

1 teaspoon dried basil, crumbled

1 teaspoon salt

½ teaspoon freshly ground black pepper

½ cup grated Asiago cheese

Preheat the oven to 350°F. Lightly grease a 3-quart casserole with olive oil. Place the potatoes into a large pot with enough water to cover. Bring to a boil over medium-high heat, reduce the heat, and simmer uncovered until the potatoes are tender. Drain, return to the pot, and set aside. In a small saucepan, heat the milk and butter over medium heat until the milk begins to steam and butter is melted. Add the milk to the potatoes and mash with a potato masher. In a small skillet, warm the olive oil over medium heat until fragrant. Add the garlic and sauté until it begins to brown. Add the oil and garlic to the potatoes, and stir in the parsley, basil, salt, pepper, and cheese. Spoon the potatoes into the casserole and bake uncovered until lightly browned, about 15 to 20 minutes. **Makes 8 to 10 servings.**

–*Deborah Coberly Goranflo, La Grange, Kentucky*

HEALTH HINT

To seal in vitamin C, add a pinch of sugar—not salt—to potato-boiling water.

Potato Pancakes With Maple Sausage

2½ cups mashed potatoes

1 large Granny Smith apple, peeled,
    cored, and grated

8 ounces maple-flavored sausage,
    browned and crumbled

2 scallions, chopped

2 large eggs

⅓ cup all-purpose flour

½ teaspoon salt

½ teaspoon freshly ground white pepper

vegetable oil, for frying

6 to 8 tablespoons sour cream (optional)

In a large bowl, combine the first eight ingredients. In a large skillet, heat 1½ tablespoons of oil on medium-low. Drop enough batter into the skillet to make 4-inch pancakes. Fry for 5 minutes on each side, or until browned. Remove and drain on paper towels. Repeat with the remaining batter, adding oil to the skillet between batches as needed. Serve immediately, with 1 tablespoon of sour cream on each pancake, if desired. **Makes 6 to 8 servings.**

–Deborah Puette, Lilburn, Georgia

Crispy Potato Quiche

1 package (24 ounces) frozen shredded
    hash browns, thawed (or substitute
    4 heaping cups shredded, blanched
    potatoes)

⅓ cup butter, melted

1 cup shredded hot-pepper cheese

1 cup shredded Swiss cheese

1 cup diced cooked ham

½ cup half-and-half

2 large eggs

¼ teaspoon seasoned salt

Preheat the oven to 425°F. Grease a 9-inch pie plate. Press the hash browns between paper towels to remove excess moisture. Press the hash browns into the pie dish, forming a solid crust. Brush the crust with melted butter, especially the top edges. Bake for 25 minutes, or until golden. Remove and reduce the oven temperature to 350°F. Spread the cheeses and ham evenly on the crust. In a separate bowl, beat the half-and-half with the eggs and salt. Pour the liquid over the cheese and ham. Bake uncovered for 30 to 40 minutes, or until a knife inserted into the center comes out clean. **Makes 8 servings.**

–Amy Kerby, Omaha, Nebraska

PASTA, POTATOES, AND RICE

Marinara Sauce

3 to 4 tablespoons olive oil
5 cloves garlic, finely chopped
2 cans (28 ounces each) Italian plum
    tomatoes
1½ tablespoons dried basil
2 teaspoons dried oregano

In a large skillet or saucepan, heat the olive oil over medium heat. Add the garlic and cook until light brown. Add the tomatoes and, using a potato masher or fork, break them into small pieces. Add the basil and oregano. Simmer, uncovered for 30 minutes or until the sauce thickens to desired consistency. **Makes about 6 cups.**

NOTE
To use as pizza sauce, cook for 45 to 60 minutes.

Alfredo Sauce

¼ cup (½ stick) butter
1 cup heavy cream
1 clove garlic, crushed
1½ cups freshly grated Parmesan or
    Gruyère cheese
¼ teaspoon ground nutmeg (optional)
¼ cup chopped fresh parsley

Melt the butter in a saucepan over medium-low heat. Add the cream and simmer for 5 minutes, then add the garlic, cheese, and nutmeg (if desired) and whisk quickly, heating through. Stir in the parsley and serve over pasta. **Makes 2½ cups.**

–Rebecca Swift

Baked Pasta With Fresh Tomatoes and Smoked Mozzarella

This dish can be prepared a day ahead, refrigerated, and brought to room temperature before baking.

4 tablespoons olive oil, divided

1 red onion, chopped

3 cloves garlic, minced

5 plum tomatoes, seeded and chopped

1 pound uncooked linguine or vermicelli

½ cup (1 stick) butter, melted and divided

8 ounces smoked mozzarella cheese, cubed

¼ cup chopped fresh Italian parsley

salt and pepper, to taste

1 cup fresh bread crumbs

Preheat the oven to 375°F. Grease a 2-quart oven-proof casserole. In a skillet, heat 3 tablespoons of olive oil, add the onion and garlic, and sauté for 5 minutes, or until the onion is transparent. Add the tomatoes and sauté for 5 minutes.

Cook the pasta in a large pot of boiling, salted water until al dente. Drain and toss with the remaining 1 tablespoon of olive oil. Place the pasta in a large mixing bowl and add ¼ cup of the melted butter, the tomato-onion mixture, cheese, and parsley. Toss well and season with salt and pepper. Pour into the casserole.

Combine the remaining ¼ cup melted butter with the bread crumbs and sprinkle on top. Bake uncovered for 20 to 25 minutes. Place under the broiler for 30 seconds to brown the bread crumbs. **Makes 6 to 8 servings.**

PASTA, POTATOES, AND RICE

Noodle Names

■ Ever wonder why pasta comes in so many shapes and sizes? To complement the sauce. Thin, delicate pastas should be used with light, thin sauces; more substantial shapes work well with heavier sauces; and sturdy shapes, such as ziti or radiatore, work best with chunky sauce. Here are some of the most common shapes in their Italian names, with translations and serving suggestions.

CAPELLINI
(angel hair)
Break up for use in soups, salads, and stir-fries; use with thin, delicate sauce

CONCHIGLIE
(shells)
Perfect for soups and salads or baked in a casserole; jumbo shells can be stuffed

DITALINI
(little thimbles)
Use in soups, salads, stir-fries, and baked dishes

FARFALLE
(bow ties, butterflies)
Use in soups and salads or with any sauce

FETTUCCINE
(small ribbons)
Break up for use in soups and salads; good for heavier cheese, meat, and tomato sauces

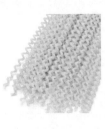

FUSILLI
(twisted spaghetti)
Break up and use in soups and salads; good in casseroles; use with any sauce

LASAGNA
(from lasania, *Latin for "cooking pot")*
Sturdy, perfect for casseroles; use with any sauce

LINGUINE
(little tongues)
Use in salads and stir-fries or with any sauce

MACARONI
(dumpling)
Use in soups, salads, and casseroles or with any sauce

MANICOTTI
(small muffs)
Perfect for stuffing; serve with any sauce

MOSTACCIOLI
(small mustaches)
Use in soups, stir-fries, and casseroles or with any sauce

ORZO
(barley)
Use in soups and casseroles, as a side dish, or with any sauce

PENNE
(quills)
Use in soups, stir-fries, and casseroles or with any sauce

RADIATORE
(radiators)
Use in soups, salads, and casseroles or with any sauce

RIGATONI
(large grooved)
Perfect with any sauce— from cheese sauce to the chunkiest meat sauce

ROTINI
(spirals or twists)
Use in soups, salads, stir-fries, and casseroles or with any sauce

RUOTE
(wagon wheels)
Use in soups, salads, and stir-fries or with any sauce

SPAGHETTI
(a length of cord)
Use in stir-fries and casseroles or with any sauce

VERMICELLI
(little worms)
A bit thinner than spaghetti; good with all sauces

ZITI
(bridegrooms)
Use in salads, stir-fries, and baked dishes; good with chunky sauces

—information courtesy National Pasta Association

HOW MUCH IS ENOUGH?

■ **Allow these amounts for each single serving of pasta.**

Long Pasta Shapes (spaghetti, linguine, fettuccine):
2 ounces uncooked = ½-inch-diameter bundle dry = 1 cup cooked

Short Pasta Shapes (elbows, macaroni, twists, shells, mostaccioli, ziti):
2 ounces uncooked = just over ½ cup dry = 1 cup cooked

Egg Noodles:
2 ounces uncooked = ½ cup dry = just over ½ cup cooked

Perfect Macaroni and Cheese

A cheddar such as Grafton or Tillamook gives this dish legendary flavor. Heat up leftovers, covered, in the microwave, rather than in the oven, so that they don't get too dry the second day.

1 pound uncooked macaroni

TOPPING:
½ cup soft bread crumbs
1 tablespoon butter

SAUCE:
3 tablespoons butter
3 tablespoons flour
2½ cups milk
salt and pepper, to taste
4 cups (1 pound) shredded cheddar
    cheese

Preheat the oven to 350°F. Grease a 3-quart casserole.

Cook the pasta in a large pot of boiling, salted water until al dente. Drain and set aside the pot.

For topping: In a small skillet, melt the butter, add the bread crumbs, and sauté for 1 to 2 minutes. Remove and set aside.

For sauce: In a heavy, medium saucepan, melt the butter over low heat. Stir in the flour with a whisk and cook for several minutes, stirring occasionally. In a separate saucepan, heat the milk to almost boiling, and add it to the butter and flour. Cook, stirring constantly, until the mixture thickens. Season with salt and pepper.

Put one-third of the macaroni in the bottom of the casserole. Cover it with one-third of the cheese, then pour one-third of the sauce over the cheese. Repeat, making two more layers. Spoon buttered bread crumbs over the top. Bake for 25 to 30 minutes. **Makes 6 to 8 servings.**

Not Your Average Tuna Casserole

A new twist on an old favorite.

1 tablespoon butter

⅓ cup chopped celery

¼ cup chopped onion

3½ cups uncooked egg noodles*

1 can (12 ounces) tuna, drained and flaked

1¼ cups fresh mushrooms, chopped

20 extra-large pitted black olives, sliced

1 cup shredded Monterey Jack cheese

dash freshly ground black pepper

1½ cups sour cream

TOPPING:

¾ cup shredded Monterey Jack cheese

6 to 8 pitted black olives, sliced

Preheat the oven to 350°F. Sauté the celery and onion in the butter to soften. Cook the noodles according to package directions, rinse, drain, and put into a large mixing bowl. Add the tuna, sautéed celery and onion, mushrooms, olives, 1 cup of cheese, and pepper and mix well. Blend in the sour cream. Spread the mixture into a 2-quart oblong casserole or baking dish. Top with ¾ cup of cheese and sliced olives and bake for 25 to 30 minutes, or until bubbly. **Makes about 6 servings.**

*You can substitute any of your favorite pasta shapes.

VARIATION

Mix tuna, celery, onion, and 1 cup of shredded cheese into the cooked noodles. Stir in ½ teaspoon of thyme and ¼ teaspoon of oregano, then add 1 cup of sour cream, ½ cup of mayonnaise, and 1 tablespoon of prepared mustard. Blend well. Spread the mixture into a baking dish. Cut a small zucchini into thin slices and tuck half of the slices into the noodle mixture. Top with the remaining slices of zucchini, several thin slices of tomato, and ¾ cup of shredded Monterey Jack cheese. Bake as above.

CHEESE BITS

When a recipe calls for shredded, crumbled, or grated cheese, use these guidelines for purchasing cheese by weight:

4 ounces regular cheese = 1 cup shredded

4 ounces blue or feta cheese = 1 cup crumbled

3 ounces hard-grating cheese = 1 cup grated

Egg Noodles With Spinach and Cheese

1 package (10 ounces) frozen chopped
    spinach, thawed
1 tablespoon olive oil
½ teaspoon dried basil
8 ounces wide egg noodles
1 cup ricotta cheese
salt and pepper, to taste
¼ cup grated Romano cheese

Squeeze excess water from the thawed spinach. Heat the oil in a skillet and sauté the spinach with the basil for 5 minutes. Cook the egg noodles according to package directions. Drain, cover, and set aside. Add the ricotta to the spinach, mix to blend, season with salt and pepper, and cook over low heat for 5 minutes, or until heated through. Toss the noodles with the spinach mixture and sprinkle with Romano cheese. **Makes 4 servings.**

Peanut Sesame Noodles

2 pounds Chinese egg noodles
½ cup sesame oil
½ cup soy sauce
3 tablespoons Chinese black vinegar
2 tablespoons peanut butter
1 tablespoon hot pepper oil
½ cup finely sliced scallions

In a large pot of boiling water, cook the noodles for about 5 minutes, or until just tender. Drain and rinse under cold water until chilled. Drain again. Put the noodles into a large bowl and set aside.

In a small bowl, use a whisk to combine the remaining ingredients. Stir the sauce into the cold noodles and mix well. If necessary, use your hands to distribute the sauce evenly. Chill overnight. **Makes 10 to 12 servings.**

Baked Ziti

At one time, this dish was known as American chop suey, for the Chinese phrase that literally means "mixed pieces" and has come to mean odds and ends. One theory holds that it was invented in New York on August 29, 1896, by cooks for the Chinese diplomat Li Hongzhang, who ate no Western food. Vary it with ground pork, peppers, or other ingredients, based on preference or availability.

8 ounces uncooked ziti or elbow macaroni

3 tablespoons olive oil

1 pound ground beef

1 cup chopped onion

½ cup chopped celery

3 cups (8 ounces) sliced fresh mushrooms

1 clove garlic, minced

1 teaspoon dried oregano

salt and pepper, to taste

1 jar (14 ounces) spaghetti sauce, or
**   2 cups homemade sauce**

1 cup (4 ounces) shredded mozzarella

Preheat the oven to 350°F. Lightly grease a 13x9-inch baking dish with olive oil. In a large pot of boiling water, cook the pasta for 5 minutes. Drain, rinse if desired, and set aside. In a large, heavy skillet, heat the oil on medium-high, add the beef and onions, and sauté, breaking up the beef as it cooks. Add the celery, mushrooms, and garlic, and cook for 3 minutes. Mix in the seasonings, then spoon the meat mixture into the pot of drained pasta and stir in the sauce. Pour the contents into the baking dish and sprinkle the cheese on top. Cover loosely with aluminum foil and bake for 35 minutes. **Makes 6 servings.**

Pasta With Tuna, Tomatoes, and Olives

Versatile, tasty, and convenient, canned tuna is a staple for a fast, uncooked sauce.

1 pound uncooked pasta

2 cans (6 ounces each) oil- or water-packed
  tuna, drained and flaked

2 cups chopped fresh tomatoes

½ cup pitted Kalamata olives

½ cup olive oil

½ cup chopped red onion

¼ cup chopped fresh basil

salt and pepper, to taste

Cook the pasta in a large pot of boiling, salted water until al dente. While the pasta cooks, make the sauce by combining the remaining ingredients in a large serving bowl. Drain the pasta and toss with the sauce. **Makes 4 to 6 servings.**

Pasta With Shrimp and Peas

This dish is as pretty as it is tasty, and fast, too—ready in the time it takes to cook the noodles.

1 box (10 ounces) uncooked ruote
  (wagon-wheel pasta)

1 tablespoon butter

1 cup sliced new baby onions or scallions

2 cups shelled green peas (2 pounds in the
  shell)

1 cup heavy cream

½ cup shredded fresh basil, or to taste

1½ tablespoons fresh lime juice, or to taste

½ teaspoon salt, or to taste

3 cups cooked, peeled, very small shrimp

Cook the ruote in a large pot of boiling, salted water until al dente. While the pasta cooks, melt the butter in a large, nonstick skillet over medium heat. Add the onion and cook for 3 minutes, or until translucent, stirring frequently. Add the peas and cream, heat to just below boiling, and cook for 3 to 4 minutes, or until the peas are bright green. Add ½ cup of the basil, then the lime juice, salt, and shrimp. Heat through, then taste and add more basil, lime juice, and/or salt, if desired. Turn off the heat, but leave the pan on the burner to keep warm until the pasta is cooked. When the pasta is ready, drain it and toss it with the sauce. **Makes 4 servings.**

Seaside Lasagna

SAUCE:

¼ cup olive oil

4 cloves garlic, finely chopped

¼ cup minced scallions

2 tablespoons butter

⅓ cup dry white wine

1 teaspoon Dijon-style mustard

1½ tablespoons fresh lemon juice

3 cups (8 ounces) sliced fresh mushrooms

1½ teaspoons dried basil

½ teaspoon dried oregano

1 pound peeled, deveined, and halved medium shrimp

¾ pound bay scallops

3 cans (6.5 ounces each) chopped clams; drain 2 cans; reserve the liquid from 1 can

2 cups grated Parmesan cheese, divided

PASTA:

8 ounces uncooked lasagna noodles

FILLING:

1 container (15 ounces) ricotta cheese

2½ cups shredded mozzarella cheese

For sauce: In a large skillet, heat the olive oil. Add the garlic and scallions and sauté for 3 to 5 minutes. Add the butter, wine, mustard, and lemon juice, stirring until the mustard is dissolved. Add the mushrooms and cook until tender. Add the basil and oregano, then the shrimp and scallops, and cook until the shrimp is pink. Add the clams and the reserved liquid. Add ½ cup of the Parmesan cheese, stir, and heat until bubbly. Set the sauce aside.

Preheat the oven to 350°F. Grease a 13x9-inch baking dish.

For pasta: Cook the lasagna in a large pot of boiling, salted water until al dente. Drain, rinse, then fill the pot—with the noodles in it—with cold water, so that they won't dry out or stick together. Set aside for assembly.

To assemble: Cover the bottom of the baking dish with sauce, add a layer of noodles, then follow with one layer each of ricotta cheese, sauce, mozzarella, a portion of the remaining Parmesan, and then noodles again. (Alternate the direction of the noodles to prevent slipping.) Repeat the layers until all of the ingredients are used, ending with sauce topped with cheese. Cover with foil and bake for 40 minutes, then cook uncovered for 10 minutes, or until the cheese on top is golden brown. Remove from the oven and let stand for 15 minutes before serving. **Makes 6 servings.**

PASTA, POTATOES, AND RICE

Shells With Crabmeat Stuffing

24 uncooked jumbo pasta shells

STUFFING:

1 pound crabmeat, cooked and chopped

1 cup cottage cheese

1 cup ricotta cheese

1 cup freshly grated Parmesan cheese

1 large egg

¼ cup finely chopped fresh parsley

¼ teaspoon freshly ground black pepper

1 tablespoon dry sherry

VELOUTÉ SAUCE:

2 tablespoons butter

2 tablespoons all-purpose flour

2 cups chicken stock, heated

pinch of nutmeg

TOPPING:

2 tablespoons seasoned dry bread crumbs

Preheat the oven to 375°F. Grease a 13x9-inch baking dish.

Cook the shells according to package directions. Drain and rinse, then fill the pot—with the noodles in it—with cold water, so that they won't dry out or stick together. Set aside.

For stuffing: In a large mixing bowl, combine the crabmeat, cheeses, egg, parsley, pepper, and sherry.

For sauce: In a medium saucepan, melt the butter and stir in the flour. Gradually whisk in the heated stock, cooking and stirring until thick and smooth. Remove from the heat and add the nutmeg.

To assemble: Stuff each shell with the crabmeat mixture and arrange in the baking dish. Pour the sauce over the stuffed shells, sprinkle bread crumbs on top, cover, and bake for 30 minutes. **Makes 6 servings.**

BON APPÉTIT

A velouté sauce, a classic in French cooking, is a white sauce that uses a light stock such as veal, chicken, or fish—instead of milk—and is thickened with butter and flour.

PASTA, POTATOES, AND RICE

USE THE RIGHT SPUD

Not just any potato can be used for any dish. For best results, use a potato that is for a specific purpose.

PURPOSE	TYPE
Baking	Blue/purple, fingerling, russet, yellow
French fries	Russet, white, yellow
Mashing	Russet, white, yellow
Pancakes	Yellow, 'Yukon Gold'
Panfrying	Red
Purées	Fingerling
Roasting	Red, russet, white, yellow
Salads, scallops, gratins	Red, white, purple
Soups, chowders	Red, white
Steaming	Blue/purple, fingerling, white, yellow

Easy Dill Potato Soufflé

2 cups mashed potatoes, at room
temperature

½ cup milk

3 large eggs, separated

1 tablespoon grated Parmesan cheese

1 tablespoon chopped fresh dill

½ teaspoon salt

⅛ teaspoon freshly ground white
pepper

Preheat the oven to 375°F. Grease a casserole. In a medium bowl, whip the milk into the potatoes using an electric mixer. In a separate bowl and using a fork, beat the egg yolks until thick and pale. Blend the yolks into the potatoes, and add the cheese, dill, salt, and pepper. Clean and dry the beaters. In a copper or stainless steel bowl, beat the egg whites at high speed until soft peaks form and fold into the potatoes. Spoon the potatoes into the casserole and bake for 30 minutes, or until the top is puffy and golden brown. **Makes 4 servings.**

MARVELOUS MASHED

■ Here are some ways to add variety to ordinary mashed potatoes and a little flair to your meal.

Cook equal amounts of parsnips and potatoes together and mash them.

Mash several cloves of roasted garlic into the potatoes.

For smooth mashed potatoes, use hot milk, not cold.

For fluffy mashed potatoes, keep the heat on low under the pan while mashing and continue stirring until all excess water has evaporated. Then blend in the milk.

Just before serving, stir in a few tablespoons of chopped fresh chives or parsley into mashed potatoes.

Roasted Garlic Mashed Potatoes

8 cloves garlic

2 teaspoons olive oil

3 cups potatoes, peeled and diced

2 teaspoons salt

½ cup cream

½ teaspoon freshly ground black
  pepper

2 tablespoons butter

Preheat the oven to 350°F. Peel the garlic cloves, toss with the olive oil, wrap in foil, and roast for 30 minutes, or until soft. Meanwhile, in a medium pan, bring 4 cups of water to a boil. Add the potatoes and salt, and simmer for 10 minutes, or until the potatoes are cooked. Drain. Mash the potatoes with the cream, roasted garlic, and pepper. Stir in the butter. **Makes 4 servings.**

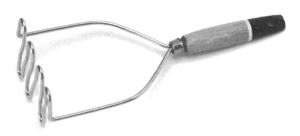

Potato Knishes

A traditional Eastern European food, a knish is a round or square of dough that is filled with potatoes, meat, or cheese. They can be baked or fried and served hot or cold, and go well with pot roast.

DOUGH:

2 cups all-purpose flour

¼ teaspoon salt

1 large egg

1 large egg white

1 tablespoon vegetable oil

oil or melted butter for coating dough

FILLING:

⅓ cup butter

½ cup minced onion

4 cups mashed potatoes

salt and pepper, to taste

For dough: In a large bowl, combine the flour and salt, mound it, and make a well in the center. Put the egg and egg white into the well and, using a fork, stir them into the flour. Add the oil, plus water as needed (a tablespoon at a time, up to ½ cup), mixing until all of the flour is moistened and the dough is slightly sticky. Knead the dough until the stickiness subsides, then shape it into a ball, coat lightly with oil, and place in a clean bowl. Cover and let stand for 30 minutes. Lightly flour the work surface, roll out the dough to form a large circle, then pull the circle gently with your fingers until the dough is very thin. Brush the surface with oil.

For filling: Preheat the oven to 400°F. In a skillet, melt the butter, add the onion, and sauté until tender. Add the mashed potatoes, combine thoroughly, and season with salt and pepper. Shape the filling into a log, place it along one edge of the dough, and roll the dough around it. Pinch together the top and bottom of the dough layers to seal, and cut into 2-inch slices, using a sharp knife. If desired, pull the dough over the filling in each slice and tuck into the knish. Bake on a greased baking sheet for 20 to 30 minutes, or until the dough is browned. **Makes 6 to 8 knishes.**

THE POTATO-IN-WATER TEST

■ To determine what kind of potatoes you have, drop one in a pot containing 11 parts water to one part salt. Waxy potatoes, best for salads, will float. Mealy potatoes, best for baking or mashing, will sink.

Potato Onion Squares

A nice change from baked or mashed potatoes at dinner or tasty served alone for brunch.

2 pounds potatoes, peeled
¼ cup (½ stick) butter
2 cups finely chopped onion
1 cup grated cheddar or Swiss cheese,
    divided
2 large eggs
1 tablespoon all-purpose flour
½ cup sour cream
½ cup milk
½ teaspoon salt
¼ teaspoon freshly ground black pepper

Preheat the oven to 375°F. Grease a 13x9-inch baking dish. Grate the potatoes, blanch them, and drain well. Squeeze out the excess moisture by hand and then press them between paper towels. In a large skillet, melt the butter, add the onion, and sauté until translucent. Add the potatoes. Cook for 4 minutes, stirring often to prevent sticking. Remove from the heat and stir in ½ cup of the grated cheese. Spread the mixture into the baking dish. In a bowl, whisk together the eggs, flour, sour cream, milk, salt, and pepper. Pour over the potato mixture and top with the remaining cheese. Bake for 45 minutes, or until golden brown. Cool slightly before cutting into squares. **Makes 8 servings.**

Scalloped Potatoes

5 to 6 medium baking potatoes, peeled
salt and pepper, to taste
¼ cup (½ stick) butter
1 cup shredded sharp cheddar cheese,
    divided
¼ cup chopped onion
2 tablespoons all-purpose flour
2 cups whole milk

Preheat the oven to 400°F. Grease an 11x7-inch baking dish. Slice the potatoes into ¼-inch-thick rounds. Layer half of the potatoes in the baking dish, season with salt and pepper, dot with butter, and add half of the cheese, the onions, and the flour. Repeat with layers of potatoes, salt and pepper, butter, onions, and flour, but not cheese. In a medium pan, heat the milk to scalding and pour over the layered potatoes. Cover with foil and bake for 45 minutes. Carefully remove the foil, sprinkle with the remaining ½ cup of cheese, and bake uncovered for another 15 minutes. **Makes 8 servings.**

Cheesy Potato Casserole

9 medium potatoes, peeled and diced

⅓ cup butter or margarine

⅓ cup all-purpose flour

2¼ cups milk

¼ cup chopped onion

¼ cup chopped fresh parsley

2 tablespoons chopped fresh chives

¼ teaspoon salt

¼ teaspoon freshly ground white pepper

1 cup grated white cheddar cheese

3 tablespoons grated Parmesan cheese

3 tablespoons dry bread crumbs

Boil the potatoes in a large pot for 25 minutes, or until tender. Drain and set aside to cool. Preheat the oven to 375°F. Grease a 13x9-inch baking dish. In a large saucepan over medium heat, melt the butter. Whisk in the flour until well blended. Gradually stir in the milk and cook, stirring constantly, until the mixture is thick and bubbly. Add the onion, parsley, chives, salt, and pepper. Gently stir in the cooked potatoes. Pour the mixture into the baking dish, sprinkle with the cheeses, and top with the bread crumbs. Bake uncovered for 20 to 25 minutes, or until heated through and the cheese is melted. **Makes 12 servings.**

WEB FAVORITE

This is one of the most downloaded recipes at Almanac.com/food. Reviewer comment: "Very good!"

Oven-Roasted Potatoes

Crispy and flavorful, these are a crowd pleaser. To increase, multiply the ingredients to serve as many as necessary.

6 large potatoes, peeled

½ cup olive oil (or use an equal amount of drippings from any roast)

salt and pepper, to taste

garlic powder, to taste (optional)

paprika, to taste

Preheat the oven to 400°F. Place a 13x9-inch baking pan in the oven to preheat (this prevents sticking). Slice the potatoes lengthwise into 1-inch-thick slices. Put the slices into a large bowl, drizzle the olive oil, and toss to coat well. Place the potatoes in a single layer in the preheated baking pan. Sprinkle with salt, pepper, and garlic powder, if using. Then sprinkle with paprika. Return the pan to the oven and roast for 15 minutes. Flip the potatoes and roast for another 15 minutes. **Makes 4 to 6 servings.**

Bakin' Bits

■ Baked potatoes—especially twice-baked and stuffed potatoes—can be a meal in themselves. Here are the methods and the mixings.

ONCE-BAKED

Preheat the oven. (See the temperature and time table below.) Wash the potatoes, rub the skins lightly with butter or oil, and sprinkle with salt. (Wrapping potatoes in foil steams them.) Pierce each deeply with a fork. Place on a baking sheet or directly on oven racks and bake until tender. Test by squeezing gently. The potato skin will be crusty and the interior slightly soft when done.

To bake a medium potato in a conventional oven, use the following temperature and time guidelines:

SET THE OVEN AT	AND BAKE FOR
325°F	90 minutes
350°–375°F	60 minutes
400°F	45 minutes

(For a larger potato, increase the time.)

TWICE-BAKED

Bake as above. When baked, halve the potato and scoop out the pulp, leaving a thin shell. Mix the pulp with the other ingredients, using one of the following recipes. Stuff the potato shells and place them on a greased baking sheet.

If the filling is cool, bake for 20 to 30 minutes at the temperature shown. If the potato and filling are both hot, baking time can be decreased to 10 to 15 minutes.

Each filling will stuff four medium baked potatoes, or eight halves.

Sour Cream and Onion Filling

½ cup sour cream
2 tablespoons butter
1 tablespoon minced onion
3 slices bacon, cooked and crumbled

Bake at 350°F.

Meat Filling

2 cups finely chopped cooked meat
1 small onion, chopped
1 clove garlic, crushed
2 teaspoons chopped fresh parsley
salt and pepper, to taste

Bake at 350°F.

Mustard Filling

2 teaspoons prepared mustard
1 small onion, minced
1 tablespoon Worcestershire sauce
½ teaspoon salt
1 cup dry bread crumbs, for topping
2 tablespoons melted butter, for topping

In a bowl, combine the first four ingredients with the potato pulp. In a separate bowl, combine the bread crumbs and butter. Stuff the potatoes and top with the bread crumbs. Bake at 350°F.

Au Gratin Filling

1 cup shredded American, cheddar, or Swiss cheese

Bake at 350°F.

Seafood Cheese Filling

1 pound cooked fish or shrimp, chopped
⅔ cup shredded cheddar or Swiss cheese
2 tablespoons butter
1 cup hot milk
2 tablespoons minced onion
½ teaspoon salt
freshly ground black pepper, to taste

Bake at 375°F.

Oyster Filling

8 large uncooked oysters
¼ cup French dressing
¼ cup (½ stick) butter, softened
¼ cup heavy cream
¼ teaspoon paprika
½ teaspoon salt
freshly ground black pepper, to taste
½ cup dry bread crumbs, for topping

In a small bowl, marinate the oysters in French dressing for 30 minutes. Drain and set aside. In a large bowl, beat the potato pulp with the butter, cream, paprika, salt, and pepper. Stuff the potato shells, but make a hollow in each half. Put one oyster in each hollow. Sprinkle with bread crumbs and bake at 350°F.

Bacon bits

Caviar

Chili and a dollop of sour cream

Chopped fresh onions, chives, or scallions

Grated cheese (cheddar, Parmesan, Gruyère, pepper Jack, Monterey Jack, etc.)

Herbed butter

Herbed gravy

Lemon butter

Marinated chopped mushrooms

Mixed dried herbs (parsley, chives, basil, dill, oregano, thyme)

Peanut butter and crumbled bacon

Plain or herbed yogurt

Poppy seeds

Salad dressings

Sour cream and chives

Toasted sesame seeds

Tomato sauce

PASTA, POTATOES, AND RICE

Rice Pilaf

This dish makes a nice accompaniment to chicken or fish.

2 cups uncooked long-grain white rice

4 chicken bouillon cubes (or substitute
4 cups of chicken stock for the water
and bouillon cubes)

¼ cup (½ stick) butter or margarine

2 teaspoons salt

1 teaspoon dried marjoram

1 teaspoon dried thyme

1 teaspoon dried rosemary

¼ teaspoon dried basil

In a large, heavy saucepan, combine all of the ingredients with 4 cups of water. Bring to a boil, reduce the heat, cover, and simmer over low heat for 15 minutes or until the rice is tender and all of the liquid has been absorbed. Fluff with a fork. **Makes 6 to 8 servings.**

Spanish Saffron Rice

2 tablespoons olive oil

1 large onion, chopped

1 green bell pepper, chopped

1 cup uncooked long-grain rice

¼ teaspoon chili powder

1 can (16 ounces) crushed tomatoes,
with juice

1 bay leaf

1 teaspoon paprika

¾ teaspoon salt

⅛ teaspoon freshly ground black pepper

¼ teaspoon saffron threads

1 tablespoon dry white wine

In a heavy saucepan, heat the oil, add the onion, and sauté for 5 minutes, or until golden. Add the bell pepper and continue cooking for 3 minutes. Stir in the rice and chili powder and cook until the rice is lightly browned. Add the tomatoes, 1 cup of water, bay leaf, paprika, salt, and pepper. Crush the saffron threads with a mortar and pestle. Blend the saffron with the wine and add to the rice. Cover tightly and simmer for 20 minutes, then uncover and cook until all of the liquid has been absorbed. **Makes 6 servings.**

Mexicali Wild Rice Casserole

2 cups cooked wild rice

2 cups whole-kernel corn

1 can (4 ounces) green chiles, drained
and diced

2 cups mild chunky salsa or picante
sauce

1 cup shredded Monterey Jack cheese

Preheat the oven to 350°F. Lightly grease a 2-quart casserole or 11x7-inch baking dish. In a medium bowl, combine the rice, corn, and chiles. Spread the mixture in the casserole. Pour the salsa over the rice mixture and sprinkle with the cheese. Cover with a lid or foil and bake for 30 minutes, or until bubbly. Uncover and bake for 5 minutes more to brown. **Makes 4 servings.**

Quick Beet Risotto

A nice accompaniment to roasted meats.

3 cups chicken broth

3 medium beets, cooked, then peeled
and diced

2 tablespoons butter

1 medium onion, chopped

1½ cups uncooked arborio rice

½ cup red wine or water

1 tablespoon balsamic vinegar

salt and pepper, to taste

Bring the broth to a boil, add the beets, and set aside. Melt the butter in a large skillet and sauté the onion until soft. Add the rice and cook for 5 minutes more. Add the wine and vinegar, stirring until absorbed. Cook for 20 to 30 minutes, adding the broth 1 cup at a time as it is absorbed, and the beets. Repeat until the rice is tender. Season with salt and pepper. **Makes 4 to 6 servings.**

Maple-Mashed Baked Sweet Potatoes

Plain baked sweet potatoes are great; this way of preparing them is sublime. Serve with turkey dishes, along with cold apple- or cranberry sauce.

4 medium, unpeeled sweet potatoes
¾ cup milk
1 tablespoon butter
2 tablespoons maple syrup
juice of ½ lemon
salt and pepper, to taste
ground cinnamon or nutmeg, for garnish

Preheat the oven to 450°F. Pierce the potatoes two or three times with a fork. Arrange them on a baking sheet and bake for 45 minutes to 1 hour, or until the pulp is tender. Slit the skin to let the steam escape. In a large skillet or saucepan, heat the milk, butter, and maple syrup; do not boil. Scoop out the sweet potato pulp (discard the skins), add it to the milk mixture, and mash (the texture will be lumpy). Stir in the lemon juice and season with salt and pepper. Put into a serving dish and dust the top with cinnamon or nutmeg. **Makes 4 to 6 servings.**

Breads, Muffins, and Pastries

THE RISING AGENT

- ■ To proof, or grow, active dry yeast: Dissolve the dry yeast in lukewarm water (105° to 115°F) to activate it. Bubbles will be evident within a few minutes, indicating that the yeast is viable.

- ■ To proof dough: Cover the dough with a clean towel or cloth and provide a warm, humid, draft-free environment to encourage optimal rising.

- ■ Rapid-rise, or instant, yeast does not need to be proofed. It can be added directly to the dry ingredients. Dough made with rapid-rise yeast needs to rise only once—after it is formed into loaves or shaped—before baking. If wet ingredients are added to rapid-rise yeast, they should be at least 105°F.

- ■ A "sponge" is the active ingredients in a prefermentation process. Typically, a sponge is all of the liquid, half of the flour, and the yeast in a bread recipe mixed together to jump-start the rising process.

FOR THE BEST BREADS

- ■ If you have part of a jar of yeast in the refrigerator that you don't plan to use right away, freeze it. It will keep there almost indefinitely.

- ■ Yeast performs best in high humidity and warm—not hot—air. When making yeast bread, place the dough in a greased ceramic bowl in a closed oven with a pan of boiling water on a lower shelf. When that water cools, replace it with more boiling water. (Do not heat the oven first. The steaming water will create a suitable environment.)

Apple Walnut Poppy Seed Coffee Cake

CAKE:
½ **cup vegetable oil**

1 **cup sugar**

2 **large eggs**

1 **teaspoon vanilla extract**

2 **cups all-purpose flour**

1 **teaspoon baking powder**

1 **teaspoon baking soda**

¼ **teaspoon salt**

3 **tablespoons poppy seeds**

1 **cup sour cream**

2 **cups peeled, cored and finely
    chopped apples**

TOPPING:
1 **cup chopped walnuts**

¾ **cup brown sugar**

1 **teaspoon ground cinnamon**

¼ **cup (½ stick) butter, softened**

For cake: Preheat the oven to 350°F. Grease and flour a 13x9x2-inch baking pan. In a large bowl, mix together the oil and sugar. Beat in the eggs and vanilla and set aside. In another bowl, sift together the flour, baking powder, baking soda, and salt. Stir in the poppy seeds. Add the dry ingredients to the oil mixture alternately with the sour cream, beginning and ending with the dry ingredients. Fold in the apples and pour the batter evenly into the baking pan.

For topping: Combine walnuts, sugar, cinnamon, and butter. Mix until crumbly and sprinkle over the batter. Bake for 35 to 45 minutes, or until a toothpick inserted in the center comes out clean. Cool in the pan for 10 minutes. **Makes 10 to 12 servings.**

–Julie DeMatteo, Clementon, New Jersey

The Old Farmer's Favorite Oatmeal Bread

2 packages (2¼ teaspoons each) active
    dry yeast

3 cups quick-cooking rolled oats

4 cups boiling water

7½ to 8 cups bread flour, divided

1 tablespoon salt

¼ cup vegetable oil

½ cup molasses

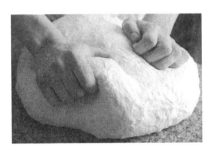

Grease three 9x5-inch loaf pans. Dissolve or proof the yeast in ¼ cup of lukewarm (105° to 115°F) water in a small bowl. Place the oats into a large bowl and pour the boiling water over them. Cool to lukewarm. Stir in 2 cups of flour and the yeast mixture. Cover, put in a warm place, and allow to rise until doubled in bulk. Punch down and add the salt, oil, molasses, and enough remaining flour to make a firm dough. Knead on a floured board until the dough is smooth and pliable. Divide and shape into three loaves, then place each in a loaf pan. Cover and allow to rise until nearly doubled. Preheat the oven to 350°F. Bake for 40 minutes, or until the bread is well browned and sounds hollow when tapped. Cool on racks before slicing. **Makes 3 loaves.**

Country Bread

An easy-to-make, no-knead bread, well suited for beginning bread bakers.

¼ cup sugar

1 cup quick-cooking rolled oats, or
    cornmeal

1 package (2¼ teaspoons) active
    dry yeast

2 teaspoons salt

2 large egg yolks

⅓ cup corn oil

1 cup dry milk powder

4 cups all-purpose flour

Grease two 9x5-inch loaf pans. Mix 1½ cups of lukewarm (105° to 115°F) water, sugar, and oats in a large bowl. Sprinkle the yeast on it and set aside for 10 minutes. Stir in the salt, egg yolks, corn oil, dry milk, and flour. Cover and let rise in a warm place for 30 minutes. Stir or work the dough with your hands for a few minutes (the dough will be sticky), then cover and let rise again. Divide the dough into two portions and place each into a loaf pan, pressing the dough into the pan with your hands. Cover and let rise until the dough reaches the top of the pan. Put a shallow pan of water on the bottom shelf of the oven. Place the bread into a cold oven, then heat the oven to 350°F. Bake for 40 to 45 minutes until the bread sounds hollow when tapped. **Makes 2 loaves.**

FOR A **SOFT UPPER CRUST**

■ Put a small dish of water in the oven while baking bread if you want a chewy crust.

Herb Cheese Bread

1 package (2¼ teaspoons) active dry yeast

1 tablespoon sugar

5 to 6 cups all-purpose flour

1 tablespoon salt

¼ cup (½ stick) butter, softened

¼ cup grated Parmesan cheese

¾ cup finely shredded sharp cheddar cheese

1 tablespoon chopped fresh parsley

1 teaspoon finely ground dried rosemary

Grease two 8x4-inch loaf pans. Dissolve the yeast in ¼ cup of lukewarm (105° to 115°F) water and sprinkle with the sugar. Let it dissolve, or proof. In a large bowl, mix 5 cups of flour with 1½ cups warm water, salt, and butter. Add the yeast and continue mixing until the dough is well blended. Turn the dough out onto a floured board and knead for at least 10 minutes, until the dough is smooth and pliable, adding flour as needed to prevent sticking. Place the dough in a greased bowl and turn to coat all sides. Cover the dough with a towel and let rise in a warm place until doubled in size (about 2 hours). Punch down the dough and turn it out onto a lightly floured board. Knead in the cheeses and herbs. Divide the dough in half and place each half in a loaf pan. Cover and let rise until the bread is slightly higher than the sides of the pans. Preheat the oven to 375°F. Bake for 30 minutes, or until the bread sounds hollow when tapped. **Makes 2 loaves.**

BREADS, MUFFINS, AND PASTRIES

Quick French Bread

1 package (2¼ teaspoons) active dry
    yeast
2 tablespoons sugar
½ teaspoon salt
1 tablespoon butter, melted
4 to 5 cups all-purpose flour
melted butter, for the top

Dissolve or proof the yeast in ½ cup of lukewarm (105° to 115°F) water and set aside. In a large bowl, stir together 1 cup warm water with sugar and salt. Add the yeast mixture and the melted butter, and stir until blended. Beat in the flour, 1 cup at a time, to form a soft dough. Turn the dough out onto a floured board and knead for 1 minute. Let the dough rest for 10 minutes. Knead again, and let it rest again for 10 minutes more. Divide the dough in half and use your hands to gently shape each half into an 8x12-inch rectangle. Starting at the long end, roll up tightly. Place the dough seam side down on an ungreased baking sheet. Using a sharp knife, slash the top every 2 inches, cover, and let rise until doubled in size. Preheat the oven to 400°F. Bake for 30 to 40 minutes, or until the bread sounds hollow when tapped. Place on racks to cool and brush the tops with melted butter. **Makes 2 loaves.**

QUICK FIX

■ **FOR GARLIC BREAD:** Cut 1 loaf of French bread into 1½-inch slices, leaving each piece attached to the loaf at the base. Cream together ½ cup (1 stick) softened butter, 2 cloves minced garlic, and 1 tablespoon minced fresh chervil or parsley. Season to taste with salt and pepper. Spread each slice with the butter mixture, wrap the loaf in foil, and bake for 20 minutes in a preheated 350°F oven.

Dinner Rolls

2 packages (2¼ teaspoons each) active dry yeast
1 cup milk
½ cup sugar
½ cup (1 stick) butter
½ teaspoon salt
1 large egg, beaten
5 to 6 cups all-purpose flour

Grease your baking sheet(s) or muffin pan(s). Dissolve or proof the yeast in ½ cup of lukewarm (105° to 115°F) water and set aside. Put the milk into a saucepan, heat to scalding, then add the sugar, butter, and salt, stirring until the butter melts. Set aside and cool to lukewarm. In a large bowl, combine the yeast and milk mixtures and blend in the beaten egg. Stir in the flour, 1 cup at a time, to form a stiff dough. Turn the dough out onto a floured board and knead until smooth. Place in a greased bowl, turn to grease the top, cover, and let rise until doubled in size. Punch down and divide into 24 to 36 pieces. Shape each piece into a ball and place on the baking sheet(s) or in the muffin pan(s). Cover and let rise until doubled. Preheat the oven to 400°F. Bake for 15 to 20 minutes, or until the rolls are browned. **Makes 2 to 3 dozen rolls.**

Fall Harvest Squash Rolls

Our thanks to Robert and Donna Kimball, owners of Beech Hill Farm, Hopkinton, New Hampshire, for sharing this recipe with us. These rolls have been served at Kimball family Thanksgiving dinners as far back as anyone can remember.

4 tablespoons dry yeast
1 cup very warm water
1⅓ cups vegetable shortening
1 cup sugar
4 large eggs
2 cups mashed winter squash
2 cups warm milk
8 cups flour, plus extra as needed
2 teaspoons salt

Dissolve the yeast in the warm water. Let sit until foamy. In a large mixing bowl, cream the shortening with the sugar. Beat in the eggs. Blend in the squash. Mix until smooth. Add the warm milk and the yeast mixture. Slowly add about 8 cups of the flour and the salt. Continue to mix until the dough pulls away from the sides of the bowl. Add more flour as needed to make a soft dough, being careful not to add too much. Let the dough rise until doubled in size, punch down, and let rise a second time until doubled.

Divide the dough into four equal parts, then divide each quarter into 12 pieces. Shape each piece into a ball and place them all in greased 9-inch cake pans, touching. Let rise until doubled. Preheat the oven to 375°F. Bake for 20 minutes or until lightly browned. Remove from the pans and let cool. **Makes 4 dozen rolls.**

Mini-Bagels

These are plain bagels. For more flavor, add the mix-ins (below) or others of your choosing.

1 cup milk

2 teaspoons sugar

¼ cup (½ stick) butter

2 teaspoons salt

1 package (2¼ teaspoons) active dry yeast

3 large eggs

4 to 5 cups all-purpose flour

¼ cup sugar, for the hot water bath

cornmeal, to prevent sticking (optional)

1 large egg white, slightly beaten, for
    brushing tops

MIX-IN FIXIN'S

■ **For seed bagels:** Put ½ cup sesame
seeds into a shallow dish. After
brushing the simmered bagel with
the egg white, dip the top of the bagel
into the seeds and proceed with
baking. Other alternatives include
poppy or caraway seeds, sea salt,
or dehydrated onion flakes.

■ **For onion bagels:** Mince two onions
and fry in 1 tablespoon vegetable
oil until crisp. Drain well. Add to the
dough, mix well, knead, and proceed
with the recipe.

■ **For cinnamon-raisin bagels:** Add
1 cup raisins and 1 teaspoon ground
cinnamon to the dough. Mix well,
knead, and proceed with the recipe.

In a saucepan, heat the milk to scalding, then add the sugar, butter, and salt, stirring until the butter is melted. Cool to luke-warm (105° to 115°F). Add the yeast, stirring until dissolved, and set aside for 10 minutes. Pour the milk and yeast mixture into a large bowl and beat in the eggs and flour, 1 cup at a time, to form a soft dough.

Turn the dough out onto a floured board and knead until smooth, adding more flour as needed to keep from sticking. Shape into a ball, place in a greased bowl, turn to grease the top, cover, and let rise until doubled in size.

Punch down the dough and with your hands pat it into a rectangle ½- to ¼-inch thick. Cut the dough into 20 equal strips. (For larger bagels, cut the dough into wider strips. Twelve strips will result in a dozen medium bagels.) Roll each strip into a thick rope, tapering the ends. Wrap the dough into a ring shape around your thumb, leaving a hole a little larger than a quarter. Tuck the ends under.

Place the rings on a floured baking sheet, cover, and let rise 30 minutes.

Preheat the oven to 400°F. Put 2 quarts (8 cups) of water and ¼ cup sugar in a large stockpot and bring it to a boil. Reduce heat to a simmer and drop in the bagels, two or three at a time. Cook for 2 minutes, turn once, and cook for 2 minutes more, or until they swell. While they are cooking, sprinkle cornmeal on an ungreased baking sheet. Remove the bagels with a slotted spoon, drain, and place on the baking sheet (the cornmeal will prevent sticking). Brush the bagels with egg white. Bake for 25 to 30 minutes, or until brown. **Makes 20 bagels.**

Cinnamon Rolls

ROLLS:

2 cups milk

½ cup brown sugar

1 package (2¼ teaspoons) active dry yeast

1 cup quick-cooking rolled oats

5 to 6 cups all-purpose flour, divided

2 large eggs, beaten

1 tablespoon salt

1 cup (2 sticks) softened butter, divided

¾ cup walnuts, chopped

½ cup raisins (optional)

1 cup sugar mixed with 1 tablespoon ground cinnamon

1 large egg yolk, beaten

FROSTING:

3 tablespoons butter, melted

1½ cups confectioners' sugar

1 to 2 tablespoons heavy cream

¼ teaspoon vanilla extract

pinch of salt

For rolls: Heat the milk to lukewarm (105° to 115°F). In a large bowl, combine the brown sugar, yeast, milk, oats, and 1½ to 2 cups of flour. The mixture should be the consistency of bubbly pancake batter. Set it aside for 20 minutes to allow the yeast to work. Add the eggs, salt, and ½ cup of the softened butter and stir well. Add enough of the flour to make a soft dough. Turn the dough out onto a floured board and knead it until it is smooth and pliable, adding more flour as needed to keep from sticking. Put the dough into a large greased bowl, cover it with a damp towel, and set it aside for at least 1 hour, letting it rise until it has doubled in size.

Grease one or two sheet pans. Divide the dough in half, and roll each half out into a 15x10-inch rectangle ½-inch thick. Spread the remaining ½ cup softened butter onto the rectangles. Distribute the walnuts and raisins (if desired) evenly, and sprinkle with most of the cinnamon sugar. Roll up the long edge of the dough, jelly-roll style, and pinch the seams closed. Slice each roll of dough into 12 pinwheel pieces and place them on the sheet pans. Brush them with egg yolk and sprinkle with the remaining cinnamon sugar. Let them rise again 45 minutes to an hour, until doubled. Preheat the oven to 350°F. Bake for 25 to 30 minutes, or until they are cooked through and lightly brown.

For frosting: Combine the frosting ingredients and spread gently over the warm rolls. **Makes 2 dozen rolls.**

Soft Pretzels

1 package (2¼ teaspoons) active dry
    yeast
2 teaspoons sugar
3½ to 4 cups all-purpose flour
1½ teaspoons salt
2 tablespoons vegetable oil
1 egg, beaten with 1 tablespoon milk,
    for a glaze
coarse salt, for topping

Lightly grease two heavy baking sheets. Place ¼ cup of lukewarm (105° to 115°F) water in a large bowl and dissolve the yeast and sugar in it. Let the yeast proof for 5 minutes, or until bubbly. Add 1 cup of lukewarm water, 3½ cups of flour, salt, and oil and stir until well combined. Turn the dough out onto a lightly floured board and knead until smooth and pliable, adding the remaining ½ cup of flour as needed to prevent sticking. Divide the dough into 24 pieces and roll each into a thin rope about 12 inches long. Make each into a pretzel shape: Form a circle, leaving enough on each end to twist one around the other. Fold the twist down the middle of the circle and spread the ends to overlap the sides. Place the pretzel on a baking sheet. When all are formed, cover them loosely with a towel and let them rest in a warm place for 15 minutes, or until puffy. Preheat the oven to 425°F. Lightly brush the egg-milk glaze over the pretzels and sprinkle them with coarse salt. Bake for 8 to 12 minutes, or until lightly browned. Cooking too long could dry the interior, making them crisp, not soft. **Makes 2 dozen pretzels.**

Homemade Pizza

A soft crust with a fresh, pizzeria flavor. If you prefer your pizza thick, make one crust instead of two.

2 tablespoons butter
1 teaspoon sugar
1 teaspoon salt
1 package (2¼ teaspoons) active dry yeast
3 cups flour
olive oil
pizza sauce (optional; recipe below)
shredded mozzarella cheese

In a 2-quart saucepan, heat 1 cup of water, butter, sugar, and salt, stirring until butter melts. Cool to lukewarm (105° to 115°F). Sprinkle yeast over mixture, and let proof for a few minutes until dissolved completely. Stir in the flour. Turn dough out onto a lightly floured board and knead briefly until it is smooth and elastic. Grease a 2-quart bowl with olive oil, put dough in the bowl, and turn to coat entirely with oil. Cover and put in a warm place to rise until doubled—about 45 minutes. Preheat the oven to 450°F. Punch dough down and divide in half. Roll out each half on a lightly floured surface to form two pizza crusts. Oil two round pans 12 to 14 inches in diameter with olive oil (or use 15x10-inch pans) and place the dough in each pan. Top with tomato sauce (optional) and sprinkle the mozzarella cheese over the top. Use any of your favorite toppings. Bake on the lowest rack of the oven for 15 to 20 minutes, or until hot and bubbling. **Makes two thin pizzas.**

Pizza Sauce

1 can (6 ounces) tomato paste
1 can (8 ounces) tomato sauce
1½ teaspoons Italian seasoning mix
3 to 4 teaspoons sugar

Mix all of the ingredients and let stand while the pizza dough is rising. **Makes enough for two pizzas.**

TOPPING SUGGESTIONS

■ With homemade pizza, it's easy to create your own combinations of sauces and toppings. Instead of tomato sauce, use pesto (for recipe, see page 72). Or, skip the sauce and layer the pizza with mozzarella and fresh tomato slices. Try goat cheese or feta instead of mozzarella and parmesan. Mix and match combinations of meat and fruit, such as ham and pineapple. The possibilities are endless.

Quick Breads and Muffins

Quick Biscuits

2 cups all-purpose flour

2 teaspoons baking powder

1 teaspoon salt

¼ cup (½ stick) butter

1 cup milk

Preheat the oven to 450°F. Sift together the flour, baking powder, and salt. Using a pastry blender, cut in the butter until the mixture is crumbly. Add the milk slowly, stirring with a fork to form a soft dough. Drop by teaspoonfuls onto an ungreased baking sheet and bake for 10 to 15 minutes. **Makes 1 dozen biscuits.**

FOR ROLLED BISCUITS:

Follow the recipe, but reduce the milk by about ¼ cup. Turn the dough out onto a floured board and knead several times. Roll out to a ½-inch thickness and cut with a 2-inch biscuit cutter or the 3½-inch rim of a clean tuna can. Place on an ungreased baking sheet and bake for 10 to 15 minutes.

Corn Bread

This bread can also be baked in a greased and preheated 8- or 9-inch cast-iron skillet.

1 cup cornmeal

1 cup all-purpose flour

1 tablespoon baking powder

2 teaspoons sugar

1 teaspoon salt

1 large egg

1½ cups milk (for lighter texture, substitute orange or cranberry juice)

¼ cup (½ stick) butter, melted

Preheat the oven to 425°F. Grease a square 8-inch baking pan. In a medium bowl, sift together the cornmeal, flour, baking powder, sugar, and salt. In a separate bowl, beat together the egg, milk, and butter. Add the wet ingredients to the dry, stirring until well blended. Pour into the pan and bake for 20 to 25 minutes. **Makes 16 squares.**

Tea Scones

Delicious served warm with butter and jam at teatime. Equally good plain or with raisins or dried cranberries.

2 cups all-purpose flour
1 tablespoon sugar
1 tablespoon baking powder
½ teaspoon salt
½ cup (1 stick) butter or margarine
1 egg
⅔ cup milk or light cream
½ cup raisins or dried cranberries (optional)

Preheat the oven to 425°F. In a mixing bowl, stir together the flour, sugar, baking powder, and salt until well blended. Cut in the butter until the mixture is crumbly. In a separate bowl, beat the egg lightly, then stir in the milk. Reserve 1 tablespoon of the egg mixture for glazing and add the remainder to the dry ingredients all at once. Stir with a fork until a soft dough forms. Fold in the dried fruit, if using. Gather the dough into a ball and turn it out onto a lightly floured surface. Knead a few times, adding a bit more flour as necessary until the dough is smooth and no longer sticky. Pat down or roll out to about a ½-inch thickness. Cut with a round cutter and place on an ungreased cookie sheet. Brush the tops with the reserved egg mixture. Bake for 12 to 14 minutes, or until golden brown. **Makes about 1 dozen scones.**

Oatcakes

1 cup all-purpose flour

2 teaspoons baking powder

½ teaspoon salt

1 cup quick-cooking rolled oats, plus
    1 tablespoon for topping

¼ cup molasses

½ cup (1 stick) butter

¼ cup sugar

Preheat the oven to 350°F. Grease an 8- or 9-inch pie plate. Combine the flour, baking powder, and salt in a medium bowl. Stir in the 1 cup of oats. Place the molasses, butter, and sugar in a small saucepan over low heat and stir until the butter is melted and the mixture is smooth. Add the butter mixture to the dry ingredients and stir to combine. Pat the dough into the pie plate. Score the dough into eight wedges and sprinkle with the remaining tablespoon of oats. Bake for 20 to 25 minutes, or until firm. Serve warm with marmalade. **Makes 8 servings.**

Boston Brown Bread

This traditional loaf is steamed on the stovetop, not baked in the oven.

1 cup cornmeal

1 cup graham flour

1 cup rye flour

1 cup molasses

1 cup buttermilk

2 teaspoons baking soda

½ teaspoon salt

1 cup raisins (optional)

Grease the insides of three round, 1-pound coffee cans. In a large bowl, combine all of the ingredients, including raisins, if desired, and stir until well blended. Fill each can with one-third of the batter. Cover the can tops tightly with foil or wax paper secured with string. Place the cans on a rack inside a large kettle or soup pot and add warm water to the kettle until the level reaches halfway up the sides of the cans. Cover the kettle with a lid and bring the water to a boil. Reduce the heat and simmer for 2½ to 3 hours, or until the bread is firm and a toothpick inserted into the center comes out clean. Add more water to the kettle during cooking, as necessary. **Makes 3 loaves.**

Banana Date Nut Bread

2 McIntosh apples, peeled, cored, and
   cut into thin slices (or ¾ cup
   unsweetened applesauce)

1 cup all-purpose flour

1 cup whole wheat flour

1 teaspoon baking soda

1 teaspoon cinnamon plus ¼ teaspoon
   ground nutmeg or 1¼ teaspoons
   five-spice powder

⅛ teaspoon salt

1 cup packed dark-brown sugar

1 cup mashed ripe bananas (about
   2 large)

½ cup low-fat buttermilk

1 large egg

1 tablespoon vegetable oil

1 teaspoon vanilla extract

⅓ to ½ cup chopped dates

½ cup ground walnuts

Preheat the oven to 350°F. Put the apple slices in a microwave-safe bowl, cover lightly, and cook on high for 2½ to 3 minutes, or until soft. Mash and set aside.

In a medium bowl, whisk together the flours, baking soda, spices, and salt. Set aside. In another medium bowl, combine the brown sugar, bananas, apples, buttermilk, egg, oil, and vanilla. Beat with an electric mixer on high speed until blended. Fold in the dates and nuts. Make a well in the center of the dry ingredients and pour in the banana mixture. Stir until just combined. Spray a 9x5x3-inch loaf pan with nonstick cooking spray. Gently pour the batter into the prepared pan. Bake for 55 to 60 minutes, or until a toothpick inserted into the center comes out clean. Remove from the oven and cool on a rack for 10 minutes before turning out onto the rack to cool completely. **Makes 1 loaf.**

Sour Cream Banana Bread

½ cup (1 stick) butter, softened

1 cup sugar

2 large eggs, beaten

½ cup sour cream

2 ripe bananas, mashed

1 teaspoon vanilla extract

2 cups bread flour

2 teaspoons baking powder

1 teaspoon baking soda

½ cup chopped pecans or walnuts

Preheat the oven to 350°F. Grease a 9x5-inch loaf pan. In a large bowl, cream the butter and sugar until light and fluffy. Add the eggs, sour cream, bananas, and vanilla and mix well. In a separate small bowl, combine the flour, baking powder, and baking soda. Add the dry ingredients to the wet and mix well. Stir in the pecans. Pour the batter into the loaf pan. Bake for 55 to 60 minutes, or until a toothpick inserted in the center comes out clean. **Makes 1 loaf.**

Pumpkin Bread

2½ cups sugar

⅔ cup canola or safflower oil

1 can (15 ounces) pumpkin, or 2 cups cooked, mashed, fresh pumpkin

4 large eggs

3⅓ cups all-purpose flour

2 teaspoons baking soda

½ teaspoon baking powder

½ teaspoon salt

1½ teaspoons ground cloves

1½ teaspoons ground cinnamon

⅔ cup milk

⅔ cup dried or fresh cranberries, or raisins

⅔ cup chopped walnuts or pecans (optional)

Preheat the oven to 300°F. Grease two 9x5-inch or three 8½x4½-inch loaf pans. In a large bowl, stir together the sugar, oil, and pumpkin. Beat in the eggs one at a time. In a separate bowl, sift the dry ingredients together, then add them to the pumpkin mixture alternately with the milk, stirring to blend. Fold in the cranberries and walnuts, if desired. Spread the batter into the loaf pans. Bake for 1 hour, 15 minutes (check at 1 hour, if using the smaller loaf pans), or until a toothpick inserted into the center comes out clean. Cool for 10 minutes before removing from the pans. **Makes 2 large or 3 small loaves.**

BREADS, MUFFINS, AND PASTRIES

Orange Nut Bread With Orange–Cream Cheese Spread

Slice the nut bread thinly and make little sandwiches using the cream cheese spread.

BREAD:

2 cups sifted all-purpose flour

½ teaspoon salt

1 teaspoon baking powder

¼ teaspoon baking soda

⅔ cup sugar

⅓ cup butter, softened

2 large eggs

**1 cup freshly squeezed orange juice
     with pulp**

½ teaspoon vanilla extract

½ teaspoon orange extract

1 cup chopped walnuts

SPREAD:

**3 packages (8 ounces each) cream
     cheese, softened**

**1 navel orange with peel, cut into
     chunks, seeds removed**

¼ cup confectioners' sugar

For bread: Preheat the oven to 350°F. Generously grease three miniature (6x3½-inch) loaf pans. Into a medium bowl, sift the flour with the salt, baking powder, and baking soda. In a large bowl, cream the sugar with the butter, then beat in the eggs, one at a time. Add the orange juice to the sugar mixture alternately with the flour mixture, stirring to combine. Add the extracts and nuts and stir well. Pour the batter into the loaf pans. Bake for 35 to 40 minutes, or until a toothpick inserted into the center comes out clean. Remove the pans from the oven. After 10 minutes, remove the loaves from the pans, cool completely, and wrap. Chill well before slicing. **Makes 3 small loaves.**

NOTE:

If desired, bake the batter in one 8½x4½-inch loaf pan for about 1 hour.

For spread: Using a food processor with a steel blade, combine the cream cheese, orange chunks, and sugar. Refrigerate for a few hours to blend the flavors. Slice the nut bread thinly and make little sandwiches using the cream cheese spread. **Makes 1½ cups.**

Zucchini Bread

2 cups shredded zucchini

3 large eggs

2 cups sugar

1 cup vegetable oil

1 teaspoon vanilla extract

3 cups all-purpose flour

1 teaspoon baking powder

2 teaspoons baking soda

1½ teaspoons ground cinnamon

½ teaspoon ground nutmeg

½ cup raisins (optional)

½ cup chopped walnuts (optional)

Preheat the oven to 350°F. Grease two 8½x4½ loaf pans. Press the zucchini between paper towels to remove any excess moisture and set aside. In a large mixing bowl, beat together the eggs and sugar. Add the oil and vanilla. In a separate bowl, combine the flour, baking powder, baking soda, cinnamon, and nutmeg. Stir the dry ingredients into the wet until well blended. Fold in the zucchini, then fold in raisins and walnuts, if using. Pour the batter into the loaf pans and bake for 1 hour, or until a toothpick inserted into the center comes out clean. **Makes 2 loaves.**

Wild Blueberry–Sour Cream Muffins

¼ cup (½ stick) butter

¾ cup sugar

2 large eggs

1⅓ cups all-purpose flour

½ teaspoon baking soda

¼ teaspoon salt

¾ cup sour cream

½ teaspoon vanilla extract

1 cup fresh wild blueberries

Preheat the oven to 425°F. Grease a standard 12-cup muffin pan or line with paper baking cups. In a large bowl, cream together the butter and sugar. Beat in the eggs one at a time. In a separate bowl, sift together the dry ingredients and add to egg mixture, alternating with the sour cream. Beat in the vanilla, then fold in the berries. Fill the cups half full. Bake for 12 to 15 minutes. Remove the muffins from the pan and cool on a wire rack. **Makes 12 muffins.**

MAKING MUFFINS

■ Stir the batter by hand; beating with an electric mixer will produce tough muffins.

■ As a general rule, the thinner the batter, the lighter the muffins will be when baked.

■ Buttermilk makes muffins moist. Whenever adding buttermilk to a recipe, add ½ teaspoon of baking soda per cup of buttermilk.

■ Almost any muffins benefit from cinnamon sugar sprinkled on top before baking. Or make a crumb topping: In a food processor, combine 1 cup flour, 1 cup brown sugar, 1 cup granola or quick-cooking rolled oats, 2 teaspoons ground cinnamon, and ½ cup (1 stick) cold butter cut into small bits. Pulse until the mixture forms fine crumbs. Spread on the tops.

■ If, after portioning the batter, you end up with any empty cups in your muffin pan, put a little water in them to keep them from scorching in the oven.

■ Muffin batter can be made and put into the greased cups in the muffin pan the night before you bake. Cover with plastic wrap and store in the refrigerator. In the morning, let the batter warm to room temperature for about 20 minutes while the oven is preheating.

Apple Cranberry Carrot Muffins

2 cups unpeeled, cored, shredded apples

1⅓ cups sugar

1 cup chopped cranberries

1 cup peeled, shredded carrots

1 cup chopped walnuts

2½ cups all-purpose flour

1 tablespoon baking powder

2 teaspoons baking soda

½ teaspoon salt

2 teaspoons ground cinnamon

2 teaspoons ground coriander

2 large eggs, beaten

½ cup safflower oil

Preheat the oven to 375°F. Grease a standard 12-cup muffin pan or line with paper baking cups. In a large bowl, thoroughly mix the apples and sugar. Stir in the cranberries, carrots, and nuts. In a medium bowl, combine the dry ingredients, then add to the apple mixture. Stir in the eggs and oil, and mix gently but thoroughly. Divide the batter evenly among the cups and bake for 25 to 30 minutes. Cool for 5 minutes in the pan before removing the muffins to cool on a wire rack. **Makes 12 muffins.**

MUFFINS AS YOU LIKE THEM

■ Use this basic recipe as a guide for inventing your own made-from-scratch muffins. Mix together the following ingredients, using your choice of the suggested alternatives, singly or in combination. Within the ranges given, vary the amounts of wet and dry ingredients to create the consistency you desire.

2 to 3 cups all-purpose flour (substitute up to 1 cup whole wheat flour, wheat bran, rolled oats, cornmeal, or crushed dry cereal)

½ teaspoon salt

½ to ⅔ cup sweetener (white or brown sugar, honey, or maple syrup)

2½ teaspoons baking powder

2 to 4 tablespoons oil or melted butter (increase to ½ cup for a more cakelike consistency)

1 cup liquid (milk, cream, orange juice, or buttermilk) Note: If you use buttermilk, add ½ teaspoon of baking soda per cup.

1 egg, slightly beaten

OPTIONAL ADDITIONS:

½ cup chopped nuts, chopped apple, mashed banana, canned pumpkin, applesauce, raisins, or other dried fruit

Preheat the oven to 400°F. Grease a standard 12-cup muffin pan or line with paper baking cups. Mix ingredients together. Fill the cups three-quarters full. Bake for 20 minutes, or until lightly browned and a toothpick inserted into the center comes out clean. **Makes 12 muffins.**

Lemon Poppy Seed Muffins

MUFFINS:

6 tablespoons (¾ stick) butter

1 cup sugar

2 large eggs

1½ cups flour

2 teaspoons baking powder

½ cup milk

grated rind of 1 lemon

½ cup poppy seeds

½ cup walnuts, finely ground (optional)

GLAZE:

⅓ cup sugar

juice of 1 lemon

For muffins: Preheat the oven to 375°F. Grease a standard 12-cup muffin pan or line with paper baking cups. In a large bowl, cream together the butter and sugar. Beat in the eggs one at a time. In a separate bowl, combine the flour and baking powder. Add the dry ingredients to the egg mixture alternately with the milk and lemon rind. Stir in the poppy seeds and ground walnuts. Fill the cups half full. Bake for 15 to 20 minutes. Remove the muffins from the pan and cool on a wire rack.

For glaze: In a small bowl, mix the sugar and lemon juice until smooth. Drizzle on the warm muffins. **Makes 10 to 12 muffins.**

Refrigerator Muffins

This batter keeps in the refrigerator for up to a week. Increase the sugar to a total of 1 cup if you prefer sweet muffins.

3 cups bran cereal, with or without raisins

¼ cup sugar

¼ cup light-brown sugar

2½ cups all-purpose flour

2½ teaspoons baking soda

1 teaspoon salt

2 large eggs

2 cups buttermilk

½ cup vegetable oil

¼ cup raisins (optional)

In a large plastic or glass container with a tight-fitting lid, mix the bran and sugars. In a separate bowl, whisk together the flour, baking soda, and salt. Add the flour mixture to the bran and stir to distribute. In a separate bowl, beat the eggs. Add the buttermilk and oil and beat lightly or whisk to blend. Pour the egg mixture over the bran and stir to combine. Add the raisins, if desired. Cover and refrigerate overnight.

Preheat the oven to 400°F. Before baking, if the batter seems thick, mix in ½ cup of buttermilk or water to thin it. Grease muffin pan(s) or line with paper baking cups. Fill the cups half full. Bake for 20 minutes, or until the tops crack yet feel firm to the touch. **Makes 18 muffins.**

Pineapple Coffee Cake

CAKE:

1½ cups sifted all-purpose flour

1 tablespoon baking powder

¼ teaspoon salt

¼ cup (½ stick) butter

¼ cup sugar

1 large egg

½ cup milk

½ cup crushed pineapple, drained

TOPPING:

½ cup brown sugar

2 tablespoons all-purpose flour

2 teaspoons ground cinnamon

¼ cup (½ stick) butter, melted

For cake: Preheat the oven to 375°F. Grease an 8- or 9-inch square baking pan. In a medium bowl, stir together the sifted flour, baking powder, and salt, and set aside. In a large bowl, cream together the butter and sugar with an electric mixer until light and fluffy. Mix in the egg and milk. Add the dry ingredients, stirring until well combined, then fold in the pineapple. Pour batter evenly into the baking pan.

For topping: In a small bowl, combine the brown sugar, flour, and cinnamon. Add the melted butter and stir to combine. Sprinkle the topping over the batter. Bake 25 to 35 minutes, or until a toothpick inserted into the center comes out clean. **Makes 9 servings.**

Sour Cream Coffee Cake

This wonderfully easy cake calls for less butter and fewer eggs than most versions.

FILLING:

2 tablespoons sugar

1 teaspoon ground cinnamon

½ cup chopped nuts

CAKE:

¾ teaspoon baking soda

1 cup sour cream

¼ cup (½ stick) butter

1 cup sugar

1 large egg

1½ cups all-purpose flour

1½ teaspoons baking powder

For filling: In a small bowl, stir together the sugar, cinnamon, and nuts and set aside.

For cake: Preheat the oven to 350°F. Grease and flour an 8- or 9-inch square baking pan. In a small bowl, stir the baking soda into the sour cream and let stand for 5 to 10 minutes. (The sour cream will increase slightly in volume.) In a large mixing bowl, cream the butter for 2 minutes with an electric mixer, then gradually add the sugar. Add the egg and beat until thoroughly combined. Add the sour cream mixture, then beat in the flour and baking powder. Beat at medium speed for 2 minutes.

Pour half of the batter into the prepared pan. Sprinkle with the filling. Spoon the remaining batter over the filling. Bake for 30 to 40 minutes, or until a toothpick inserted into the center comes out clean. Let stand for 10 minutes before removing from the pan. **Makes 9 servings.**

Comforting Gingerbread

½ cup corn oil

¼ cup light-brown sugar

2 cups all-purpose flour

1 cup whole wheat flour

½ cup milk

2 large eggs, slightly beaten

½ cup dark molasses

2 teaspoons ground ginger

Preheat the oven to 350°F. Grease an 8- or 9-inch square baking pan. In a large mixing bowl, combine the oil and brown sugar. In another bowl, sift the flours together, then add to the brown sugar mixture and stir until well blended. Add the milk, eggs, and molasses and stir to blend. Fold in the ginger. Pour into the pan. Bake for 30 minutes, or until a toothpick inserted into the center comes out clean. Serve warm with applesauce or whipped cream, or dusted with confectioners' sugar. **Makes 9 servings.**

CHAPTER

11

Desserts

(continued on next page)

Desserts *(continued)*

Cakes

The 2000 Old Farmer's Almanac *Recipe Contest: "Layer Cakes"*

Old-Fashioned Buttermilk Wedding Cake

CAKE:

1 cup (2 sticks) butter or margarine, softened

3 cups sugar

4 cups cake flour

1 teaspoon baking soda

2 teaspoons baking powder

¼ teaspoon salt

2 cups buttermilk

1 teaspoon vanilla extract

½ teaspoon butter flavoring

½ teaspoon almond extract

6 large egg whites

FROSTING:

8 ounces cream cheese, softened

3 cups confectioners' sugar

2 teaspoons vanilla extract

Preheat the oven to 350°F. Grease and flour three 9-inch round cake pans.

For cake: In a large bowl and with an electric mixer, cream the butter and sugar until fluffy. Add the flour, baking soda, baking powder, and salt. Pour in the buttermilk and begin mixing slowly. Continue to mix until well blended. Add the flavorings and stir. Wash and dry the beaters.

In a separate bowl, beat the egg whites until stiff. Fold the egg whites into the cake batter. Divide the batter evenly among the prepared pans. Bake for 20 minutes at 350°F, then lower the heat to 300°F and bake for about 25 minutes more, or until a toothpick inserted into the center comes out clean. Remove the cakes from the oven and cool on racks. After 10 minutes, remove the cakes from the pans and continue cooling on racks.

For frosting: Combine all of the ingredients in a mixing bowl and beat until smooth. When the cake is completely cooled, frost the layers and assemble. **Makes 12 to 16 servings.**

–Diane Niebling, Overland Park, Kansas

DESSERTS

Peachy Almond Cake

CAKE:

1 cup (2 sticks) butter, softened

2 cups sugar

4 large eggs

3 cups all-purpose flour

3½ teaspoons baking powder

½ teaspoon salt

1¼ cups milk

1 teaspoon vanilla extract

1 teaspoon almond extract

FILLING:

1 cup (7-ounce package) almond paste

2 ripe peaches, peeled, pitted, and sliced

1 cup peach preserves, softened in
     microwave oven or stirred, divided

FROSTING:

2 cups heavy cream

½ cup confectioners' sugar, or to taste

½ teaspoon almond extract, or to taste

1 teaspoon vanilla extract, or to taste

caramel sauce (optional)

peach slices (optional)

mint sprigs (optional)

Preheat the oven to 350°F. Grease and flour two 9-inch round cake pans.

For cake: In a large bowl and with an electric mixer, cream the butter and sugar until fluffy. Add the eggs, one at a time, beating briefly after each and then until the mixture is as light as whipped cream. In another bowl, sift together the flour, baking powder, and salt, and set aside.

In a small bowl, blend the milk and extracts. Alternately add the dry ingredients and the milk to the butter mixture, stirring to blend after each. Spread the batter equally in the prepared pans and bake for 30 to 40 minutes, or until a toothpick inserted into the center comes out clean. Remove the cakes from the oven and cool them on wire racks.

For filling: Place one cake layer on a serving plate. Divide the almond paste in half and roll each portion into a 9-inch round (roll the paste between two layers of waxed paper or plastic wrap). Place one sheet of almond paste over the first cake layer. In a small bowl, mix the peach slices with ¾ cup of the peach preserves and spread over the almond paste. Add the second cake layer and brush with the remaining ¼ cup peach preserves. Top with second round of almond paste.

For frosting: Whip the cream until stiff, then add the sugar and extracts to taste, stirring to blend. Frost the cake with the whipped cream and refrigerate until serving time. If desired, drizzle a little caramel sauce on the dessert plates before putting the cake on it and garnish each serving with a few peach slices and a sprig of fresh mint. **Makes 8 to 10 servings.**

–TerryAnn Moore, Oaklyn, New Jersey

DESSERTS

CAKE MISTAKES

■ If you're having a problem with your cake, here are some possible reasons why.

IF THE CAKE . . .	IT COULD BE DUE TO . . .
Has peaks or cracks	Too much flour, a too-hot oven
Is sunken	Too little flour, too much sugar, too much fat, a too-cool oven, underbaked
Is too dark or too pale	A too-hot or a too-cool oven, underbaked or overbaked, wrong size pan
Tastes flat, bitter, or unpleasant	Poor-quality ingredients
Is coarse	Too much fat, eggs beaten too much, mixed too little, a too-cool oven
Is too dense	Eggs beaten too much or too little, mixed too much, a too-hot oven
Is crumbly	Mixed too little
Has tunnels	Mixed too little, a too-hot oven
Has a hard, thick crust	Too much flour, too much sugar, a too-cool oven, overbaked
Is dry	Too much flour, too little fat, eggs beaten too much, overbaked
Is soggy	Too little flour, too much fat, mixed too little, underbaked
Is tough	Too much flour, too little fat, mixed too much, a too-hot oven, overbaked

BATTER MATTER

■ Prepare cake pans with butter and flour—before you mix the batter. Use waxed paper cut to fit and buttered, as well as butter on the bottom and sides of the pan.

■ Sift dry ingredients. Sifted flour is aerated and fluffed, making it lighter and easier to incorporate with the other ingredients.

The 2000 Old Farmer's Almanac *Recipe Contest: "Layer Cakes"*

Millennium Chocolate Cake With Mocha Frosting

CAKE:

⅔ cup butter, softened

1¾ cups sugar

2 large eggs

1 teaspoon vanilla extract

2½ ounces unsweetened baking chocolate, melted and cooled

2½ cups sifted cake flour

1¼ teaspoons baking soda

½ teaspoon salt

1¼ cups sour milk or buttermilk

FROSTING:

6 cups confectioners' sugar

1 cup (2 sticks) unsalted butter, softened

½ cup unsweetened cocoa powder

⅔ cup strong brewed coffee (use part coffee-flavored liqueur, if desired)

1 tablespoon vanilla extract

Preheat the oven to 350°F. Grease two 9-inch round cake pans, then line the bottoms with waxed or parchment paper. Grease the paper well. Dust with flour and shake out the excess.

For cake: In a large bowl and with an electric mixer, cream the butter and sugar until fluffy. Add the eggs and vanilla, and beat on high speed for 5 minutes, scraping the bowl occasionally. Add the chocolate and stir to blend.

In a separate bowl, whisk the flour with the baking soda and salt. Add the flour to the cake batter alternately with the sour milk, mixing well after each addition. Divide the batter equally between the two prepared pans and bake for 30 to 35 minutes, or until a toothpick inserted into the center comes out clean. Remove the cakes from the oven and let them cool in the pans on wire racks for 10 minutes. Then invert the cakes from the pans to cool completely on the racks. Carefully peel off the waxed paper.

For frosting: In a medium bowl and with an electric mixer, beat the confectioners' sugar with the butter until smooth. Add the cocoa, coffee (and liqueur, if using), and vanilla, and beat on low speed until well blended. Beat for 1 minute more at medium speed. Chill for 20 to 30 minutes, or until the mixture reaches spreading consistency. Frost the layers and assemble. **Makes about 12 servings.**

–Josephine D. Piro, Easton, Pennsylvania

HOW TO ○ SOUR MILK

■ To make sour milk, add one tablespoon of lemon juice or distilled white vinegar to 1 cup of milk. Let it stand for 5 minutes before adding to a recipe.

DESSERTS

NO-SKILL, ALL-FRILL, DECORATING IDEAS

- ■ Fresh flowers lend an easy elegance.

- ■ Sweet, ripe berries or chopped nuts add color, flavor, and style.

- ■ Store-bought candies and cookies add instant glitz, especially to children's cakes.

- ■ Chocolate shavings, made with a frozen chocolate candy bar (dark or white) and a vegetable peeler, dress up a plain vanilla frosting.

- ■ Chocolate leaves (see page 239 for directions).

THIRD PRIZE

The 2004 Old Farmer's Almanac *Recipe Contest: "Apples"*

Easy Three-Bowl Apple Cake

4 apples, peeled, cored, and diced

1¾ cups sugar

1½ tablespoons lemon juice

3 cups all-purpose flour

2 teaspoons baking soda

2 teaspoons cinnamon

dash of salt

2 large eggs, beaten

1 cup oil

1½ teaspoons vanilla extract

Preheat the oven to 350°F. Grease a 13x9-inch baking pan. In bowl 1, combine the apples, sugar, and lemon juice and mix well. In bowl 2, sift together the flour, baking soda, cinnamon, and salt. In bowl 3, lightly mix the beaten eggs, oil, and vanilla. Combine bowl 1 (the apple mixture) and bowl 3 (the egg mixture) and add to bowl 2 (the dry ingredients). Mix well (the batter will be stiff). Spread the batter into the prepared pan. Bake for 45 minutes, or until browned or a toothpick inserted near the center comes out clean. **Makes about 20 servings.**

–*Helen D. Lomupo, Gilboa, New York*

Oatmeal Date Cake With Cinnamon–Cream Cheese Frosting

CAKE:

1½ cups boiling water

1 cup rolled oats

1½ cups all-purpose flour

1 teaspoon baking soda

1 teaspoon cinnamon

½ teaspoon grated nutmeg

½ cup (1 stick) butter or margarine,
    softened

1 cup granulated sugar

1 cup brown sugar

2 large eggs

1 teaspoon vanilla extract

⅓ cup chopped dates

FROSTING:

8 ounces cream cheese, softened

½ cup (1 stick) butter, softened

4 cups confectioners' sugar, sifted

2 teaspoons vanilla extract

2 teaspoons cinnamon

For cake: Pour the boiling water over the rolled oats, stir, and let stand for about 40 minutes. Preheat the oven to 350°F. Grease and flour two 8-inch round cake pans. In a medium bowl, whisk together the flour, baking soda, cinnamon, and nutmeg and set aside. In a large bowl and with an electric mixer on medium speed, beat the butter. Add the sugars and beat until fluffy. Add the eggs, one at a time, beating after each. Add the vanilla and the cooled oat mixture and stir to blend well. On low speed, beat in the flour mixture a little at a time. Add in the dates and stir until well blended. Pour an equal amount of batter into each cake pan and bake for 40 minutes, or until a toothpick inserted into the center comes out clean. Remove the cakes from the oven and let them cool on racks in the pans for 10 minutes. Invert the cakes onto the racks and continue cooling.

For frosting: In a large bowl and with an electric mixer, whip the cream cheese and butter together until fluffy. Add the sugar, vanilla, and cinnamon. Mix until smooth. Frost the layers and assemble. **Makes 10 to 12 servings.**

–Jennifer Walsh, Creston, Iowa

DESSERTS

Triple-Lemon Layer Cake

CAKE:

1 cup (2 sticks) butter or margarine,
    softened

2 cups sugar

4 large eggs

3 cups all-purpose flour

¼ teaspoon salt

1 cup buttermilk

1 teaspoon vanilla extract

1 tablespoon lemon extract

1 teaspoon baking soda

1 tablespoon vinegar or lemon juice

FILLING:

1½ cups sugar

¼ cup cornstarch

½ cup lemon juice

2 large egg yolks, well beaten

2 tablespoons butter

FROSTING:

⅓ cup butter, softened

4 cups confectioners' sugar

2 tablespoons milk

1 tablespoon white corn syrup

1 tablespoon lemon extract

1½ to 3 cups frozen whipped topping,
    thawed

Preheat the oven to 350°F. Grease and flour two 8- or 9-inch round cake pans.

For cake: In a large bowl and with an electric mixer, cream the butter and sugar until fluffy. Add the eggs, one at a time, beating well after each. In a separate bowl, mix together the flour and salt. Add it to creamed mixture alternately with the buttermilk, stirring to blend after each addition. Add the vanilla and lemon extracts and stir to blend. In a separate small bowl, dissolve the baking soda in the vinegar. Add it to the creamed mixture, stirring to combine. Pour an equal amount of batter into each prepared pan and bake for 30 to 40 minutes, or until a toothpick inserted into the center comes out clean. Cool for 10 minutes and remove from the pans. Cool completely, then cut each layer in half horizontally.

For filling: In a saucepan, mix the sugar and cornstarch. Add the lemon juice, egg yolks, and 1 cup of water. Cook on medium-high heat until thick, stirring constantly. Bring to a boil for 1 minute. Stir in the butter. Cool completely. Spread the filling thinly on the tops of three cake layers and stack the layers. Place the fourth layer on top.

For frosting: In a large bowl and with an electric mixer, beat the butter, confectioners' sugar, milk, corn syrup, and lemon extract until fluffy. Fold the whipped topping into the creamed mixture a little at a time, stirring until you have the desired consistency for spreading. Frost and assemble the cake. Refrigerate until ready to serve. **Makes 10 to 12 servings.**

–Fara Murray, Carrollton, Texas

DESSERTS

German Chocolate Cake

CAKE:

½ cup boiling water

1 bar (4 ounces) sweet cooking chocolate

2 cups sugar

1 cup (2 sticks) butter, softened

4 large eggs, separated

1 teaspoon vanilla extract

2¼ cups all-purpose flour or 2½ cups cake flour

1 teaspoon baking soda

1 teaspoon salt

1 cup buttermilk

FROSTING:

5 large egg yolks

1 can (12 ounces) evaporated milk

1½ cups sugar

1 cup (2 sticks) butter

1½ teaspoons vanilla extract

2 cups flaked coconut

1½ cups chopped pecans

Preheat the oven to 350°F. Grease three 8- or 9-inch round cake pans and line the bottoms of the pans with waxed or parchment paper.

For cake: In a mixing bowl, pour the boiling water over the chocolate. Stir until the chocolate is melted and set aside to cool. In a medium bowl and with an electric mixer, beat the sugar and butter until light and fluffy, then add the egg yolks one at a time, beating after each. Add the melted chocolate and vanilla and beat on low speed to blend. In a separate bowl, mix together the flour, baking soda, and salt. Add the dry ingredients to the egg mixture alternately with the buttermilk, beating after each addition until the batter is smooth. Wash and dry the beaters.

In a separate bowl, beat the egg whites until stiff, then fold the egg whites into the batter. Pour an equal amount of batter into each baking pan. Bake for 35 to 40 minutes, or until a toothpick inserted near the center comes out clean. Cool for 10 minutes, then remove the cakes from the pans and cool them completely on wire racks.

For frosting: Wash and dry the beaters. In a two-quart saucepan and with an electric mixer, beat the egg yolks and evaporated milk. Stir in the sugar, butter, and vanilla. Bring to a boil over medium heat, stirring constantly, and cook for 10 to 12 minutes, or until thick. Remove the pan from the heat and stir in the coconut and pecans. Beat the frosting until it is a spreadable consistency. Frost the tops of the layers, assemble the cake, and frost the sides. **Makes 10 to 12 servings.**

–Karen Parish-Foster and Kim Aikens, Whittaker, Michigan

DESSERTS

Best Chocolate Cake

Use the Mocha Frosting recipe on page 232 or your favorite chocolate frosting.

3 ounces unsweetened baking chocolate

1⅓ cups strong coffee, divided

¾ cup (1½ sticks) butter

2¼ cups packed brown sugar

2 large eggs

1 teaspoon vanilla extract

2 cups sifted all-purpose flour

1 teaspoon baking soda

½ teaspoon salt

Preheat the oven to 350°F. Grease two 9-inch cake pans. Line each one with waxed paper. Butter the waxed paper. In a saucepan, melt the chocolate in ⅓ cup coffee over very low heat, stirring constantly. Set aside to cool. In a medium bowl and with an electric mixer, cream the butter and brown sugar. Add the eggs, one at a time, beating after each. Add the vanilla and chocolate and beat well. In a separate bowl, combine the dry ingredients. Add alternately to butter mixture with 1 cup coffee, mixing just enough to blend. Pour the batter into the prepared pans. Bake for 30 minutes, or until a toothpick inserted into the center comes out clean. (Do not remove the cake too soon or it will fall.) Cool the cakes for 10 minutes in the pans. Remove them from the pans (the layers are fragile; handle carefully) and cool them on a rack. Frost and assemble the cake. **Makes 12 to 16 servings.**

Great-Grandmother's Sponge Cake

CAKE:

4 large eggs

2 cups sugar

2 cups all-purpose flour

2 teaspoons baking powder

2 teaspoons vanilla extract

¼ teaspoon salt

1 cup hot milk

¼ cup (½ stick) butter, melted

FROSTING:

2 cups whipping cream

½ cup sugar

2 cups fresh berries (any variety)

Preheat the oven to 350°F. Grease and flour a 10-inch tube pan.

For cake: In a large bowl and with an electric mixer, beat the eggs and sugar until fluffy. In a separate bowl, sift the flour with the baking powder. Add the flour to the egg mixture, stirring to blend. Add the vanilla, salt, milk, and butter and stir to combine. Pour the batter into the prepared pan. Bake for 45 minutes, or until a toothpick inserted into the center comes out clean. Cool and cut in half horizontally.

For frosting: In a large bowl, whip the cream with the sugar. Frost the bottom layer of the cake with half of the cream and arrange 1 cup of berries on it. (If using strawberries, slice before placing. Raspberries and blackberries may be mashed before spreading, if desired.) Assemble the cake and frost the top with the remaining cream and berries. **Makes 12 servings.**

DESSERTS

The World's Best Cheesecake

CRUST:

2 cups crushed graham crackers

½ cup (1 stick) melted butter

¼ cup crushed walnuts

FILLING:

3 packages (8 ounces each) cream cheese, softened

1½ cups sugar

5 large eggs

3 tablespoons lemon juice

TOPPING:

1 pint (2 cups) sour cream

½ cup sugar

1 teaspoon vanilla extract

Preheat the oven to 350°F.

For crust: In a medium bowl, combine the graham crackers, melted butter, and walnuts. Using your fingers, press the mixture evenly across the bottom and up the sides of a 10-inch springform pan.

For filling: In a large bowl and with an electric mixer, cream the cream cheese and sugar. Add the eggs, one at a time, beating thoroughly after each. Beat in the lemon juice. Pour the filling over the crust. Bake for 40 to 45 minutes, without opening the oven door. Remove the cheesecake and reduce the heat to 300°F.

For topping: Put all of the ingredients into a small bowl and mix to blend thoroughly. Spread the topping over the cheesecake. Return the cake to the oven and bake for 15 minutes. Remove the cheesecake from the oven and cool it on a rack for several hours. Refrigerate overnight. **Makes 10 to 12 servings.**

TOPPERS FOR CHEESECAKE

- Fresh fruit in season, such as blueberries, raspberries, and blackberries, as well as sliced kiwifruit, strawberries, and peaches. Arrange the fruit in overlapping rings or rows.

- Fruit preserves. Heat 1 cup of preserves until thin, then drizzle over the top of the cheesecake. Garnish with fresh berries or sliced fruit.

- Canned or homemade fruit pie fillings such as cherry, pineapple, or blueberry. Spread a layer of filling evenly over the top of the cheesecake.

- Chocolate shavings or chocolate leaves (recipe on page 239).

AN EASY WAY TO CRUSH GRAHAM CRACKERS

- Place a few graham crackers into a zipper-sealed plastic bag, push out the air, and seal the bag. Put the bag on a countertop or other hard surface and roll over it a few times with a rolling pin. Repeat the process until you have the correct amount of crushed crackers.

DESSERTS

HOW TO MAKE CHOCOLATE LEAVES

■ Collect 12 fresh, nontoxic leaves about the size of a rose leaf. Keep a bit of the stem attached. Wash them thoroughly with warm soapy water, rinse completely, and pat dry between two paper towels.

Over low heat, melt about 3½ ounces of good-quality chocolate. Use a pastry brush to brush the melted chocolate to a thickness of about ⅛-inch onto the underside of each leaf. Place each leaf chocolate side up on a cookie sheet lined with waxed paper. Place the cookie sheet in the refrigerator for 15 to 20 minutes, or until the chocolate is firm. Then, with the chocolate side down, hold the leaf stem and carefully peel the leaf away from the chocolate, working quickly so that the chocolate doesn't melt. Place the chocolate leaves in a waxed-paper–lined container and keep refrigerated until ready to use. Makes 12 chocolate leaves.

The Best-Ever Carrot Cake

The secret ingredient in this cake is pineapple.

CAKE:

1¾ cups sugar

¾ cup vegetable oil

1 teaspoon vanilla extract

4 large eggs

2 cups all-purpose flour

½ teaspoon ground nutmeg

1½ teaspoons cinnamon

2 teaspoons baking powder

1 teaspoon baking soda

2 cups lightly packed shredded carrots

1 can (8 ounces) pineapple tidbits, drained

¾ cup chopped walnuts

FROSTING:

2 packages (3 ounces each) cream cheese, softened

6 tablespoons (¾ stick) butter, softened

1 teaspoon minced orange peel

2 to 2¼ cups sifted confectioners' sugar

Preheat the oven to 350°F. Grease and flour a 13x9-inch baking pan.

For cake: In a medium bowl and with an electric mixer, beat together the sugar, oil, and vanilla until just combined. Add the eggs, one at a time, and beat after each. In a separate bowl, combine the flour, nutmeg, cinnamon, baking powder, and baking soda. Add to the wet ingredients and stir to blend. Add the carrots, pineapple, and nuts and stir only until combined. Pour the batter into the prepared pan. Bake for 45 minutes, or until a knife inserted near the center comes out clean. Remove the pan from the oven, place it on a rack to cool.

For frosting: In a medium bowl and with an electric mixer, beat the cream cheese, butter, orange peel, and 2 cups of the confectioners' sugar until smooth. Adjust the amount of confectioners' sugar to desired consistency. Frost the cake. Makes 15 to 20 servings.

DESSERTS

Pies

A FEW POINTERS ABOUT MAKING PIES

- When mixing dough, slip one hand into a plastic bag and use it as a mitten. That way, when the phone rings, you can slip off the bag and pick up the receiver with a clean hand.

- Fill a sugar shaker with flour to shake out when you're rolling pastry.

- To keep pie dough from sticking to your countertop, roll out the crust between two sheets of lightly floured wax paper.

- To avoid a soggy bottom crust in your fruit pie, get the filling into the piecrust and into the oven quickly.
  If there is extra juice in the mixing bowl, don't pour it into the piecrust.

- To avoid a tough piecrust, don't over mix or overwork the dough.

- For easy cleanup after baking pies, use a cookie sheet covered with aluminum foil to catch any juices that may run over the edge.

- When cutting a cream or custard pie, wet the knife with hot water to make a clean cut that won't tear the filling.

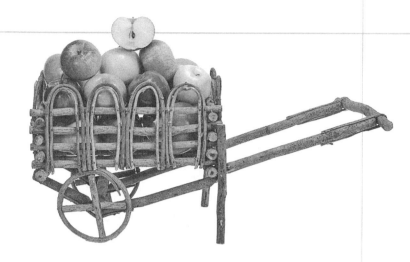

The 1991 Old Farmer's Almanac *Recipe Contest: "Apples"*

Upside-Down Apple Pie

½ cup currants or raisins

2 tablespoons apple juice

¼ cup (½ stick) butter or margarine,
  softened

1 cup pecan halves

⅔ cup dark-brown sugar

1 unbaked 9-inch double piecrust

6 to 8 cups pared and thinly sliced
  tart apples

2 tablespoons all-purpose flour

½ cup sugar

2 tablespoons lemon juice

1 teaspoon cinnamon

1 teaspoon nutmeg

Soak the currants in apple juice until plump (30 minutes to 1 hour). Preheat the oven to 450°F. Grease the bottom and sides of a 9-inch glass pie plate with the soft butter. Press the pecan halves in any pattern, round side down, into the butter. Pat the brown sugar over the pecans and butter. Carefully cover with the bottom piecrust. In a large bowl, mix the apples, flour, sugar, lemon juice, and spices. Add the currants and juice. Fill the piecrust, and top with the remaining crust. Crimp the edges and cut slits in the top of the crust. Bake for 10 minutes. Reduce heat to 350°F and bake for 45 minutes more. Remove the pie from the oven and cool it on a rack for 5 minutes. Gently loosen the edges of the pie with a knife, carefully place a large serving plate on top, and invert the pie. **Makes 6 to 8 servings.**

–Joan Kammire, Cary, North Carolina

DESSERTS

Old-Fashioned Chocolate Fudge Pie

FILLING:

¾ cup (1½ sticks) unsalted butter, cut
    into chunks

3 ounces unsweetened chocolate,
    broken up

3 extra-large eggs, plus 1 extra-large
    egg yolk

1½ cups sugar

6 tablespoons all-purpose flour

¼ teaspoon salt

2 teaspoons vanilla extract

1 fully baked 10-inch piecrust, or
    1 10-inch graham-cracker crust,
    baked 10 minutes

TOPPING:

2 cups heavy whipping cream

3 tablespoons sifted confectioners' sugar

1 teaspoon vanilla extract

Preheat the oven to 325°F.

For filling: In a heavy saucepan over low heat, melt the butter and chocolate, stirring occasionally to blend. Set aside to cool. In a large bowl and with an electric mixer, beat the eggs and egg yolk until light-colored or pale yellow. Add the sugar, flour, and salt, and beat well to combine. Whisk in the cooled chocolate. Add the vanilla and stir. Pour the filling into the baked piecrust and bake for 40 minutes, or until a knife inserted 2 to 3 inches from the edge can be withdrawn cleanly. (Small bubbles may appear over the surface of the baked pie, and cracks may form.) Remove the pie from the oven and cool it on a rack.

For topping: In a large bowl and with an electric mixer, whip together the topping ingredients. Spread the topping on the pie. Chill for at least 1 hour. **Makes 8 to 10 servings.**

–Laurie Charkowsky, Cranford, New Jersey

DESSERTS

Basic Piecrust

3 cups pastry or all-purpose flour
pinch of salt
1 cup shortening
½ to ¾ cup ice water

In a large bowl, combine the flour and salt. Cut in the shortening until the mixture is crumby. Toss the dough with water. Mix to combine but do not over mix. Roll out the dough on a lightly floured surface. Place in a pie plate and fill as desired. Cover with the top crust. **Makes enough for two single-crust pies or one double-crust pie.**

Tender, Flaky Pastry

Before canned shortening, there was lard. Some cooks still prefer it.

2 cups all-purpose flour
½ teaspoon salt
⅔ cup lard
6 tablespoons ice water, more or less

In a large bowl, combine the flour and salt, whisking to blend. Cut in the lard until the particles are about the size of peas. Add ice water, a tablespoon at a time, until the dough just holds together. Separate the dough into two balls, one slightly larger (for the bottom crust), and flatten them to about 1 inch high. Wrap the dough in plastic and chill for at least 1 hour.

Roll out the dough on a lightly floured surface. Place in a pie plate and fill as desired. Cover with the top crust. **Makes one double crust for a 9-inch pie**. (Recipe can be halved to make a single piecrust.)

THE BEST BAKING AND COOKING APPLES IN NORTH AMERICA

■ Almost any apple can be enjoyed when eaten fresh. But when faced with how to use apples in the kitchen, consider these recommendations:

VARIETY	APPEARANCE	FLAVOR CHARACTERISTICS	BEST USES
'Braeburn'	tall shape, bright color	tart, sweet, aromatic	sauce
'Cortland'	larger than 'McIntosh'	tart, crisp	pies, sauce, fruit salads
'Fuji'	red skin, firm	sweet, juicy	baking
'Gala'	yellow-orange skin with red striping (resembles a peach)	mild, sweet, juicy, crisp	dried, cider
'Granny Smith'	green skin	tart, moderately sweet, crisp	baking
'Jonagold'	yellow top, red bottom	tangy-sweet	pie, sauce
'Jonathan'	bright-red on yellow	mild to tart, juicy, crisp	sauce
'McIntosh'	red skin	spicy, sweet, aromatic, juicy	sauce
'Newtown Pippin'	greenish-yellow skin	sweet-tart, crisp	pie, sauce, cider
'Rhode Island Greening'	grass-green skin, tending toward yellow/orange	very tart	pie
'Rome Beauty'	thick skin	mildly tart, crisp	baking, cider
'Winesap'	sturdy, red skin	very juicy, sweet-sour, winey, aromatic	sauce, pie, cider

HOW MUCH IS ENOUGH?

1 pound of apples = 2 large, 3 medium, or 4 to 5 small apples

1 pound of apples = 3 cups peeled and sliced apples

Classic Apple Pie

What's more all-American than apple pie?

12 cups apples, peeled, cored, and sliced
    (10 to 12 large apples)

¾ cup sugar

1 tablespoon lemon juice

1 teaspoon nutmeg

1 teaspoon cinnamon

1 unbaked Basic or Tender, Flaky piecrust
    (see page 243)

1 tablespoon butter

Preheat the oven to 425°F. Prepare enough apple slices to fill a 10-inch pie plate heaping full. (Use the pie plate to measure by filling it with slices.) When you have enough, put the apples into a large bowl. Add the sugar, lemon juice, and spices and toss well to coat. Roll out the bottom crust and line the pie plate with it. Return the apple mixture to the plate, pressing the apples firmly in place. Dot the apples with butter. Roll out the top crust, place it on top of the apples, and seal the edges firmly. Cut vents into the top crust. Bake for 20 minutes. Reduce the heat to 400°F and bake for 20 minutes more. Reduce the heat again to 375°F and cook for 20 minutes more, or until the crust is nicely browned, and the apples feel done when you put a knife through a vent. (If you use McIntosh apples, the pie will be done in less than an hour.) **Makes 10 to 12 servings.**

Pumpkin Pie

Spicy and full of flavor, this pie goes well with ice cream, fresh whipped cream, or a wedge of cheddar.

1 cup brown sugar, firmly packed

¾ teaspoon salt

¾ teaspoon ground nutmeg

½ teaspoon ground cinnamon

½ teaspoon ground cloves

¼ teaspoon ground ginger

1½ cups cooked or canned pumpkin purée

1 cup milk, scalded

3 large eggs

1 unbaked 10-inch piecrust

Preheat the oven to 400°F. In a large mixing bowl, combine the brown sugar, salt, and spices. Add the pumpkin and stir to combine. Gradually add the milk, stirring to blend. Separate one of the eggs, put the white into a large bowl, and set it aside. Put the egg yolk into a medium bowl, add the two remaining eggs, and beat to combine with an electric mixer. Add the eggs to the pumpkin. Wash and dry the beaters. In a separate bowl, beat the egg white until stiff. Fold the egg white into the pumpkin mixture. Pour the filling into the piecrust. Bake for 35 to 45 minutes, or until set. **Makes 8 servings.**

DESSERTS

Any Berry Pie

Depending on the season or supply, experiment: Combine two or more kinds of berries.

CRUST:

2¼ cups all-purpose flour

¼ teaspoon salt

½ cup (1 stick) butter or margarine, chilled

5 to 7 tablespoons ice water

FILLING:

2½ cups fresh or thawed frozen berries

½ cup sugar

2 tablespoons flour or 1 tablespoon
    cornstarch

1 teaspoon cinnamon, ground ginger, or
    nutmeg

⅛ teaspoon salt

2 tablespoons (¼ stick) melted butter, 1
    beaten egg yolk, or ⅛ cup milk

For crust: In a large bowl, combine the flour, salt, and butter. Cut the butter into the mixture until it resembles coarse meal. Toss with ice water, stirring the mixture quickly. Gather the dough into a ball, wrap it in plastic, and chill it for 1 hour or more.

For filling: Preheat the oven to 425°F. Separate the dough into two pieces. On a lightly floured surface, roll out the larger piece as the bottom crust and place it into the pie plate. Pour in the fruit and sprinkle it with sugar, flour, spice, and salt. Roll out the remaining dough and place it on top of the fruit. Seal and flute the edges, and cut decorative slits in the top to allow steam to escape. Brush with the butter, beaten egg yolk, or milk, if desired. Bake for 40 minutes, or until the fruit is cooked and the crust is golden brown. **Makes 6 to 8 servings.**

Strawberry Chiffon Pie

A smooth, cool treat for a hot summer day.

1½ cups (about 1 quart) crushed, fresh
    strawberries

¾ cup sugar

1 tablespoon lemon juice

1 tablespoon (about 2 packets) unflavored
    gelatin

¼ cup cranberry or cranapple juice

2 cups whipping cream, divided

1 baked 9-inch piecrust

strawberry halves, for garnish

Combine the strawberries, sugar, and lemon juice in a bowl and let stand for about 30 minutes. In a small bowl, combine the gelatin and juice. Set the bowl in a larger bowl filled with hot water. Stir gently until all of the gelatin is dissolved. Stir the gelatin mixture into the berries. Refrigerate until partially set. In a large bowl, whip 1 cup of cream. Fold the whipped cream into the berry mixture. Pour the filling into the baked piecrust and chill until firm. When ready to serve, whip the remaining 1 cup of cream and spread or pipe it on the top of the pie. Decorate with strawberry halves. **Makes 6 to 8 servings.**

DESSERTS

PIE, PLEASE

Lena Beachy and Louella Mast, the "pie ladies" of Plain City, Ohio, were featured in The 2001 Old Farmer's Almanac. *Between them, they had more than 110 years of pie-making experience and shared the distinction of making as many as 53,000 pies per year for a restaurant in the heart of Ohio's Mennonite country. Here's their advice for a perfect pie, with a recipe.*

- Fruit pies are the easiest to make. Custard and butterscotch pies are the hardest because the ingredients must be cooked to a certain consistency, then cooled quickly. This takes practice.

- Use only fresh or frozen fruit, not canned.

- Add ½ teaspoon of lemon juice to a fruit filling to bring out the taste of the fruit and help the fruit keep its color.

- Make the top piecrust slightly thinner than the bottom crust to help maintain the structure of the pie.

- Be creative with the vent holes in the top crust (they have to be made to allow steam to escape). Make artistic markings, such as small leaves for an apple pie or a heart for a cherry pie.

- Bake a pie only on the center rack of the oven.

- If you're using canned whipped topping on a pie, improve the texture and taste: Put it into a bowl, add a small amount of heavy cream and a pinch of sugar, and whip the cream with a whisk.

- To keep the bottom crust of a cream pie from getting soggy, add the filling just before serving.

Louella's Custard Pie

Louella fills the piecrust only about half full, then moves the pie to the oven rack and adds the rest of the filling using a cup. She prefers glass pie plates to metal ones.

4 large eggs
1 cup sugar
½ teaspoon salt
1 teaspoon all-purpose flour
1 teaspoon vanilla extract
3 cups milk, scalded
1 unbaked 9-inch piecrust
cinnamon, for sprinkling

Preheat the oven to 425°F. Into a medium bowl, separate one of the eggs, whip or beat the white until stiff, and set aside. In a separate bowl, beat the yolk and the remaining three eggs. Add the sugar, salt, flour, and vanilla and stir well. Add the scalded milk. Stir in the beaten egg white. Pour the batter into the piecrust. Sprinkle with cinnamon. Bake for 10 minutes, then at 350°F for about 20 minutes, or until the filling is set. **Makes 8 servings.**

DESSERTS

Lemon Meringue Pie

FILLING:

1 cup sugar

2 tablespoons all-purpose flour

3 tablespoons cornstarch

¼ teaspoon salt

juice and zest from 1 lemon

2 tablespoons (¼ stick) butter

4 egg yolks, beaten

1 baked 9-inch piecrust

MERINGUE:

4 egg whites

6 tablespoons sugar

Preheat the oven to 350°F.

For filling: In a medium saucepan, whisk together the sugar, flour, cornstarch, and salt. Add 1½ cups of water, lemon juice, and zest and stir to mix. Cook over medium-high heat, stirring frequently, until the mixture comes to a boil and appears clearer. Stir in the butter. Place the egg yolks in a small bowl and gradually whisk in ½ cup of the hot sugar mixture. Whisk the egg yolk mixture back into the remaining sugar mixture. Bring to a boil and continue to cook while stirring constantly until thick. Remove from the heat. Stir and allow to cool before pouring the filling into the baked piecrust.

For meringue: In a large glass or metal bowl, whip the egg whites until foamy. Add the sugar gradually and continue to whip until stiff peaks form. Spread the meringue over the lemon filling, sealing the edges at the crust. Bake for about 10 minutes, or until the meringue is golden brown. **Makes 8 servings.**

DESSERTS

No-Bake Peanut Butter Pie

CRUST:
¼ cup finely chopped roasted peanuts
1 cup graham cracker crumbs
⅓ cup melted butter

FILLING:
1¼ cups creamy peanut butter
1 package (8 ounces) cream cheese, softened
1 cup confectioners' sugar, divided
2 tablespoons (¼ stick) butter, melted
1¼ cups chilled whipping cream
1 tablespoon vanilla extract

TOPPING:
½ cup whipping cream
4 ounces semisweet chocolate, chopped

For crust: In a medium bowl, combine the ingredients and, using your fingers, press the crust into a 9-inch pie plate. Put the crust in the freezer while preparing the filling.

For filling: In a large bowl and with an electric mixer, beat the peanut butter, cream cheese, ½ cup confectioners' sugar, and butter. Wash and dry the beaters. Put the whipping cream, the remaining confectioners' sugar, and vanilla into a medium bowl and beat until peaks form. Fold the cream into the peanut butter mixture. Spoon the filling into the chilled crust. Refrigerate until firm.

For topping: In a small saucepan on medium-high heat, cook the cream until almost boiling. Reduce the heat to low. Add the chocolate and stir constantly until it melts. Remove the pan from the heat and cool slightly. Pour the topping over the filling to cover completely and evenly. Refrigerate for at least 1 hour before serving. **Makes 8 servings.**

DESSERTS

Cookies and Bars

German Hazelnut Cookies

4 cups all-purpose flour, divided

3 cups (6 sticks) cold, unsalted butter

3 cups confectioners' sugar

3½ cups ground hazelnuts or walnuts, divided

3 large eggs, well beaten

juice and grated peel of 1 lemon

1 egg beaten with 1 tablespoon water, for glaze

Measure 3 cups of flour into a bowl and cut in the butter as for pastry. Stir in the confectioners' sugar, and then 3 cups of the nuts. Add the eggs, lemon juice, and peel and mix thoroughly. Wrap the dough tightly in plastic wrap and chill for at least 2 hours.

Preheat the oven to 350°F. Grease two cookie sheets. Remove a small amount of dough from the refrigerator (keep the rest of the dough refrigerated). With some of the remaining flour, dust a board or counter surface. Roll out the portion to a ¼-inch thickness on the board. Dust the top of the dough with flour to prevent sticking. Using cookie cutters, cut out shapes and place them on a cookie sheet. (Note: The dough can also be dropped by teaspoonfuls; cookies will flatten into wafers as they bake.) Brush the cookies gently with the egg-water mixture and sprinkle with pinches of remaining ground nuts. Bake for 10 to 15 minutes, or until golden. **Makes about 5 dozen cookies.**

–Betsy P. Race, Euclid, Ohio

QUICK FIX

Allow a cookie sheet to cool completely before filling it with the next batch.

DESSERTS

The 1989 Old Farmer's Almanac *Recipe Contest: "Holiday Cookies and Bars"*

Apricot Almond Bars

TOPPING:

1½ cups sugar

3 cups sliced, blanched almonds

4 large egg whites

2 tablespoons all-purpose flour

½ teaspoon cinnamon

¼ teaspoon freshly grated nutmeg

BARS:

2½ cups all-purpose flour

½ cup sugar

1 cup (2 sticks) butter

2 large egg yolks

APRICOT GLAZE:

½ cup apricot preserves

CHOCOLATE GLAZE:

3 ounces semisweet chocolate

1 ounce unsweetened chocolate

Preheat the oven to 350°F. Line a 15½x10½x1-inch jelly-roll pan with foil.

For topping: Combine all of the ingredients in the top of a double boiler over hot water on medium-high heat. Cook, stirring occasionally, until the mixture reaches 110°F on a candy thermometer. Remove from the heat and set aside.

For bars: In a large bowl, combine the flour and sugar. Cut in the butter until the mixture is crumbly. Add the egg yolks. With your hands, work the batter into a smooth dough and press it into the prepared pan. Prick the dough with a fork in several places. Bake for 15 minutes. Remove the bars from the oven and spread with the almond topping. Return the bars to the oven and bake for 20 minutes more.

For apricot glaze: Put the apricot preserves into a small saucepan. Add 1 tablespoon of water and cook over medium heat until boiling, stirring occasionally. Strain the preserves through a fine sieve, reserving the juices and discarding the chunks. Brush the glaze over the bars immediately after the pan comes out of the oven. Cool the pan on a rack. When the bars have cooled, cut them into 2-inch squares.

For chocolate glaze: In the top of a double boiler over hot water on medium-high heat, melt the two types of chocolate together. Using a small spoon, drizzle the glaze over the squares and allow to set. **Makes about 6 dozen bars.**

—Carolyn Rosen, Nashville, Tennessee

DESSERTS

COOKIE BITES

■ For chewy cookies, be careful not to overcream the butter and sugar, and underbake the batter a bit.

■ For firm cookies, allow the cookies to "cook" on the cookie sheet for a minute or two out of the oven after baking, before transferring them to a cooling rack.

■ Cookies baked on a cookie sheet lined with parchment paper slide off the sheet easily, and stop cooking as soon as they're out of the oven.

■ Separate crisp and soft cookies so that their respective textures will be preserved. Well packed, your homemade cookies will keep fresh in the kitchen for about a week.

■ Layer soft cookies between sheets of waxed paper in containers with tight lids to retain moisture. Add an apple slice if necessary to add humidity.

■ Store crisp cookies in a container with a loose-fitting lid.

SECOND PRIZE

The 1993 Old Farmer's Almanac *Recipe Contest: "Chocolate"*

Chocolate Peppermint Creams

COOKIES:

3 cups all-purpose flour
1¼ teaspoons baking soda
½ teaspoon salt
¾ cup (1½ sticks) butter
1½ cups brown sugar, packed
12 ounces semisweet chocolate chips
2 large eggs

FILLING:

3 cups confectioners' sugar
⅓ cup butter, softened
¼ teaspoon peppermint extract, or to taste
¼ cup milk

Preheat the oven to 350°F. Grease your cookie sheets.

For cookies: In a medium bowl, sift the flour, baking soda, and salt together. Put the butter, brown sugar, and 2 tablespoons water into a large saucepan over low heat and stir as the butter melts. Add the chocolate chips and stir as the chocolate melts. Remove the pan from the heat and set aside to cool slightly. Add the eggs to the chocolate mixture and, with an electric mixer, beat to blend. Add the flour mixture and stir to combine. Drop by heaping teaspoonfuls onto the prepared cookie sheets. Bake for 8 to 10 minutes. Remove from the oven, transfer to racks, and allow to cool.

For filling: In a large bowl and with an electric mixer, cream all of the filling ingredients until smooth.

Sandwich pairs of cookies together with 1 teaspoon of filling. **Makes about 3 dozen sandwich cookies.**

–Roselie A. Aiello, Mount Shasta, California

DESSERTS

The 1989 Old Farmer's Almanac *Recipe Contest: "Holiday Cookies and Bars"*

Chocolate Orange Delights

BARS:

3 ounces unsweetened chocolate

¾ cup (1½ sticks) butter, softened

1 cup brown sugar

1 cup sugar

½ cup sour cream

2 eggs

2 teaspoons grated orange peel

2 cups sifted flour

1 teaspoon baking soda

½ teaspoon salt

1 cup chopped walnuts or pecans

2 cups chocolate chips

GLAZE:

3 ounces semisweet chocolate

1 teaspoon orange extract

4 tablespoons butter

candy sprinkles (optional)

Preheat the oven to 375°F. Lightly grease your cookie sheets.

For cookies: In the top of a double boiler over hot water on medium-high heat, melt the unsweetened chocolate. Set it aside to cool. In a large bowl and with an electric beater, cream the butter and sugars thoroughly. Add the sour cream, eggs, orange peel, and melted chocolate and beat well. Add the flour, baking soda, and salt and stir to combine. Add the nuts and chocolate chips and mix. Drop the batter by rounded teaspoonfuls onto the cookie sheets. Bake for 12 to 15 minutes. Remove from the oven and transfer the cookies to wire racks to cool.

For glaze: In a small saucepan over low heat, melt the semisweet chocolate. Add the orange extract and stir to combine. Add the butter, 1 tablespoon at a time, and stir until smooth. Spread on cookies. If desired, decorate with candy sprinkles before the glaze sets. **Makes about 6 dozen cookies.**

–Frances E. Callahan, Chester, Vermont

DESSERTS

Classic Sugar Cookies

3½ cups all-purpose flour
¼ teaspoon salt
1 cup (2 sticks) unsalted butter, softened
⅔ cup sugar
1 large egg, lightly beaten
1 tablespoon light corn syrup
2 teaspoons vanilla extract

In a medium bowl, mix together the flour and salt. In a large bowl and with an electric mixer, cream the butter and sugar. Add the egg, corn syrup, and vanilla and beat to combine. Add the flour mixture, one-third at a time, and mix until thoroughly incorporated. Shape the dough into two flat disks, wrap each in plastic, and chill for 1 to 2 hours, or until it is firm enough to roll out. Preheat the oven to 375°F. Cut two pieces of waxed paper the size of your rolling surface. Unwrap each dough disk and roll it out between the papers until it is ¼-inch thick. Using a cookie cutter or drinking glass, cut out cookies. Transfer them to a cookie sheet with a spatula, leaving about 1 inch between them. Bake for 8 to 10 minutes. **Makes 3 to 4 dozen cookies.**

Best Butter Cookies

1 cup (2 sticks) butter, softened
1 cup sugar
1 egg
2 tablespoons orange juice
1 tablespoon vanilla extract
2½ cups all-purpose flour
1 teaspoon baking powder

In a large bowl, cream the butter and sugar. Add the egg, orange juice, and vanilla and beat well. Add the flour and baking powder and stir to blend. Cover the dough with plastic wrap and put it into the refrigerator to chill for 2 to 3 hours, or until firm. Preheat the oven to 375°F. Cut two pieces of waxed paper the size of your rolling surface. Roll out portions of the dough between the papers to ¼-inch thick, keeping the remainder chilled. Using a cookie cutter or drinking glass, cut out cookies. Using a spatula, place the cookies onto ungreased cookie sheets. Bake for about 8 minutes, or until lightly browned. Cool completely before frosting. **Makes about 4 dozen.**

Creamy-Flavored Frosting

1 cup confectioners' sugar
2 tablespoons melted butter or margarine
1 tablespoon milk
1 teaspoon flavored extract (vanilla, orange,
**   or raspberry)**
4 drops food coloring (optional)

Just before you are ready to frost the cookies, combine all the ingredients in a small bowl and beat with a fork until smooth and creamy. Spread thinly onto cooled cookies; decorate further with nonpareils, chocolate sprinkles, or colored sugar, if desired. Allow the frosting to dry before stacking or covering the cookies. **Makes enough to frost about 3½ dozen small cookies.**

NOTE:

If using orange extract, combine 2 drops of yellow food coloring and 2 drops of red to make orange frosting. If using raspberry extract, use 4 drops of red food coloring for pink frosting. For vanilla, leave the frosting creamy white.

Egg Paint

1 egg yolk
liquid or paste food coloring

In a small cup or bowl, stir together the egg yolk and a small amount of liquid or paste food coloring to obtain the desired color.

Using a paintbrush, decorate the unbaked cookies with egg paint, freehand or with a stencil. Bake at 375°F for 8 to 10 minutes, or until the cookies begin to brown on the edges. Remove the cookie sheet from the oven and place it on a wire rack to cool for 5 minutes. Transfer the cookies onto the rack to finish cooling.

STORAGE FIX

When storing or freezing frosted cookies, very delicate cookies, soft cookies, or bars, place layers of waxed paper between them.

Aunt Sophie's Magic Cookies

2 cups (4 sticks) butter, softened
4 cups all-purpose flour
1 pint vanilla ice cream, softened
¾ cup sugar
¼ cup pecans or walnuts, chopped fine
2 tablespoons cinnamon

Cut the butter into the flour. Add the ice cream and blend it into the mixture with your hands. (Add more flour if necessary to make the dough easy to handle.) Wrap the dough in plastic wrap and refrigerate overnight. The dough will become hard.

When you're ready to bake, preheat the oven to 350°F. In a small bowl, combine the sugar, nuts, and cinnamon. Sprinkle some of the sugar mixture onto a pastry cloth or smooth (not terry cloth) dish towel. On top of the sugar mixture, roll out a small piece of the dough to form a 4- to 5-inch circle that is ⅛-inch thick. Turn the dough over once during rolling so that both sides are covered with the sugar mixture. Cut the circle into quarters and roll each from the outside to the center. Repeat until all the dough and sugar mixture are used. Bake on a cookie sheet for 20 minutes or until browned. **Makes 6 to 7 dozen cookies.**

Oatmeal–Chocolate Chip Cookies

1 cup (2 sticks) butter or margarine,
    at room temperature
½ cup sugar
½ cup brown sugar
1 teaspoon vanilla extract
1 large egg
2 cups all-purpose flour
½ teaspoon salt
1 teaspoon baking powder
1 teaspoon baking soda
2 cups quick-cooking rolled oats
2 cups chocolate chips
½ cup chopped nuts (optional)

Preheat the oven to 400°F. Lightly grease your cookie sheets. In a large bowl and with an electric mixer, cream the butter and sugars until smooth. Add the vanilla and egg and mix to blend. In a separate bowl, combine the flour, salt, baking powder, and baking soda. Add to the butter mixture and stir to combine. Add the oats and mix to blend. Stir in the chocolate chips and nuts. Drop by spoonfuls onto cookie sheets and bake for 10 minutes, or until lightly browned. **Makes 4 dozen cookies.**

Perfect Macaroni and Cheese
(see page 186)

Easy Dill Potato Soufflé
(see page 193)

Herb Cheese Bread
(see page 207)

Mild and Meaty Lasagna

(see page 298)

Peachy Almond Cake
(see page 230)

Crescent City Banana Bundles
(see page 262)

Strawberry Chiffon Pie
(see page 246)

Upside-Down Apple Pie

(see page 241)

Fran's Chowchow
(see page 285)

Carrot Cookies With Orange Butter Frosting

COOKIES:

½ cup shortening

½ cup (1 stick) butter or margarine

¾ cup sugar

2 eggs

1 cup cooked and mashed carrots

2 cups flour

2 teaspoons baking soda

½ teaspoon salt

¾ cup shredded coconut

FROSTING:

1½ cups confectioners' sugar

3 tablespoons butter or margarine

2 teaspoons grated orange peel

1 tablespoon orange juice

Preheat the oven to 375°F. Lightly grease your cookie sheets.

For cookies: Into a medium bowl, put the shortening, butter, sugar, and eggs and mix thoroughly. Add the carrots and stir to blend. Add the flour, baking soda, and salt and mix. Add the coconut and stir. Drop by teaspoonfuls onto a cookie sheet, leaving about 2 inches between them. Bake for 8 to 10 minutes, or until no imprint remains when touched lightly. Remove from the oven and transfer to a rack to cool. Cool completely before frosting.

For frosting: In a medium bowl and with an electric beater, beat all of the ingredients together until smooth. If needed, add a few drops of water to thin the frosting enough for spreading. **Makes 5 dozen cookies.**

Gingerbread Men

1 cup brown sugar
1 cup dark molasses
1 cup (2 sticks) butter
1 teaspoon baking soda
1 teaspoon cinnamon
2 teaspoons ground ginger
½ teaspoon salt
4 cups flour

In a large saucepan over medium-high heat, bring brown sugar, molasses, and butter to a boil. Remove from heat and let cool slightly. Dissolve the baking soda in ⅓ cup of water and add it to the molasses mixture. Add the remaining ingredients and stir until well blended. Wrap the dough in plastic wrap and chill for at least 8 hours.

Preheat the oven to 350°F. Lightly grease a cookie sheet. Roll out the dough to ⅛-inch thickness on a floured board. Cut with a gingerbread-man cookie cutter. Bake for 12 to 15 minutes, or until crisp and golden. Allow the cookies to cool before decorating. **Makes about 4 dozen cookies.**

Best Brownies

Everyone has a favorite brownie recipe, but these are hard to beat.

1 cup (2 sticks) butter, softened
2 cups sugar
1 tablespoon corn syrup
⅔ cup cocoa
4 large eggs
1 teaspoon vanilla extract
1½ cups all-purpose flour
1 teaspoon baking powder

Preheat the oven to 350°F. Grease a 13x9-inch baking pan. Into a large bowl, put the butter, sugar, corn syrup, cocoa, eggs, and vanilla and stir to blend. In a separate bowl, combine the flour and baking powder. Add the flour to the batter, mixing well. Pour the batter into the prepared pan and bake for about 30 minutes, or until the top is shiny and the center is set. Allow to cool in the pan before cutting into squares. **Makes 24 brownies.**

Pumpkin Cheesecake Bars

These luscious bars have a hint of cinnamon, ginger, and nutmeg.

CRUST:

1 package (⅓ pound) graham crackers

⅓ cup packed light-brown sugar

½ teaspoon cinnamon

5 tablespoons unsalted butter, melted

FILLING:

1 package (8 ounces) cream cheese, softened

⅔ cup packed light-brown sugar

1 large egg

1 egg yolk

1 teaspoon vanilla extract

1 tablespoon all-purpose flour

½ teaspoon each cinnamon, ground ginger, and nutmeg

¾ cup canned pumpkin

⅓ cup heavy cream

Preheat the oven to 350°F. Butter a 9-inch square pan.

For crust: Break the crackers into a food processor. Add the brown sugar and cinnamon, and process to a fine meal. Add the melted butter and process again. Press the crust into the bottom of the pan and slightly up the sides. Bake for 10 minutes. Remove from the oven and set aside to cool. Reduce the oven temperature to 325°F.

For filling: In a large bowl and with an electric mixer, cream the cream cheese, brown sugar, egg, and egg yolk. Add the vanilla and stir to blend. Add the remaining ingredients and stir until smooth. Pour the filling into the crust and bake for 45 minutes. Remove from the oven and cool on a rack. Refrigerate for at least 4 hours before slicing. **Makes 9 bars.**

DESSERTS

Peanut Butter and Jelly Bars

Kids love these as breakfast-on-the-run or for after-school snacks. Substitute your favorite flavor of jam or jelly.

½ cup smooth peanut butter

7 tablespoons margarine, softened

1 cup packed brown sugar

1¼ cups flour

1¼ cups quick-cooking oats

¾ cup strawberry jam or jelly

Preheat the oven to 300°F. In a large bowl and with an electric mixer, cream the peanut butter, margarine, and brown sugar until the mixture is light and fluffy. Add the flour and oats and mix well. Press half of the mixture into an 8x8-inch baking pan. Gently spread the jam over the mixture. Layer the remaining oat mixture over the jam and press lightly. Bake for about 40 minutes. Cool and cut into bars. **Makes 16 bars.**

Lemon Squares

CRUST:

2 cups all-purpose flour

½ cup confectioners' sugar

1 cup (2 sticks) margarine

FILLING:

4 large eggs, beaten

2 cups sugar

⅓ cup lemon juice*

¼ cup all-purpose flour

½ teaspoon baking powder

confectioners' sugar for dusting (optional)

Preheat the oven to 350°F.

For crust: Put the flour and confectioners' sugar into a large bowl and mix. Cut in the margarine. Press the crust into a 13x9-inch baking pan. Bake for 25 minutes.

For filling: Put all of the ingredients into a large bowl and stir to combine. Pour the filling onto the baked crust. Return the pan to the oven and bake for 25 minutes more. Sprinkle with confectioners' sugar, if desired. Cut into squares when cool. **Makes 24 squares.**

*NOTE: If desired, add 2 tablespoons of fresh-grated lemon zest to the filling. Or, substitute key lime juice for lemon juice, and omit the lemon zest.

DESSERTS

Chocolate Hazelnut Dream Bars

BARS:

1 cup whole skinless hazelnuts

¼ cup sugar

2 tablespoons cocoa powder

½ cup (1 stick) butter

1½ teaspoons hazelnut liqueur

1 large egg, slightly beaten

1¼ cups vanilla wafer crumbs

½ cup flaked coconut

1 ounce white chocolate, melted,
   for garnish

FROSTING:

⅓ cup butter

2 tablespoons hazelnut liqueur

3 cups sifted confectioners' sugar

2 to 3 tablespoons half-and-half

Preheat the oven to 350°F.

For bars: Spread the hazelnuts on a cookie sheet and toast in a the oven for 10 minutes, or until golden brown. Reserve 36 for garnish. Chop the rest fine. Put the sugar and cocoa into a heavy saucepan and stir to combine. Add the butter, hazelnut liqueur, and egg. Cook over low heat, stirring constantly, until the butter melts and the mixture thickens. Remove the pan from the heat. Stir in the chopped hazelnuts, vanilla wafer crumbs, and coconut. Press the mixture firmly into an 9-inch square pan. Cover the pan with plastic wrap and chill for 20 minutes.

For frosting: In a large bowl and with an electric mixer at medium speed, cream the butter. Add the hazelnut liqueur and stir. Gradually add the confectioners' sugar, alternating with the half-and-half and beating between each addition. (Begin and end with the confectioners' sugar.) Beat until mixture reaches spreading consistency. Spread the frosting over the cooled hazelnut bars. Cover with plastic wrap and chill for 25 minutes. Cut the bars into 1½-inch squares. To garnish, dip the reserved hazelnuts into the white chocolate and place one on each square. Store in the refrigerator. **Makes 36 bars.**

Fruit Desserts

Crescent City Banana Bundles

BUNDLES:

2 cans (8 ounces each) refrigerated
   crescent dinner rolls

4 medium firm-ripe bananas

8 teaspoons brown sugar, divided

8 tablespoons coarsely chopped pecans,
   divided

8 tablespoons white chocolate chips,
   divided

SAUCE:

½ cup (1 stick) butter

½ cup brown sugar

2 tablespoons orange juice or rum

6 tablespoons coarsely chopped pecans

Preheat the oven to 375°F.

For bundles: Divide the crescent rolls into 8 rectangles and press the perforated edges to seal. On a lightly floured surface, roll each rectangle to a 6x6-inch square. Peel the bananas and cut them in half crosswise. Cut each half into ½-inch slices and put into the center of each square. Sprinkle each pile of bananas with 1 teaspoon brown sugar, 1 tablespoon pecans, and 1 tablespoon white chocolate chips. Bring up the corners and sides of the rolls and pinch them together in the center to form a bundle. Place each one on an ungreased cookie sheet. Bake for 17 to 20 minutes, or until golden brown.

For sauce: In a small saucepan over medium-high heat, bring the butter, brown sugar, and orange juice to a boil. Add the pecans and boil for 1 to 2 minutes, or until slightly thickened. Reduce the heat but keep the sauce warm. Put a bundle on each plate with a scoop of ice cream, if desired. Spoon sauce over everything. **Makes 8 servings.**

–Julie DeMatteo, Clementon, New Jersey

DESSERTS

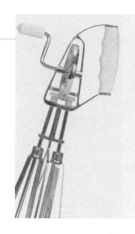

FIXES

■ If cream has been around for a while and is more likely to turn to butter instead of whipped cream, add ⅛ teaspoon of baking soda before whipping.

■ For best results, add vanilla and sugar to whipped cream just before it becomes stiff.

■ Cream will whip better and egg whites will beat faster if you add a pinch of salt.

SECOND PRIZE

The 1995 Old Farmer's Almanac *Recipe Contest: "Family-Tradition Ethnic Desserts"*

Serbian Plum Dumplings

When my grandmother left Serbia for the United States in the early 1920s, she brought very little with her, but one thing she did have was this recipe for plum dumplings.

1½ pounds potatoes (about 5 medium), peeled, cooked, and mashed

2 large eggs, beaten

1 teaspoon salt

2 cups (approximately) all-purpose flour

½ cup sugar

1 teaspoon cinnamon

14 small purple plums, pitted

¼ cup (½ stick) butter, melted

¼ cup toasted bread crumbs

Put the potatoes, eggs, and salt into a large bowl and mix well. Add the flour, ½ cup at a time, and work enough into the potato mixture to make a smooth, firm dough. In a separate bowl, mix the sugar and cinnamon. Fill the cavity of each plum with 1 teaspoon of the cinnamon-sugar mixture. Pat a piece of potato dough into a round cake about 2½ inches wide and ¼-inch thick. Put one sugared plum in the center, fold the dough over the plum, and pinch the edges to seal, making a round dumpling. Repeat with the remaining plums and dough. Drop the dumplings, one at a time, into a large pot of boiling, salted water. Return the water to a boil and cook gently for 5 minutes. Lower the heat and simmer for about 15 minutes more. Scoop out the dumplings with a slotted spoon and place in serving bowl. Drizzle with melted butter, sprinkle with bread crumbs, and serve hot. **Makes 14 dumplings.**

–Marcelle LaMaster-Skelton, Bloomington, Indiana

Lemon Cream and Raspberry Tart

CRUST:

⅓ cup packed dark-brown sugar

½ cup toasted and finely ground pecans

½ cup all-purpose flour

½ teaspoon cinnamon

½ teaspoon ground ginger

¼ teaspoon salt

6 tablespoons cold unsalted butter, cut into
    small pieces

FILLING:

6 ounces cream cheese, softened

½ cup lemon curd, at room temperature

TOPPING:

12 ounces raspberries (fresh or frozen)

Preheat the oven to 375°F.

For crust: Into a food processor or blender, put all of the crust ingredients and pulse until combined, about 40 seconds. Press the crust evenly into the bottom and up the sides of a 9-inch round tart pan with a fluted rim. Bake in the center of the oven for 20 minutes. Remove from the oven and cool in the pan on a rack.

For filling: In a food processor or mixer, whip the cream cheese until it is light and fluffy. Gradually add the lemon curd and whip until mixture is combined. Fill the cooled crust with the lemon cream and top with raspberries. **Makes 8 servings.**

–Veronica Betancourt, Antioch, California

DESSERTS

■ HONEY LEMON SAUCE

Serve with sliced strawberries, peaches, or blueberries.

2 tablespoons honey

1 tablespoon fresh or bottled lemon juice

1 cup plain yogurt

dash of cinnamon

Stir the honey and lemon juice into the yogurt, then season with cinnamon. **Makes 1 cup.**

THIRD PRIZE

The 1995 Old Farmer's Almanac *Recipe Contest: "Family-Tradition Ethnic Desserts"*

Norwegian Fruit Soup (Søt Suppe)

This recipe came from Norway in 1913, when my husband's parents arrived in this country. Any combination of dried fruits may be used, and every year my recipe changes.

½ pound dark raisins

½ pound light raisins

1 pound small prunes, pitted

3 cinnamon sticks, broken up

1 tablespoon whole cloves

4 tablespoons instant tapioca

½ cup sugar

1 seedless orange, peeled, thinly sliced, and quartered

1 to 2 cups applesauce

1 cup orange juice or water, as needed

Put 6 cups of water, the raisins, prunes, cinnamon sticks, cloves, and tapioca into a saucepan. Slowly bring the liquid to a boil, stirring occasionally. Cook gently until the tapioca is transparent. Add the sugar, orange slices, and applesauce. Add enough orange juice to thin the soup to a desired consistency. Serve warm or chilled alone in bowls or over sponge cake or ice cream. **Makes 8 servings.**

—Mary Linstad, Porterfield, Wisconsin

DESSERTS

Summer Peach Crisp

FILLING:

¼ **cup flour**

⅓ **cup sugar**

½ **teaspoon cinnamon**

¼ **teaspoon nutmeg**

⅛ **teaspoon ground ginger**

8 **cups peeled and sliced ripe peaches or**
    nectarines

¼ **cup peach nectar or orange juice**

TOPPING:

⅔ **cup packed brown sugar**

½ **cup rolled oats**

½ **cup sliced almonds, toasted**

½ **cup all-purpose flour**

3 **tablespoons sugar**

½ **cup (1 stick) butter**

Preheat the oven to 400°F.

For filling: In a large bowl, stir together the flour, sugar, cinnamon, nutmeg, and ginger. Add the peach slices and nectar. Toss to coat. Spread filling into an ungreased 8-inch square baking dish.

For topping: Put the brown sugar, oats, almonds, flour, and sugar into a bowl and stir to blend. Using a pastry blender, two knives, or your fingers, cut in the butter until the mixture resembles coarse crumbs. Sprinkle the topping over the filling and bake for 30 to 35 minutes, or until the fruit is tender and the topping is golden. Serve warm or cold, with ice cream, if desired. **Makes 10 servings.**

–Mike Potoroka, Goodeve, Saskatchewan

Spiced Pear Shortcake

3 large pears, peeled, cored, and sliced

3 tablespoons butter

3 tablespoons sugar

6 shortcake biscuits

whipped cream, seasoned with ground
    ginger to taste

Sauté the pear slices in butter, adding sugar when the fruit begins to soften. Cook just until tender. Spoon the fruit over split shortcake biscuits and top with spiced whipped cream. **Makes 12 half-biscuit servings.**

Shortcake Biscuits

2 cups all-purpose flour

3 tablespoons sugar

2½ teaspoons baking powder

½ teaspoon salt

6 tablespoons (¾ stick) cold, unsalted
    butter

½ cup milk

¼ cup sour cream

1 large egg

½ teaspoon vanilla extract

1 large egg, beaten with 1 tablespoon
    milk, for egg wash

sugar, for sprinkling

Preheat the oven to 425°F. Lightly grease a cookie sheet. Into a large bowl, sift together the flour, sugar, baking powder, and salt. Cut in the butter until it is the size of split peas. In a separate bowl, whisk together the milk, sour cream, egg, and vanilla. Add the wet ingredients to the dry and stir briskly just until gathered into a sticky dough. Cover the bowl with plastic wrap and let it rest for 5 minutes.

Flour the palms of your hands. Then, take a portion of dough slightly smaller than a tennis ball and roll it between your palms to form a smooth ball. Make six balls. Place them onto the cookie sheet, brush them with the egg wash, and sprinkle them with sugar. Bake for 15 to 20 minutes, or until golden brown. Remove the biscuits from the oven and cool them on a rack. To serve, split in half edgewise and add your favorite fresh fruit, with a dollop of whipped cream on top. Garnish with a pinch of nutmeg, cinnamon, or ginger. **Makes 6 biscuits.**

Strawberry Shortcake

1 quart fresh strawberries
½ cup confectioners' sugar
6 shortcake biscuits
cream or ice cream, to taste
cinnamon, to taste

Slice the strawberries into a medium bowl and toss gently with the sugar. Let the berries sit for at least an hour to get really juicy. Spoon the berries over split shortcake biscuits and garnish with cream or ice cream and a pinch of cinnamon. **Makes 12 half-biscuit servings.**

Blueberry Buckle

BATTER:
¼ cup (½ stick) butter
¾ cup sugar
1 large egg
½ cup milk
2 cups all-purpose flour
2 teaspoons baking powder
¼ teaspoon salt
2 cups fresh blueberries
1 to 2 spoonfuls all-purpose flour

TOPPING:
¼ cup (½ stick) soft butter
½ cup sugar
⅓ cup all-purpose flour
½ teaspoon cinnamon

Preheat the oven to 375°F. Grease and flour a 9-inch square pan.

For batter: In a large bowl and with an electric mixer, cream the butter and sugar. Add the egg and beat thoroughly. Stir in the milk. In a separate bowl, mix together the flour, baking powder, and salt. Add to the batter, mixing well. In a small bowl, toss the blueberries with the flour, then add them to the batter and stir to blend. Spread the batter in the prepared pan.

For topping: In a medium bowl, cream the butter, sugar, flour, and cinnamon until well blended and crumbly. Sprinkle the topping over the batter. Bake for 45 to 50 minutes. Serve warm with whipped cream. **Makes 9 servings.**

Blueberry Crunch

This is best when made with fresh-picked blueberries.

1 cup quick-cooking oatmeal
1 cup firmly packed brown sugar
½ cup all-purpose flour
½ cup powdered milk
½ teaspoon salt
½ teaspoon cinnamon
½ cup shortening
1½ cups blueberries

Preheat the oven to 350°F. Grease a 9-inch square baking pan. Into a large bowl, put the oatmeal, brown sugar, flour, powdered milk, salt, and cinnamon and mix thoroughly. Add the shortening and mix until the ingredients are coarsely blended. Spread half of the mixture in the prepared pan. Spread the blueberries over the crumb mixture. Sprinkle the remaining crumbs over the blueberries. Bake for 40 to 45 minutes, or until bubbling. Remove from the oven and set aside to cool slightly. Serve topped with ice cream. **Makes 9 servings.**

Chilled Lemon Soufflé With Blueberries

SOUFFLÉ:
2 packages (3 ounces each) lemon gelatin
    mix
2 cups boiling water
2 cups lemonade
¼ cup lemon juice
2 teaspoons grated lemon rind
1 pint heavy cream, whipped

SAUCE:
2 cups blueberries, crushed
½ cup sugar
1 teaspoon vanilla extract

Prepare a 3-inch collar of waxed paper that is long enough to wrap around the interior of your soufflé dish.

For soufflé: Put the gelatin into a medium bowl and pour the boiling water over it. Stir until the gelatin is dissolved. Add the lemonade, lemon juice, and lemon rind and stir to blend. Refrigerate the gelatin until it is slightly thickened. Remove the gelatin from the refrigerator and, using an electric mixer, beat it until it is fluffy and thick. Fold the gelatin into the whipped cream. Pour the mixture into a 1½-quart souffle dish, filling it to within an inch of the top. Place the collar of waxed paper around the inside of the dish, then pour in the rest of the soufflé. Refrigerate until firm.

For sauce: In a small bowl, combine the blueberries, sugar, and vanilla, stirring to blend. Remove the soufflé from the refrigerator. Remove the collar before serving. Spoon sauce over individual servings. **Makes 8 servings.**

DESSERTS

Puddings and Flan

The 1995 Old Farmer's Almanac *Recipe Contest: "Family-Tradition Ethnic Desserts"*

Cardamom-Scented Carrot Rice Pudding (Gajar Ki Kheer)

This recipe is originally from Pakistan and is a favorite everyday dessert.

1 quart half-and-half
1 quart milk
½ cup short-grain or pearl rice
6 carrots, peeled and grated
1 cup sugar, or more to taste
1 to 1½ teaspoons ground cardamom
blanched, slivered almonds

In a large pan over medium-high heat, bring the half-and-half, milk, and rice to a boil. Reduce the heat to low and simmer for 30 minutes, stirring often. In a separate pan, bring 6 cups of water to a boil. Blanch the carrots in the boiling water for 3 minutes and drain well. Add the carrots to the rice mixture. Add the sugar and cardamom and stir to blend. Cook until the mixture has thickened slightly, about 15 minutes. Remove from the heat and cool. Serve in individual bowls and sprinkle with almonds. **Makes 8 to 10 servings.**

–Farah Ahmed, Sunnyvale, California

STICKY SITUATIONS

■ You can soften raisins, dates, and other dried fruit that have become hard by soaking them in cool water for 1 hour or boiling-hot water for 30 minutes. Drain before using.

■ When dates have cemented themselves into a solid block, remove them from their packaging and put them on a cookie sheet. Preheat the oven to 350°F and put the dates into the oven for 5 minutes. The dates will loosen up.

■ To keep sticky dates from adhering to a knife, freeze them for two hours before chopping them.

Indian Pudding

4 cups milk, divided

¼ cup (½ stick) butter, plus extra for coating the baking dish

½ cup yellow or white cornmeal

½ cup light-brown sugar

½ cup molasses

1 teaspoon salt

1 teaspoon ground ginger

1 teaspoon cinnamon

½ cup raisins (optional)

Preheat the oven to 325°F. Butter a 2-quart baking dish. Have a pan that will hold the baking dish and hot water (for baking). In a saucepan, bring 2 cups of milk just to a boil. Put the cornmeal into the top of a double boiler over hot water on medium-high heat and pour the scalded milk over it, stirring constantly. Cook for about 15 minutes, stirring frequently, until the cornmeal is smooth. Add the remaining ingredients (including raisins if desired) except for the leftover milk, and stir until smooth. Pour the mixture into the prepared dish, and pour the remaining 2 cups of milk over the top. Set the baking dish into the pan and add enough hot water to about 2 inches up the side of the baking dish. Bake for 3 hours, or until the pudding is firm. **Makes 8 servings.**

Bread Pudding

This dish is good served warm or cold with whipped cream.

2 cups milk

2 tablespoons butter

6 pieces stale white bread, cut into cubes

2 eggs

½ cup sugar

1 teaspoon vanilla extract

¼ teaspoon salt

¾ cup raisins

Preheat the oven to 350°F. Grease the bottom and sides of a 2-quart glass casserole. Combine the milk and the 2 tablespoons of butter in a saucepan and heat just until the milk is scalded. Layer the bread cubes in the bottom of the casserole. In a separate bowl, beat the eggs slightly, then add the sugar, vanilla, salt, and raisins. Mix well. Stir into the milk mixture, then pour over the bread cubes. Place the casserole in a pan of hot water and bake for 50 to 60 minutes. **Makes 6 to 8 servings.**

Rice Pudding

4 extra-large eggs
⅔ cup sugar
¼ teaspoon salt
1 teaspoon vanilla extract
4 cups milk
1 cup cooked rice
½ cup raisins (optional)
cinnamon and nutmeg, for sprinkling

Preheat the oven to 325°F. Grease a 13x9-inch baking dish. Pour ½-inch of water into a shallow pan that is large enough to hold the prepared baking dish. In a large bowl and with an electric mixer, beat the eggs well. Add the sugar, salt, vanilla, and milk and beat well. Then add the rice and raisins, if desired. Pour the pudding into the prepared dish and sprinkle the top with cinnamon and a dash of nutmeg. Place the dish into the larger pan; the water should come about halfway up the outside of the dish (add more water, if necessary). Bake until the custard is just firm and lightly browned on top, 45 to 60 minutes. **Makes 6 to 8 servings.**

Almond-Crusted Cherry Pudding

FILLING:
**2 cans (14.5 ounces each) red tart
   cherries, drained**
¼ cup sugar
2 teaspoons cornstarch
½ teaspoon almond extract
¼ teaspoon cinnamon

TOPPING:
½ cup flour
½ cup sugar
½ teaspoon baking powder
¼ cup (½ stick) margarine
1 egg
**⅓ cup slivered almonds, plus extra for
   garnish, if desired**

Preheat the oven to 375°F.

For filling: In a large bowl, mix together the cherries, sugar, cornstarch, almond extract, and cinnamon with 2 tablespoons of water. Pour into a 9½-inch square ungreased baking dish.

For topping: In a small bowl, stir together the flour, sugar, and baking powder. Cut in the margarine with a fork or pastry cutter until the mixture is crumbly. Add the egg and mix until a stiff batter forms. Drop by spoonfuls evenly over the cherry filling, then sprinkle with the almonds. Bake for 35 to 40 minutes. Serve warm with whipped cream or vanilla ice cream. Garnish with more almonds if desired. **Makes 6 to 8 servings.**

This is one of the most popular recipes at Almanac.com/food. Reviewer comments at the site include: "Truly a five-star, good-eatin' recipe"; "Should be called 'A Touch of Heaven'!"; "So easy and tastes GREAT!"

Grape-Nuts Pudding

4 cups (1 quart) milk, scalded
1 cup Grape-Nuts cereal
4 large eggs
½ cup sugar
dash of salt
1 tablespoon vanilla extract
ground nutmeg, to taste

Preheat the oven to 350°F. Grease a 2-quart casserole. In a large bowl, pour the scalded milk over the Grape-Nuts and allow to stand for 5 minutes. In a small bowl, beat the eggs, sugar, salt, and vanilla. Add to the soaked Grape-Nuts. Pour into the casserole dish. Sprinkle generously with nutmeg. Set the casserole dish into a pan of hot water and bake for 45 to 55 minutes or until a knife inserted in the center comes out clean. **Makes 6 to 8 servings.**

Custard Flan

4 eggs
3 tablespoons sugar
2 cups milk or milk and cream
1 teaspoon vanilla extract
¼ cup sugar

Preheat the oven to 300°F. Lightly grease six small custard cups. Break the eggs into a large bowl and beat until they are light and fluffy. Add the 3 tablespoons of sugar and beat until the mixture is a lemon color. Add the milk and vanilla and beat again to mix thoroughly. Set aside.

In a small saucepan over medium heat, melt the ¼ cup of sugar, stirring constantly, until it forms a caramel-like syrup (which will be extremely hot, so caution is advised). Immediately pour the syrup into the custard cups. Pour the milk mixture into the custard cups to within ½-inch of the tops. Set the cups into a large pan and fill the pan with water to about ¾ of an inch from the tops of the cups. Bake for about 1 hour. Flans are done when a knife inserted into the center comes out clean. Remove custard cups from the pan and cool on a wire rack. Refrigerate until well chilled. To serve, run a knife around the edge of each cup, place a small dessert plate upside down over each cup, and turn the cup and plate over. **Makes 6 servings.**

DESSERTS

Jack's Christmas Cake

This rich, buttery cake freezes well, travels well, and looks great sliced and served on a plate with Christmas cookies.

1 cup (2 sticks) butter or margarine

1 box (16 oz.) confectioner's sugar

2 teaspoons vanilla extract

5 eggs

3 cups flour

2 cups chopped walnuts

1 cup whole glazed red cherries

1 cup whole glazed green cherries

Preheat the oven to 350°F. Grease and flour a 10-inch tube pan. In a large bowl, cream the butter with the sugar until it is light and fluffy.

Add the vanilla and eggs and mix well. Add the flour, and stir until well blended. Stir the walnuts and cherries into the batter. Pour the batter into the prepared pan and bake for 1 hour and 20 minutes or until a toothpick inserted into the center comes out clean. Cool the cake on a wire rack before removing from the pan. Before serving, sprinkle with confectioner's sugar. **Makes 20 servings.**

DESSERTS

CHAPTER

Canning and Preserving

When Putting Things By...

. . . the containers are as important as the contents:

■ Use only jars that are specifically designed for home canning, such as Mason or Ball jars. Most canning jars are sold with two-piece lids—a round screw lid and a removable flat metal disk that has a rubber-type sealing compound around the outer edge. The screw lid can be reused if it is cleaned well and does not rust. To ensure a tight seal, do not reuse the lids with a sealing compound.

■ Before every use, thoroughly wash empty jars in hot water and detergent and rinse well. To sterilize empty jars just before filling, put them right side up in a large pot. Fill the pot and jars with water to 1 inch above the tops of the jars. Boil for 10 minutes. Turn off the heat and keep the jars in the hot water until ready to use, taking out one at a time as needed.

■ For a strong seal, it's important to fill each jar to the proper level, leaving the right amount of air space, called headspace, between the top of the food or liquid and the inside of the jar lid. In general, allow ¼-inch of headspace for jams, jellies, juices, pickles, and relishes; ½-inch of headspace for acid foods such as tomatoes and fruits; and 1-inch of headspace for low-acid foods such as meats and most vegetables. (If tomatoes are mixed with meats or other vegetables, count the mixture as low-acid.)

■ After the food has been placed into a jar, remove all air bubbles by sliding a nonmetallic spatula in an up-and-down motion around the sides of the jar a few times.

■ When the jars are filled, wipe them clean and seal. Label and date the jars and store them in a clean, cool, dark, dry place. Do not store near heat or direct sunlight or in extreme cold. Under these conditions, food will lose quality and may spoil. Dampness may corrode metal lids and break seals.

THE TOOLS YOU'LL USE

Knives (for cutting and preparing fruits and vegetables)

Cutting board

Jars, screw lids, and new tops

Jar funnel (for pouring and packing liquid and small food items into canning jars)

Jar lifter (for removing hot jars from canning bath)

Tongs (for removing treated lids from hot water)

Clean cloths (for wiping jar rims and spills)

Timer or clock (for monitoring food-processing time)

Hot pads or mitts (for handling hot jars)

Large pot, boiling-water canner, or pressure canner

PROPER CANNING PRACTICES

■ THE BOILING-WATER BATH

In this procedure, jars of food are completely covered with boiling water and heated for a specific amount of time. (Follow the directions provided by your pot's manufacturer.) Use this method to safely can tomatoes, fruits, jams, jellies, and pickles with high acidic content. Acidic foods are usually safe for about 18 months.

■ THE PRESSURE CANNER

In this procedure, jars of food are set in 2 to 3 inches of water in a pressure canner and cooked at a high temperature for a specific amount of time. (Follow the directions provided by the manufacturer of your pressure canner.) Use this method to safely can many foods with a low acidic content and a pH of 4.6 and higher, including meat, seafood, poultry, dairy products, and vegetables.

■ WHAT'S THE DIFFERENCE?

Mainly this: In the boiling-water bath process, food is heated to 212°F, which kills many harmful microorganisms. The spores of *Clostridium botulinum* survive, however, enabling the bacteria to grow again in low-acid foods. During the pressure-canning method, the temperature of the food reaches 240°F, completely destroying the spores.

SHELF LIFE

■ Canned foods will keep best if stored in a cool, dry place. For optimum nutritional value, use them within 1 year.

SECRET INGREDIENTS

Ever wonder why some home-canned goods are uncannily delicious? Here are some clues:

■ The best fruits and vegetables are fresh, firm, and free of spoilage. Avoid any fruits or vegetables that have been waxed. Measure or weigh amounts carefully; the proportion of fresh food to other ingredients will affect the flavor.

■ Use canning or pickling salt. Using plain table salt may cause the pickles to turn too dark or a white sediment to form in the jar.

■ White distilled and cider vinegars of 5 percent acidity are recommended. Use white vinegar when a light color is desirable, as with fruits and cauliflower.

■ White granulated and brown sugars are used most often. Sugar serves as a preserving agent, contributes flavor, and aids in gelling. Corn syrup and honey can be used to replace part of the sugar, but too much will mask the fruit flavor and alter the gel structure. Do not try to reduce the amount of sugar in traditional recipes. Too little sugar prevents gelling and may allow yeasts and molds to grow.

HOW MUCH IS ENOUGH?

■ Quantities needed (in pounds) per quart canned:

FRUIT	POUNDS	VEGETABLE	POUNDS
Apples	2½ to 3	Asparagus	2½ to 4½
Blackberries	1½ to 3½	Beans	1½ to 2½
Blueberries	1½ to 3	Beets	2 to 3½
Cherries	2 to 2½	Cauliflower	3
Grapes	4	Corn	3 to 6
Peaches	2 to 3	Cucumbers	1½
Pears	2 to 3	Peas	3 to 6
Raspberries	1½ to 3	Peppers	3
Strawberries	1½ to 3	Spinach	2 to 3
		Tomatoes	2½ to 3½

Old-Fashioned Strawberry Preserves

2 pounds strawberries, hulls removed
4 cups white sugar
¼ teaspoon cream of tartar

In a large pot, combine all of the ingredients and simmer slowly until the sugar dissolves. Continue cooking for 15 to 20 minutes. Remove from the heat. Let stand 24 hours, then pack into sterilized jars, seal, and process. **Makes 2 half-pint jars.**

Raspberry Jam

1 quart (3½ cups) raspberries
7 cups sugar
1 bottle liquid pectin

Crush a layer of berries in a large pot. Then add the remaining berries and sugar. Bring the mixture to a boil over high heat, stirring constantly. Allow to boil for 1 minute. Add the pectin and boil for 1 minute more. Remove from the heat, stir, and skim. Pack into sterilized jars, seal, and process. **Makes 6 half-pint jars.**

Spiced Blueberry Jam

2 pounds (4½ cups) blueberries
7 cups sugar
½ teaspoon ground cinnamon
½ teaspoon ground cloves
juice or grated rind of 1 lemon
1 bottle liquid pectin

In a large pot, combine the berries, sugar, spices, and lemon rind and cook, bringing to a boil for 2 minutes. Stir as needed to prevent scorching. Remove from the heat and add the pectin. Skim off the foam. Pack into sterilized jars, seal, and process. **Makes 8 half-pint jars.**

For processing tips, see pages 276–277.

CANNING AND PRESERVING

Rose Hip Jam

Rose hips are rich in vitamin C. Pick them when they are red-ripe.

4 cups rose hips

4 apples, peeled and cored

5 cups sugar

Wash the rose hips and snip off the stem and blossom ends. Place the rose hips into a large pot with 1 quart of water and bring to a boil. Cook, covered, for about 20 minutes, or until tender. Strain, then discard seeds and skins. In a separate pan, cook the apples until soft, then add the rose hip mixture and sugar. Cook over low heat to dissolve the sugar, then bring the mixture to a boil. Continue cooking until it begins to jell. Remove from the heat. Pack into sterilized jars, seal, and process. **Makes 6 half-pint jars.**

Blackberry Jam

6 cups blackberries

6 cups sugar

1 cup orange juice

4 tablespoons lemon juice

1 tablespoon grated orange peel

In a large pot, combine the berries with ½ cup of water and cook until heated through. Remove from the heat and, when cool to the touch, rub the berries through a sieve into a large pot. Discard the seeds and skins in the sieve. Add the remaining ingredients to the pot. Cook over low heat until thick. Remove from the heat. Pack into sterilized jars, seal, and process. **Makes 6 six-ounce jars.**

For processing tips, see pages 276–277.

Pepper Jam

36 sweet red or green peppers, seeded
    and chopped fine
2 tablespoons salt
2 cups white vinegar
6 cups sugar

Sprinkle salt over the peppers and let stand for a few hours or overnight. Drain. Put the peppers into a large pot and add the vinegar and sugar. Stir to combine. Cook over medium heat, stirring until the jam comes to a boil. Reduce the heat and continue to cook, stirring occasionally, for about 1 hour, or until thick. Remove from the heat. Pack into sterilized jars, seal, and process. **Makes 8 pint jars.**

Mother's Mustard Pickles

This is a good way to use leftover vegetables from the garden.

2 cups pickling salt
1 quart sliced cucumbers
2 quarts sliced green tomatoes, cut up
1 quart small button onions
1 cauliflower, broken into small pieces
4 green peppers, seeded and chopped
4 red peppers, seeded and chopped
1 small bunch celery, finely chopped
½ cup all-purpose flour
4 tablespoons ground mustard
1 teaspoon turmeric
1½ cups brown sugar
2 quarts white vinegar
several whole cloves
2 sticks cinnamon

In a large pot, make a brine from 4 quarts of water and the salt. Heat, add the vegetables, and leave overnight. In the morning, heat the vegetables well in the brine; drain. Mix the flour, mustard, turmeric, and brown sugar with enough cold water to make a smooth paste. In a large pot, heat the vinegar, add the flour mixture, and cook, stirring constantly, until smooth. Add the vegetables, a few whole cloves, and the cinnamon sticks. Allow to scald thoroughly. Remove from the heat. Pack into sterilized jars and process in a boiling-water bath for 10 minutes; start counting the processing time when the water starts to boil. **Makes 6 quart jars.**

Processing times given are for elevations less than 1,000 feet. For every additional 1,000 feet of elevation, add 1 minute to time.

PICKLING PROPORTIONS

1 tablespoon fresh herbs = 1 teaspoon crushed dried herbs
1 pound pickling salt = 1⅓ cups
1 pound granulated sugar = 2 cups
1 pound brown sugar = 2¼ to 2¾ cups, firmly packed
1 pound honey = 1½ cups

IN A PICKLE?

IF THE PROBLEM IS...	THE POSSIBLE CAUSE IS...
Soft and slippery pickles	Pickles were stored in a warm spot. The brine was too weak. The jars didn't seal properly. The cucumbers were not covered with brine.
Dark pickles	The water was too hard. Ground spices or too many spices were used. The canning lids were corroded.
Shriveled pickles	The brine was too salty. The cucumbers were not fresh. The pickles were overprocessed.
White sediment in the jar	Table salt was used. The temperature during fermentation was not controlled.

Bread and Butter Pickles With Red Pepper

5 cups sliced cucumbers

1 large onion

1 green pepper, seeded and sliced

1 red pepper, seeded and sliced

4 tablespoons pickling salt

1 pint white vinegar

1 cup brown sugar

1 teaspoon mustard seed

½ teaspoon turmeric

½ teaspoon celery seed

In a large pot, cover the cucumbers, onion, and peppers with 8 cups of water and the salt. Let stand 3 hours, then drain, discarding the liquid. Add the vinegar, brown sugar, mustard seed, turmeric, and celery seed and boil until clear. Remove from the heat. Pack into sterilized jars, seal, and process in a boiling-water bath for 10 minutes; start counting the processing time when the water starts to boil. **Makes 4 pint jars.**

Sliced Cucumber Pickles

3 large cucumbers, sliced

1 green pepper, seeded and finely chopped

3 onions, sliced

salt

1 cup sugar

1 teaspoon turmeric

1 teaspoon mustard seed

several whole cloves

cider vinegar

In a large pot, sprinkle the vegetables with salt and let stand 3 hours. Drain well, discarding the liquid, and return the vegetables to the pot. Add the sugar and spices. Cover the contents with vinegar and heat through but do not boil. When the ingredients are just at the boiling point, remove the pot from the heat and pack the pickles and juice into sterilized jars. Seal and process in a boiling-water bath for 5 minutes; start counting the processing time when the water starts to boil. **Makes 2 quart jars.**

For processing tips, see pages 276–277.

CANNING AND PRESERVING

Kosher-Style Dill Pickles

30 to 36 pickling cucumbers (3 to 4 inches
    long)

3 cups vinegar

6 tablespoons pickling salt

1 small bunch fresh dill or ½ teaspoon
    dried dill per jar

½ to 1 clove garlic per jar, blanched and
    sliced

½ tablespoon mustard seed per jar

Wash the cucumbers in cold water. In a large pot, make a brine from the vinegar, 3 cups of water, and salt and bring to a boil. In the bottom of a sterilized quart jar, place a generous layer of dill (seed heads, leaves, and stems are all suitable), ½ to 1 clove of garlic, and ½ tablespoon mustard seed. Pack the cucumbers vertically into the jar until it is about half full, then add more dill and fill the remainder of the jar with cucumbers. Repeat, using all of the cucumbers and jars. Fill the jars to within ½-inch of the top with the boiling brine. Seal and process in a boiling-water bath for 15 minutes; start counting the processing time when the water starts to boil. Note: Pickles may shrivel after the processing but will later plump in the sealed jars. **Makes 2 quart jars.**

Pickled Peppers

When you only want a few, this recipe will do nicely.

1 teaspoon pickling salt

1 tablespoon sugar

2 cloves garlic

4 cups seeded, sliced peppers (sweet red,
    yellow, and green, and a few hot
    peppers if desired)

1¼ cups white vinegar

1 cup boiling water (approximate)

Place the salt, sugar, and garlic in a sterilized quart jar. Pack the peppers firmly into the jar, with the skins facing out. Pour in the vinegar. Fill the jar to within ½-inch of the top with boiling water. Seal and process in a boiling-water bath for 5 minutes; start counting the processing time when the water starts to boil. Set aside to cool undisturbed for 12 hours. **Makes 1 quart.**

Fran's Chowchow

1 gallon chopped green tomatoes

1 gallon chopped cabbage

½ gallon chopped onions

1 bunch celery

6 sweet peppers, seeded

6 hot peppers, seeded

¾ cup salt

4 cups white sugar

2¼ cups brown sugar

2 quarts cider vinegar

1 box pickling spice

Using a food processor fitted with a coarse blade, grind all of the vegetables. Put the vegetables into a pot and sprinkle the salt over the mixture. Let stand for 2 hours. Drain, discarding the liquid. Put the vegetables into a large kettle. Add the sugars, vinegar, and spice. Bring to a boil, reduce heat, and simmer for 1 hour, stirring occasionally. Remove from the heat. Pour the hot relish into sterilized jars, seal, and process in a boiling-water bath for 10 minutes; start counting the processing time when the water starts to boil. **Makes 8 half-pint jars.**

Christmas Relish

12 medium zucchini

2 green peppers, seeded

2 sweet red peppers, seeded and chopped

4 cups onions, coarsely ground

⅓ cup salt

1 teaspoon turmeric

1 teaspoon curry powder

1 teaspoon celery seed

1 tablespoon cornstarch

½ teaspoon pepper

3 cups cider vinegar

4½ cups sugar

Using a food processor fitted with a coarse blade, grind the zucchini, green and red peppers, and onions. In a large enamel pot, mix the vegetables with the salt and let stand overnight. In the morning, drain, rinse with cold water, and drain again, discarding the liquid each time. Return the vegetables to the pot. In a separate bowl, mix together the remaining ingredients and add to the vegetables. Bring the relish to a boil, and continue boiling for 20 minutes. Remove from the heat. Pour into sterilized jars, seal, and process in a boiling-water bath for 10 minutes; start counting the processing time when the water starts to boil. **Makes 7 pint jars.**

For processing tips, see pages 276–277.

CANNING AND PRESERVING

Hot Dog Relish

6 medium green tomatoes
2 large onions, peeled
½ head cabbage, cored
6 green peppers, seeded
¼ cup salt
3 cups vinegar
3 cups sugar
1 tablespoon mustard seed
1 tablespoon celery seed
1 teaspoon turmeric
3 sweet red peppers, seeded and finely
chopped

Put the tomatoes, onions, cabbage, and green peppers through the coarse blade of a food processor. Transfer the cut vegetables to a large bowl, mix with the salt, and let stand overnight. In the morning, rinse and drain well. In a large pot, combine the vinegar, sugar, 1 cup of water, and spices and boil for 5 minutes. Add the vegetable mixture and the red peppers and simmer for 10 minutes. Remove from the heat. Fill sterilized jars, seal, and then process in a boiling-water bath for 10 minutes; start counting the processing time when the water starts to boil. **Makes 6 pint jars.**

Peach Chutney

½ cup chopped onion
½ pound seedless raisins
1 small clove garlic, peeled
4 pounds fresh peaches, peeled, pitted,
and chopped
2 tablespoons chili powder
⅔ cup chopped crystallized ginger
2 tablespoons mustard seed
1 tablespoon salt
1 quart white vinegar
3⅜ cups brown sugar

Using the fine blade on a food grinder, chop the onions, raisins, and garlic. Combine all of the ingredients in a kettle. Bring the mixture to a slow boil and continue cooking for about 1 hour, or until the chutney is thick and a rich brown color, stirring occasionally to prevent scorching. Remove from the heat. Fill sterilized jars, seal, and process in a boiling-water bath for 10 minutes; start counting the processing time when the water starts to boil. **Makes 3 pint jars.**

For processing tips, see pages 276–277.

The Old Farmer's Almanac Everyday Cookbook

Tangy Cranberry Apple Chutney

12 sour apples, peeled, cored, and chopped

1 cup seedless raisins, chopped

1 pint cider vinegar

2 cups chopped cranberries

2 cups sugar

juice of 4 lemons

1 red pepper, seeded and minced

2 green apples, minced

½ teaspoon cayenne pepper

1 tablespoon ground ginger

Place the chopped sour apples into a pot and add the remaining ingredients. Stir together and simmer until the mixture is thick. Remove from the heat. Pack into sterilized jars, seal, and process in a boiling-water bath for 10 minutes; start counting the processing time when the water starts to boil. **Makes about 4 pint jars.**

Rhubarb Chutney

Serve this tangy condiment with chicken or turkey. It also complements the flavors of a spicy curry.

2 cups diced rhubarb (about ¾ pound, untrimmed)

1 tart apple, peeled, cored, and chopped

½ cup light-brown sugar

¼ cup cider vinegar

½ cup raisins

1 tablespoon lemon juice

1 teaspoon ground ginger

½ teaspoon ground cumin

Combine all of the ingredients in a heavy enamel pot. Bring them slowly to a boil, then reduce the heat and simmer for about 10 minutes, or until the rhubarb and apple are very soft but still hold their shape. (Do not allow them to turn into mush.) Remove from the heat. Cool to lukewarm or chill in the refrigerator before serving. **Makes 2½ cups.**

NOTE:

The chutney will keep for a week in the refrigerator. To store for a longer time or to present as a gift, pack the chutney into sterilized half-pint canning jars and process in a boiling-water bath for 10 minutes; start counting the processing time when the water starts to boil.

Tomato Ketchup

½ bushel (about 23 pounds) ripe tomatoes

⅓ cup salt

1 tablespoon whole cloves, tied in a
    cheesecloth bag

2½ teaspoons ground nutmeg

1 tablespoon ground mace

½ teaspoon cayenne pepper, or to taste

1 quart cider vinegar

Press the tomatoes through a sieve until all of the pulp is out. Put the pulp into a porcelain or enamel kettle and bring it to a boil. Add the remaining ingredients and cook for 1½ hours, stirring occasionally to prevent sticking. Remove from the heat. Remove the cheesecloth bag. Fill sterilized jars, seal, and process in a boiling-water bath for 5 minutes; start counting the processing time when the water starts to boil. **Makes 8 quart jars.**

Green Tomato Mincemeat

6 cups peeled, cored, and chopped
    apples

6 cups chopped green tomatoes

4 cups brown sugar

1⅓ cups vinegar

3 cups seedless raisins

3 teaspoons ground cinnamon

1 teaspoon ground cloves

¾ teaspoon ground allspice

¾ teaspoon ground mace

¾ teaspoon pepper

2 teaspoons salt

¾ cup (1½ sticks) butter

In a large kettle, mix the apples with the tomatoes and drain. Add the remaining ingredients, except the butter, and gradually bring to a boil. Boil until thick, stirring occasionally. Remove from the heat. Add the butter, stir to blend, then pack into sterilized jars, seal, and process in a boiling-water bath for 20 minutes; start counting the processing time when the water starts to boil. **Makes 8 pint jars.**

For processing tips, see pages 276–277.

MINCING WORDS

Holiday Mincemeat

3 pounds lean beef, finely chopped

2 pounds suet, chopped

3½ quarts apples, peeled, cored, and finely chopped

3 pounds seedless raisins, chopped

2 pounds currants

1¼ pounds citron, cut into small pieces

½ cup chopped candied orange peel

½ cup chopped candied lemon peel

½ cup lemon juice

½ cup orange juice

2 tablespoons salt

4 cups sugar

1 cup black coffee

2 cups cider

1¼ teaspoons ground cloves

1 teaspoon ground allspice

2 teaspoons ground cinnamon

1 cup currant jelly

½ cup sherry

4 cups brandy

Mix all of the ingredients, except the sherry and brandy, and simmer over low heat for about 2 hours, stirring occasionally. Remove from the heat. When cool, but not cold, add the sherry and brandy and stir to blend. Transfer to an earthenware crock and let stand for at least a week to allow flavors to blend. Pack in sterilized jars, seal, and process under pressure. **Makes 12 quart jars.**

Family Favorites

Everyone has recipes that have been passed down through generations and that define special occasions. This chapter consists of favorite recipes from employees of Yankee Publishing Inc. We hope that you enjoy every bite.

Dad's Celebratory Waffles

It's always a treat when Dad makes these waffles. The light orange flavor melds wonderfully with maple syrup.

2½ cups all-purpose flour, sifted before
    measuring
½ teaspoon cinnamon
5 teaspoons baking powder
¾ teaspoon salt
2 tablespoons sugar
grated zest of 1 orange
5 large eggs, separated
8 tablespoons vegetable oil
3 cups milk

Preheat the waffle iron and grease it, if necessary. In a large bowl, resift the flour with the cinnamon, baking powder, salt, and sugar. Mix in the orange zest. In a separate bowl and with a hand beater or electric mixer, beat the egg yolks thoroughly. Add the oil and milk and stir to blend. Form a "well" in the center of the dry ingredients and pour the liquid ingredients into it. Beat the batter until no lumps remain. Wash and dry the beaters. In a separate bowl, beat the egg whites until stiff but not dry. Fold the whites into the batter until barely blended. Ladle the batter onto the waffle iron and cook for 4 to 5 minutes, or until steam has almost completely stopped releasing from the sides. **Makes 4 generous servings.**

–Heidi Stonehill, senior associate editor, The Old Farmer's Almanac

Helvi's "Pannukakku" (Finnish Oven Pancake)

My mother-in-law served this hot with a strong cup of coffee.

4 tablespoons butter
6 medium eggs
1 cup all-purpose flour
4 cups milk
½ teaspoon salt
½ cup sugar
1 cup fruit (sliced apples, fresh or frozen
    blueberries, or other)
extra sugar

Preheat the oven to 400°F. Put the butter into a large cast iron skillet or ovenproof pan. Place the skillet or pan into the oven until the butter melts. Remove the hot skillet carefully. In a medium bowl, mix the remaining ingredients, except for the fruit and extra sugar, until well blended. Pour all of the batter into the hot, buttered skillet and place the fruit on top. Sprinkle with sugar. Bake for 30 minutes, or until the pancake is puffy and the top is brown. Slice and serve warm as a breakfast dish or warm or cold as a dessert. **Makes about 8 servings.**

–Mare-Anne Jarvela, senior editor, The Old Farmer's Almanac

Cherry Party Pinwheels

These fun hors d'oeuvres are as attractive as they are addictive.

16 ounces cream cheese, softened

¼ medium onion (or to taste), minced

3 tablespoons sweet pickle relish or minced pickle of any kind, drained

8 to 10 maraschino cherries, stems removed, minced and drained

1 teaspoon Dijon-style or any prepared mustard

salt and pepper, to taste

1 packet ranch dressing mix (optional)

3 vegetable (spinach recommended) tortillas or wraps (9-inch) or equivalent

In a medium bowl, combine the first six ingredients and the ranch dressing, if desired, and mix well. Spread one-third of the mixture evenly on each of the tortillas, staying about ¾ of an inch from the edge. Carefully roll up each tortilla, wrapping it as firmly as possible. Wrap the tortilla "log" snugly and completely in plastic wrap. Refrigerate for at least six hours, or overnight. Remove the log from the refrigerator. Remove and discard the plastic wrap. Using a serrated knife, carefully slice off the irregular ends of each log, leaving bluntly flat ends. (Eat the cuttings or discard.) Carefully slice the logs into ½- to ¾-inch disks, or pinwheels. Arrange on a platter and refrigerate, covered with plastic wrap, until ready to serve. **Makes about 30 pinwheels.**

–Jack Burnett, copy editor, The Old Farmer's Almanac

Parsley Pesto

A friend served this once, and now it's a snack staple on crackers or bread or with celery or carrot sticks. Experiment with the ingredient quantities.

4 to 6 cloves garlic

¼ cup pine nuts or walnuts, toasted

1 hard-boiled egg (yolk optional)

1 bunch curly-leaf parsley, washed (stems optional)

2 to 3 tablespoons olive oil, or more for desired consistency

1 tablespoon cider vinegar or fresh lemon juice

Put the garlic and nuts into a blender or food processor and chop fine. Add the egg and chop fine. Add the parsley, olive oil, and vinegar and process until well chopped and mixed, stopping as needed to scrape down the sides of the bowl. If the pesto seems thick, add more olive oil and process again. **Makes about 1½ cups.**

–Janice Stillman, editor, The Old Farmer's Almanac

Cream Cheese, Egg, and Olive Spread

My mother-in-law stuffed celery with this spread every Thanksgiving and Christmas. That tradition continues at our house, but we also use it on crackers and in sandwiches.

6 hard-boiled eggs, peeled and finely chopped

16 ounces cream cheese, softened

20 to 30 green olives with pimiento, coarsely chopped

dash of freshly ground black pepper

Chop the eggs while still warm. In a large bowl, thoroughly blend together the cream cheese, eggs, olives, and pepper. Refrigerate until ready to serve and use within a few days. **Makes about 3 cups.**

–*Margo Letourneau, art director,* The Old Farmer's Almanac

Eggplant Dip (Caponata)

Sometimes referred to as Italian caviar, this dip is commonly served at weddings and other festive gatherings. Serve warm or cold with crackers or on crusty bread.

2 medium tomatoes, peeled, seeded and finely chopped

¼ cup olive oil

2 stalks celery, finely chopped

1 large sweet onion, finely chopped

1 eggplant, peeled, finely chopped

1 large clove garlic, minced

½ cup black olives, pitted and sliced

1 teaspoon dried basil

1 teaspoon salt

¼ teaspoon pepper

2 teaspoons sugar

1 teaspoon balsamic vinegar

In a strainer, drain the tomatoes for 10 minutes. In a large skillet, heat the oil. Add the celery and onion and sauté for about 5 minutes, or until tender. Stir in the eggplant and garlic and sauté for 5 minutes more. Add the tomatoes, olives, basil, salt, pepper, sugar, and vinegar. Simmer for 15 to 20 minutes. Refrigerate in a nonreactive container for at least 2 hours to allow flavors to blend. **Makes about 4 cups, depending on the size of the eggplant.**

–*Carol Loria, wife of Leonard Loria, former art director,* Yankee *Magazine*

Sally's Sweet Bulgur Salad

I wanted to introduce grains into my family's diet, so I served tabouli with bulgur—but nobody liked it. Over the years, by adding sugar and other ingredients, a winner evolved.

SALAD:

1 cup cracked bulgur (available at
    natural food stores)

¾ cup chopped dried cherries or
    cranberries

¾ cup chopped pecans

¾ cup chopped fresh parsley

¾ cup chopped fresh chives

¾ cup chopped fresh mint

DRESSING:

½ cup fresh lemon juice

1 generous teaspoon sugar

½ cup olive oil

For salad: Put the bulgur into a large bowl and just cover it with boiling water. Set aside for 2 hours. Then drain well and pat dry, if necessary. Mix in all of the chopped ingredients.

For dressing: In a separate bowl or jar, combine the lemon juice and sugar. Stir or shake until the sugar is dissolved. Slowly mix in the olive oil. Pour the dressing over the salad before serving. **Makes about 8 servings.**

–Sally Hale, wife of Judson D. Hale Sr., editor in chief and chairman of the board of Yankee Publishing Inc.

Scalloped Oysters

This recipe, a favorite at our Thanksgiving and Christmas dinners, was passed down to me by my mother, Reta L. Huberlie of Peterborough, New Hampshire, who celebrated her 102nd birthday in 2005.

1 quart shucked oysters (small, if possible)

3 sleeves Ritz crackers, crumbled

½ cup (1 stick) unsalted butter

1½ cups heavy cream

freshly ground black pepper (optional)

paprika, to taste

Preheat the oven to 350°F. Generously grease a 13x9-inch casserole. Rinse the oysters, drain, and remove any bits of shell. Layer the crackers and oysters, dotting each layer with butter and a splash of cream and sprinkling with pepper, if desired. End with cream and crackers. Sprinkle with paprika. Bake for 30 to 45 minutes, or until bubbly and lightly browned on top. **Makes 12 to 15 servings.**

–Sally Hale

Heidi's Cheesy Potatoes

This recipe has had several variations, but is a favorite in our family no matter what form it takes. It's good as a side dish or as the main meal, and can be made ahead of time and refrigerated until needed (in which case, reheat before serving).

6 medium to large potatoes ('Yukon Gold' recommended), peeled

1 pint sour cream

½ teaspoon pepper

8 to 12 ounces cottage cheese

6 to 9 ounces precooked boneless ham steak cut into chunks (optional)

1 cup shredded Monterey Jack cheese

1 cup shredded sharp cheddar cheese

1 box (5.5 ounces) large-cut, Italian-flavor croutons

paprika, to taste

Preheat the oven to 350°F. Slice the potatoes to a ½- to ¼-inch thickness. Put the potatoes into a large saucepan, cover with water, and cook on medium-high heat until they are fork-tender. Drain and set aside. In a small bowl, mix together the sour cream and pepper. Place half of the potatoes in a layer on the bottom of a 2-quart casserole. Spoon half of the cottage cheese on top of the potatoes. Dot with half of the ham, if using. Add half of both cheeses. Sprinkle the croutons on top. Spread half of the sour cream over the croutons. Repeat to form another layer. Sprinkle with paprika. Bake uncovered for 30 minutes, or until hot and bubbly, slightly brown at the edges, and the cheese is melted. **Makes 8 to 10 servings.**

–Heidi Stonehill

Turkey Chili

There's nothing better on a cold winter day than a house full of friends and a bowl full of chili. My friends request this hearty (and healthy) dish all the time.

1¼ pounds ground turkey

1 small onion, finely chopped

1 red bell pepper, finely chopped

3 cloves garlic, minced

1 can (28 ounces) crushed tomatoes

1 can (15 ounces) dark red kidney beans, drained and rinsed

1 can (8 ounces) tomato sauce

1 generous tablespoon chili powder

½ teaspoon dried basil

¼ teaspoon freshly ground black pepper

2 cups cooked rice

In a large saucepan, sauté the turkey, onion, pepper, and garlic until the meat is no longer pink and the onion is tender. Drain. Add the crushed tomatoes, kidney beans, tomato sauce, chili powder, basil, and black pepper and stir. Bring to a boil, then reduce heat, cover, and simmer for 35 minutes. Serve over rice. **Makes 4 servings.**

–Sarah Perreault, assistant editor, The Old Farmer's Almanac

Nana's Pot Roast

My nana made this on Sundays in the winter. If the gravy isn't thick enough, add a flour slurry (see page 128) to bring to desired consistency. It can also be prepared in a slow cooker.

2 tablespoons vegetable oil

flour, to dust beef

3 pounds bottom beef round rump roast

1 package dry onion soup mix

1 can (14.5 ounces) cream of mushroom
  soup

3 large carrots, peeled and cut into 1-inch
  pieces

3 to 4 medium potatoes, cut into 1 inch
  cubes

2 stalks celery, cut into 1-inch pieces

10 to 12 boiling onions

Preheat a Dutch oven over medium-high heat. Add the oil. Meanwhile, dust the roast with flour. When the oil comes just to the smoking point, add the roast and brown it on all sides. In a separate bowl, combine 1½ cups water, dry soup mix, and mushroom soup. Add this to the Dutch oven, then add the vegetables. Cover tightly. Place in a 300°F oven and cook for 2 to 2½ hours, or until the internal temperature of the meat reaches 140°F. **Makes 6 servings.**

IF YOU'RE USING A SLOW COOKER

Prepare the ingredients as above. Brown the roast in a skillet, then put it into the slow cooker with the soup mixture and vegetables. Cook on low for 8 hours. Note: The vegetables will be soft. If you prefer crunchy vegetables, steam or blanch them separately prior to serving, adding 2 tablespoons of beef base for slow-cooked flavor.

–Paul Belliveau, director, production and new media, Yankee Publishing Inc.

Paella

My great-grandmother brought this recipe from Valencia, Spain, to Mexico, where my grandmother made it often, especially on Mother's Day, when the whole family got together. When I moved to New England, I added lobsters, steamers, and scallops to the recipe. Don't scrimp on the saffron; it makes the dish.

3 large artichokes

¾ cup olive oil, divided

3 green arbol chiles or 1 pablano chile, stemmed and chopped rough

3 cloves garlic, cut in half

½ red onion, finely chopped

½ celery stalk, finely chopped

½ carrot, finely diced

½ red bell pepper, seeded and finely chopped

1 pound chicken breasts, cut into 1-inch cubes

2 pounds pork (lean tenderloin or chops), cut into 1-inch cubes

2 links smoked chorizo, cut into ¼-inch sections

1 teaspoon salt

½ teaspoon pepper

2½ cups of white rice

8 cups (approximately 4 cans) chicken, vegetable, beef, or fish stock, divided

2 to 3 tablespoons saffron threads (15 to 20 threads total)

10 large cooked shrimp

10 large steamers

1 cup sea scallops

2 lobster tails or 1 can (11.3 ounces) frozen lobster meat, thawed and drained

10 to 25 mussels

1 cup red wine

1 jar (6 ounces) roasted red bell peppers, cut into strips

1 jar (6.5 ounces) artichoke hearts, with liquid

salt and freshly ground black pepper, to taste

fresh parsley sprigs, for garnish

Cut the artichokes in half and put them into a large pot. Cover with water. Cook for 30 minutes, then set aside to cool. In a large paella dish or deep frying pan, heat ½ cup of the oil over low heat. Sauté the chiles and garlic cloves until the chiles start to blister. Add the onion to the pan. Sauté the onion for 5 minutes, or until it begins to soften and caramelize. Add the celery, carrots, and red bell pepper and cook for 5 minutes more. Add the chicken, pork, chorizo, and remaining ¼ cup of oil and cook, stirring to prevent sticking. Add the salt and pepper. Cook on medium heat for about 15 minutes. Add the rice, 6 cups of stock, and the saffron. Stir and cover with a tight-fitting lid. Leave on the stove for about an hour, or until the rice absorbs the liquid. Add the shrimp, steamers, scallops, lobster, mussels, and remaining 2 cups of stock. Stir in the wine. Cover and simmer for 15 minutes more. Add the artichokes, artichoke hearts, and roasted red bell pepper strips. Cook, uncovered, for 5 minutes more. Remove from the heat, and let stand for 10 minutes before serving. Adjust the salt and pepper, if necessary. Garnish with fresh parsley sprigs. **Makes 10 to 12 servings.**

–Gil Martinez, former assistant art director, Yankee *Magazine*

Mild and Meaty Lasagna

A favorite on Christmas Eve and at our family gatherings, this can be made the day before, refrigerated, and brought to room temperature before baking.

1 pound lean ground beef

1 pound ground pork

½ cup onion, finely chopped

2 cloves garlic, minced

2 teaspoons dried basil

1 teaspoon dried oregano

1 teaspoon garlic salt

12 to 15 lasagna noodles, cooked with
⠀⠀¼ cup olive oil

1 pound shredded fresh mozzarella,
⠀⠀divided

10 ounces shredded fresh Parmesan,
⠀⠀divided

1 pound ricotta cheese (do not substitute
⠀⠀cottage cheese)

5 cups tomato sauce (see recipe below
⠀⠀or use prepared)

Preheat the oven to 350°F. In a large frying pan, sauté the beef and pork with the onion, garlic, spices, and garlic salt. Use a fork to crumble the meats as they brown. Drain and set aside. Rinse the lasagna noodles and put them into a pan of cold water. Reserve one-quarter of the mozzarella and Parmesan cheeses. In the bottom of a lasagna pan or large baking pan, place three lasagna noodles side by side. Begin the assembly: Over the noodles, spread one-third of the meat mixture; on top of that, spread one-third of the remaining mozzarella and Parmesan and one-third of the ricotta; and on top of that, spread one-third of the sauce. Repeat two times, ending with sauce to cover completely. Sprinkle the reserved mozzarella and Parmesan on top. Place a loose foil tent over the lasagna and bake for 40 minutes. Remove the foil tent and continue baking until the cheese on top is slightly browned, about 20 minutes more. **Makes 12 to 15 servings.**

BASIC TOMATO SAUCE

There is nothing like the fresh taste of homemade sauce, but if time is not on your side, a good-quality prepared sauce will do fine.

½ cup onion, finely chopped

3 large cloves garlic, minced

¼ cup olive oil

3 pounds ripe tomatoes, peeled, seeded,
⠀⠀and finely chopped

1½ teaspoons dried basil

1½ teaspoons dried oregano

½ teaspoon crushed hot red pepper flakes

1 teaspoon salt

dash of freshly ground black pepper

1 can (6 ounces) tomato paste, plus 2 cans water

Sauté the onion and garlic in the olive oil until the onion is translucent. Put the tomatoes, basil, oregano, red pepper flakes, salt, and black pepper into a large saucepan. Add the onion and garlic and mix thoroughly. Stir in the tomato paste and water. Cover and simmer over medium-low heat for 1 hour, stirring occasionally, or until the sauce thickens. **Makes about 5 cups.**

–Margo Letourneau

A FEW HINTS

ABOUT HAM

- Preheat the oven to 325°F.

  For a bone-in half ham (5 to 8 pounds), allow 18 to 20 minutes per pound.

  For a boneless half ham (3 to 4 pounds), allow 25 to 30 minutes per pound.

  For a whole ham (10 to 15 pounds), allow 18 to 20 minutes per pound.

  For a shank or butt portion (usually 3 to 4 pounds), allow 35 minutes per pound.

  In all cases involving ham, the internal temperature should be 160°F to be considered "done."

Edna's Ham Glaze

My grandmother had a knack for making delicious ham. Here is one of her secrets.

½ cup brown sugar

1 tablespoon red-wine vinegar

⅛ teaspoon ground cloves

⅛ teaspoon ground mustard

1 cup (8 ounces) ginger ale

In a small bowl, mix together the brown sugar, vinegar, cloves, and mustard. Add the ginger ale, a little at a time, to create a consistency that is thick enough to cling to the ham. Set aside the remaining ginger ale. Place the ham on the bottom of a roasting pan and spread the glaze over it. Pour the remaining ginger ale into the bottom of the pan. Bake the ham, basting occasionally from the drippings. **Makes about ¾ cup of glaze, enough for a 5- to 10-pound ham.**

–Heidi Stonehill

Crispy Teriyaki Tuna Steaks

Easy to prepare, this recipe can easily be doubled.

2 tablespoons wasabi (Japanese horseradish) powder

2 tablespoons soy sauce

2 tablespoons honey

1 teaspoon peeled and minced fresh ginger

2 fresh tuna steaks, each about ¾-inch thick and 4 ounces

1 cup crispy rice cereal

2 tablespoons sesame seeds

1 tablespoon canola oil

1 teaspoon sesame oil

1 tablespoon green onion, thinly sliced, for garnish

In a small bowl, stir the wasabi, soy sauce, honey, and ginger into a thin paste. Dip the tuna steaks into paste and let marinate for 10 minutes. Meanwhile, put the crispy cereal and sesame seeds into a plastic bag and, with a rolling pin, coarsely crush the cereal mixture. Drop the tuna steaks into the bag, one at a time, and shake to coat evenly. Discard the extra marinade paste and cereal mixture. Heat the canola oil in a heavy skillet on medium-high heat, then add the sesame oil after the pan is hot (to avoid smoke). Cook the tuna in the hot skillet, searing each side for about 2 minutes, or until done medium-rare. Garnish with green onions. **Makes 2 servings.**

–Carol Loria

Rulltårta (Swedish Jelly Roll)

My mother made this quick jelly (or applesauce) roll when unexpected company dropped by.

3 large eggs

¾ cup sugar

1 cup all-purpose flour

1 teaspoon baking powder

1 teaspoon ground cardamom

½ cup jelly or applesauce

1 tablespoon sugar

sugar or cinnamon/sugar mix, for topping

Preheat the oven to 475°F. Line a large cookie sheet or a jelly-roll pan with wax paper. In a large bowl and with an electric mixer, beat the eggs and sugar until fluffy. In a separate bowl, combine the flour, baking powder, and cardamom before gently adding that to the egg mixture. Spread the batter in the prepared pan. Bake for 5 minutes. Remove the cake from the oven and sprinkle with 1 tablespoon of sugar. Cut a second piece of wax paper slightly larger than your pan and spread it on your work area. Turn the cake upside down onto the paper. Peel off the wax paper from the bottom of the cake and discard. While the cake is still warm, spread the jelly or applesauce over the cake and carefully roll it into a log. Sprinkle with sugar or sugar/cinnamon mix. Slice to serve. **Makes 8 to 10 servings.**

–Mare-Anne Jarvela

Apple Kuchen

In my family, this recipe is known as "Memere's famous kuchen."

KUCHEN:
¾ cup (1½ sticks) margarine
1 cup sugar
2 large eggs
2 cups all-purpose flour
2 teaspoons baking powder
½ cup milk
1 teaspoon vanilla extract
4 apples, peeled, cored, and sliced

TOPPING:
½ cup (1 stick) margarine
1 cup sugar
1 cup all-purpose flour

For kuchen: Preheat the oven to 350°F. Grease a 13x9-inch pan. In a large bowl, cream the margarine and sugar. Add the eggs and stir to blend. In a separate bowl, sift the flour with the baking powder. Measure the milk into a separate bowl and add the vanilla. Alternatively add the flour mixture and milk to the sugar mixture, stirring to blend after each addition. Spread the batter into the prepared pan and top with apple slices.

For topping: In a saucepan over medium heat, melt the margarine. Remove from the heat. Add the sugar and flour and work with a fork until it is crumbly. Sprinkle over the kuchen. Bake for 45 minutes, or until a toothpick inserted into the center comes out clean. **Makes 12 servings.**

–Sarah Perreault

Hungarian Kifli Coffee Cake

My father's Czechoslovakian mother used to make this at Christmas and Easter. My mother continued the tradition every Christmas. Now, my siblings and I make it, with variations in the amount of filling or the thickness of the dough. For me, it defines Christmas morning.

FAMILY FAVORITES

FILLING:

3 cups ground walnuts

⅓ cup sugar

⅓ cup golden raisins

1 teaspoon cinnamon

DOUGH:

2¾ cups all-purpose flour

3 tablespoons sugar

1 teaspoon baking powder

pinch of salt

¾ cup (1½ sticks) butter

1 large egg

¾ cup sour cream

juice of ½ lemon

1 large egg, beaten

Preheat the oven to 350°F. Grease and flour a cookie sheet.

For filling: In a large bowl, combine all of the filling ingredients and set aside.

For dough: In a separate large bowl, mix together the flour, sugar, baking powder, and salt. Using a fork or two knives, cut the butter into the flour mixture until it is the texture of cornmeal. Make a hole in the center of the flour mixture and into it put the egg, sour cream, and lemon juice. Mix the batter by hand until it is completely blended and forms a slightly sticky dough. Divide the dough into two balls of equal size. Lightly flour your work surface and roll out each ball into a rectangle that is approximately 12x10 inches and ¼-inch thick. Spread half of the filling over the dough, leaving a 1-inch border on all sides. With the long side facing you, roll up the dough. Tuck the ends under, so that the filling doesn't spill out, and place the roll, seam side down, on the prepared sheet. Repeat with the remaining dough. Brush with the beaten egg and bake for about 40 minutes, or until golden. **Makes 2 coffeecakes.**

FILLING VARIATION

3 cups ground poppy seeds*

¼ cup honey

¼ cup milk

Commercially prepared poppy seed butter (available in most supermarkets) can be used instead. In that case, do not add any honey or milk; use it alone.

–Martie Majoros, research editor, The Old Farmer's Almanac

Snow Pudding

Years ago, when my mother made it, the recipe for this airy, elegant confection (so named because it is as white as snow) appeared on pamphlets that were included in boxes of gelatin packets. Years later, when I wanted to make it myself, the recipe no longer appeared on the pamphlets, presumably because it contains raw egg whites. Fortunately, a copy remained in Mom's recipe drawer. Let it snow!

PUDDING:

½ cup cold water

1 envelope unflavored gelatin

1½ cups hot water

¼ cup lemon juice

¾ cup sugar

1 large egg (separated)

SAUCE:

½ teaspoon cornstarch

¼ cup sugar

1 cup milk

¼ teaspoon vanilla extract

For pudding: Put the cold water into a large mixing bowl and sprinkle the gelatin over it. Allow it to set for 1 minute. Add the hot water, lemon juice, and sugar and stir until the gelatin and sugar dissolve. Refrigerate the pudding until it is thick, but not firm (6 to 8 hours). In a separate bowl and with an electric mixer, beat the egg white until it forms soft peaks. Remove the gelatin from the refrigerator and fold the egg white into it. Return to the refrigerator until ready to serve.

For sauce: In a saucepan, stir together the egg yolk, cornstarch, and sugar. Add the milk and cook over medium heat, stirring constantly until slightly thick. Remove from heat, stir in the vanilla, and set aside to cool. Spoon the sauce over individual servings of pudding. **Makes 4 to 6 servings.**

–Janice Stillman

Coconut Ginger Torte

Mom taught me how to make this early in life, and it never fails to impress.

TORTE:

4 large eggs

1 can (14 ounces) condensed milk

3 cups (7 ounces) unsweetened coconut
   flakes

⅓ cup diced crystallized ginger

¼ cup sugar

TOPPING:

1 cup of ginger marmalade

2 fresh apricots, cut into thin slices, for garnish

Preheat the oven to 350°F. Butter and flour a 9-inch pie plate.

For torte: In a blender, combine the eggs, condensed milk, coconut, ginger, and sugar and process until smooth. Pour the mixture into the prepared pie plate and bake for 45 minutes, or until a toothpick inserted into the middle comes out clean. Remove from the oven and set on a rack. When it is cool to the touch, invert it onto a serving plate.

For topping: Spread marmalade on the top. Garnish with apricot slices. **Makes 8 to 10 servings.**

VARIATION

Instead of coconut, use finely chopped pecans, almonds, or pistachios and spread melted milk or dark chocolate over the top.

–Gil Martinez

Nisu (Finnish Coffee Bread)

My mother makes this at Christmas and throughout the year. Sometimes she adds cherries on top.

BREAD:

2 cups milk

½ cup (1 stick) butter

⅔ cup sugar

1½ teaspoons salt

1 tablespoon dry yeast

2 eggs

2 teaspoons ground cardamom

6 to 7 cups all-purpose flour

1 large egg, beaten

sugar

FROSTING:

½ cup (1 stick) butter, softened

8 ounces cream cheese, softened

2 teaspoons vanilla extract

4 cups confectioners' sugar

chopped nuts (optional)

For bread: In a saucepan over medium heat, scald the milk, then add the butter, sugar, and salt. Stir to blend and set aside to cool to lukewarm. In a large bowl, combine ¼ cup of lukewarm (105° to 115°F) water and yeast and stir gently to dissolve. Add the eggs and slightly beat them. Add the milk mixture and cardamom and mix well. Add enough flour (2 to 3 cups) to make a batter. Mix until the dough is smooth and elastic (about 5 minutes). Slowly add the remaining flour, one cup at a time, stirring well after each addition, until the dough is smooth and glossy in appearance and leaves the sides of the bowl.

Turn the dough out onto a lightly floured surface and knead for 5 minutes. Place the dough into a greased bowl and turn the dough to grease the top. Cover with a towel and let rise until doubled in size.

Preheat the oven to 350°F. Lightly grease three cookie sheets. Turn out the dough onto a lightly floured surface, divide into three portions to make three loaves, then divide each portion into three pieces. Using the palm of your hand, gently roll each piece into a "rope" about 14 inches long. Braid three ropes together to make one loaf. Pinch the ends and tuck them under. Repeat with the remaining dough. Place each braid on a cookie sheet. Cover and let rise about 30 minutes. Brush the braids with the beaten egg and sprinkle with sugar. Bake for 18 to 20 minutes. Allow to cool. Frost, if desired.

For frosting: In a medium bowl and with an electric mixer, cream together the butter, cream cheese, and vanilla. Gradually add the sugar and beat until smooth. Spread the frosting on each braid. Sprinkle with chopped nuts, if desired. **Makes three 16-inch loaves.**

–Lisa Traffie, former Internet design coordinator, Yankee Publishing Inc.

How to Make a Family Heirloom Cookbook

Everyone treasures family photo albums and some families put similar value on recipe collections. Surprise the members of your family with a keepsake cookbook. Start by soliciting favorite recipes from grandparents, aunts, uncles, cousins, nieces, nephews—everyone in the family. Ask them to include a few comments about the recipe, such as where it came from, what makes it special, and any relevant advice (e.g., substitutions or alternate ingredients). Consider asking for copies of family photos, with or without the dish displayed prominently.

Later, on a computer or typewriter, rekey each recipe in an attractive format, clearly indicating who sent it. (The computer will allow you to be creative with type fonts and sizes.) Print the recipes on colored paper, slip them into clear plastic binder sheets, and organize them with a table of contents and chapter dividers in a three-ring binder or photo album. Use the photos (or copies of family pictures that you have) to illustrate the book.

Make a copy of the cookbook for each family member, personalizing each edition with the recipient's name on the cover and any other information that makes it memorable.

–Susan Gross, production director, The Old Farmer's Almanac

Cranberry Fluff

This is a standard at our Thanksgiving and Christmas dinners. Cranberries stain, so be careful!

2 cups raw cranberries, crushed or finely chopped

2 cups mini marshmallows

¾ cup sugar

2 cups diced, unpeeled apples

1 cup grapes, sliced into quarters or halves

½ to 1 teaspoon salt

½ cup coarsely chopped walnuts

1 cup heavy cream

In a large bowl, mix together the cranberries, marshmallows, and sugar. Refrigerate overnight. In the morning, add the apples, grapes, salt, and walnuts. In a separate bowl, whip the cream until it forms stiff peaks but is not dry. Gently fold the whipped cream into the fruit and nut mixture. Place the fluff into a glass bowl and refrigerate until ready to serve—no more than a few hours. **Makes about 10 servings.**

–Lisa Traffie

Apple Crisp Pudding

I love apples and autumn! This recipe, which was passed down from my nana to my mother and in turn to me, is a seasonal tradition.

5 cups apples, peeled, cored, and sliced

1 teaspoon cinnamon

1 cup sugar

¾ cup all-purpose flour

½ cup (1 stick) butter, softened

Preheat the oven to 375°F. Grease a 13x9-inch pan. Arrange the apple slices in the pan. In a separate bowl, combine ½ cup of water with the cinnamon, then pour the liquid over the apples. In a small bowl and using a fork or your fingers, combine the sugar, flour, and butter together until it is crumbly. Sprinkle the crumbs on top of the apples. Bake for 30 to 40 minutes, or until the pudding is light brown in color. **Makes 6 servings.**

Sarah Johnson, former associate copy editor, Yankee *Magazine*

Here are two recipes that can help.

Baked Beans for 50

Cook beans in quantity for family reunions, church suppers, or even events for your whole (well, small) town!

6 pounds dry beans

1 pound salt pork

2 medium onions, chopped

1 cup sugar

2 cups molasses

5 tablespoons salt

2 tablespoons dry mustard

1½ teaspoons pepper

1 pint boiling water

Put the beans into a large pot and cover them with water. Soak them overnight. In the morning, parboil the beans in the soaking water until the skins crack when blown upon, about 2 hours. Drain.

Preheat the oven to 275°F. Score the salt pork rind. Cut off a small portion and place it in the bottom of a large baking dish. Add the onions to the baking dish. Add about half of the beans, the larger piece of salt pork, and then the rest of the beans. Mix the remaining ingredients with the boiling water and pour the mixture over the beans. Add more boiling water to cover the beans. Bake for 12 hours, adding more boiling water as necessary.

–courtesy Maine Department of Agriculture

FAMILY FAVORITES

Spaghetti and Meatballs for 8 to 32

TO SERVE:	8	16	24	32
SAUCE:				
peeled tomatoes (28-ounce cans)	1	2	3	4
ground beef, pounds	½	1	1½	2
large onions, chopped	1	2	3	4
cloves garlic, minced	7	14	21	28
tomato paste (6-ounce cans)	2	4	6	8
water (28-ounce cans)	1	2	3	4
water (6-ounce cans)	2	4	6	8
boneless pork cutlets, pounds	½	1	1½	2
mushrooms (4-ounce cans)	1	2	3	4
sugar, tablespoons	1	2	3	4
dried oregano, basil, marjoram, and rosemary, teaspoons each	½	1	1½	2
salt and pepper, teaspoons each	½	1	1½	2
red wine, cups	½	1	1½	2
MEATBALLS:				
ground beef, pounds	1½	3	4½	6
medium onions, chopped	1	2	3	4
seasoned bread crumbs, cups	½	1	1½	2
chopped parsley, teaspoons	½	1	1½	2
grated Parmesan cheese, teaspoons	1	2	3	4
large eggs	1	2	3	4
salt and pepper	to taste			
SPAGHETTI:				
1 pound package	1	2	3	4

For sauce: Heat tomatoes and crush with a potato masher. Brown the ground beef and add to the tomatoes. Sauté the onions and garlic and add to the sauce. Add the tomato paste. Fill the used tomato cans (both sizes) with water and add to the sauce. Blend well and bring to a boil. Brown the pork cutlets and add to the sauce, along with the remaining sauce ingredients. Reduce to a simmer. When the meatballs are ready, add them to the sauce and simmer for 3 hours or longer, until the sauce is thick.

For meatballs: Mix all of the ingredients together (a dough hook is helpful) and roll into balls. In a saucepan over medium heat, brown the meatballs on all sides.

For spaghetti: Cook spaghetti according to the directions on the package.

–courtesy Unitarian Universalist Church, Peterborough, New Hampshire

Reference

PAN SIZES AND EQUIVALENTS

■ You don't need to own pans in every size; you can substitute one for another. However, you must keep in mind that if you change the pan size, you may have to change the cooking time. For example, if a recipe calls for using an 8-inch round cake pan and baking for 25 minutes, and you substitute a 9-inch pan, the cake may bake in only 20 minutes because the batter forms a thinner layer in the larger pan. (Use a toothpick inserted into the center of the cake to test for doneness. If it comes out clean, the cake has finished baking.)

Also, specialty pans such as tube and Bundt pans distribute heat differently; you may not get the same results if you substitute a regular cake pan for a specialty one, even if the volume is the same. Here's a plan for those times when you don't have the correct-size pan:

PAN SIZES	VOLUME	SUBSTITUTE
9-INCH PIE PAN	**4 cups**	**8-inch round cake pan**
8x4x2½-INCH LOAF PAN	**6 cups**	**Three 5x2-inch loaf pans** **two 3x1¼-inch muffin tins** **12x8x2-inch cake pan**
9x5x3-INCH LOAF PAN	**8 cups**	**8x8-inch cake pan** **9-inch round cake pan**
15x10x1-INCH JELLY-ROLL PAN	**10 cups**	**9x9-inch cake pan** **two 8-inch round cake pans** **8x3-inch springform pan**
10x3-INCH BUNDT PAN	**12 cups**	**Two 8x4x2½-inch loaf pans** **9x3-inch angel food cake pan** **9x3-inch springform pan**
13x9x2-INCH CAKE PAN	**14 to 15 cups**	**Two 9-inch round cake pans** **Two 8x8-inch cake pans**

■ If you are cooking a casserole and don't have the correct-size dish, substitute a baking pan. Again, think about the depth of the ingredients in the dish and lengthen or shorten the baking time accordingly.

CASSEROLE SIZE	PAN SUBSTITUTE
1½ quarts	9x5x3-inch loaf pan
2 quarts	8x8-inch cake pan
2½ quarts	9x9-inch cake pan
3 quarts	13x9x2-inch cake pan
4 quarts	14x10x2-inch cake pan

WEIGHTS, MEASURES, AND EQUIVALENTS

▨ WHEN CONVERTING COMMON HOUSEHOLD MEASURES . . .

3 teaspoons = 1 tablespoon

16 tablespoons = 1 cup

1 cup = 8 ounces

2 cups = 1 pint

2 pints = 1 quart

4 quarts = 1 gallon

▨ METRIC CONVERSIONS

½ teaspoon = 2 mL

1 teaspoon = 5 mL

1 tablespoon = 15 mL

¼ cup = 60 mL

⅓ cup = 75 mL

½ cup = 125 mL

⅔ cup = 150 mL

¾ cup = 175 mL

1 cup = 250 mL

1 liter = 1.057 U.S. liquid quarts

1 U.S. liquid quart = 0.946 liter

1 U.S. liquid gallon = 3.78 liters

1 gram = 0.035 ounce

1 ounce = 28.349 grams

1 kilogram = 2.2 pounds

1 pound = 0.45 kilogram

▨ WHEN MEASURING VEGETABLES . . .

ASPARAGUS: 1 pound = 3 cups chopped

BEANS (STRING): 1 pound = 4 cups chopped

BEETS: 1 pound (5 medium) = 2½ cups chopped

BROCCOLI: ½ pound = 6 cups chopped

CABBAGE: 1 pound = 4½ cups shredded

CARROTS: 1 pound = 3½ cups sliced or grated

CELERY: 1 pound = 4 cups chopped

CUCUMBERS: 1 pound (2 medium) = 4 cups sliced

EGGPLANT: 1 pound = 4 cups chopped (6 cups raw, cubed = 3 cups cooked)

GARLIC: 1 clove = 1 teaspoon chopped

LEEKS: 1 pound = 4 cups chopped (2 cups cooked)

MUSHROOMS: 1 pound = 5 to 6 cups sliced = 2 cups cooked

ONIONS: 1 pound = 4 cups sliced = 2 cups cooked

PARSNIPS: 1 pound unpeeled = 1½ cups cooked, puréed

PEAS: 1 pound whole = 1 to 1½ cups shelled

POTATOES: 1 pound (3 medium) sliced = 2 cups mashed

PUMPKIN: 1 pound = 4 cups chopped = 2 cups cooked and drained

SPINACH: 1 pound = ¾ to 1 cup cooked

SQUASH (SUMMER): 1 pound = 4 cups grated = 2 cups salted and drained

SQUASH (WINTER): 2 pounds = 2½ cups cooked, puréed

SWEET POTATOES: 1 pound = 4 cups grated = 1 cup cooked, puréed

SWISS CHARD: 1 pound = 5 to 6 cups packed leaves = 1 to 1½ cups cooked

TOMATOES: 1 pound (3 or 4 medium) = 1½ cups seeded pulp

TURNIPS: 1 pound = 4 cups chopped = 2 cups cooked, mashed

WHEN MEASURING FRUIT . . .

APPLES: 1 pound (3 or 4 medium) = 3 cups sliced

BANANAS: 1 pound (3 or 4 medium) = 1¾ cups mashed

BERRIES: 1 quart = 3½ cups

DATES: 1 pound = 2½ cups pitted

LEMON: 1 whole = 1 to 3 tablespoons juice; 1 to 1½ teaspoons grated rind

LIME: 1 whole = 1½ to 2 tablespoons juice

ORANGE: 1 medium = 6 to 8 tablespoons juice; 2 to 3 tablespoons grated rind

PEACHES: 1 pound (4 medium) = 3 cups sliced

PEARS: 1 pound (4 medium) = 2 cups sliced

RHUBARB: 1 pound = 2 cups cooked

STRAWBERRIES: 1 quart = 3 cups sliced

WHEN CONVERTING CAN SIZES . . .

CAN NAME	FL. OZ.	CUPS	mL
#10	103.70	12.96	3067
#5	56.00	7.00	1656
#3 cylinder	46.00	5.75	1360
#2.5	28.50	3.56	843
#2	20.00	2.50	591
#303	15.60	1.95	461
#211 cylinder	12.00	1.50	355
#1 picnic	10.50	1.30	311
8 ounces	8.30	1.04	245
6 ounces	5.75	0.72	170

MINIMUM TEMPERATURES FOR MEAT AND POULTRY

WHEN IS IT DONE?

■ When cooking meat and poultry, interior temperature is a critical factor for safety and for flavor. To be certain of the correct doneness, use an instant-read thermometer, which will give a reading quickly but is not ovenproof and must not be left in the meat while cooking. Use the thermometer toward the end of the minimum cooking time and allow it to remain in the meat for only 15 seconds at a depth of 2 inches, or to the indicator mark on the thermometer's stem. Follow these guidelines for accurate readings:

■ **For roasts, steaks, and thick chops, insert the thermometer into the center at the thickest part, away from bone, fat, and gristle.**

■ **For whole poultry, insert the thermometer into the inner thigh area near the breast but not touching bone.**

■ **For ground meat (such as meat loaf), insert the thermometer into the thickest area.**

■ **For thin items such as chops and hamburger patties, insert the thermometer sideways.**

INTERNAL MINIMUM TEMPERATURES FOR MEAT AND POULTRY

PRODUCT	MINIMUM FAHRENHEIT
Beef (roasts, steaks, and chops)	
Rare (some bacterial risk)	140°
Medium	160°
Well-done	170°
Casseroles	160°
Chicken	
Ground	170°
Whole	180°
Breasts, roasts	170°
Parts (thighs, wings)	Cook until juices run clear
Duck	180°
Goose	180°
Gravies, sauces, and soups	Bring to a boil
Ground beef, lamb, pork, and veal	160°

PRODUCT	MINIMUM FAHRENHEIT
Ham	
Fresh (raw)	160°
Precooked (to reheat)	140°
Lamb (roasts, steaks, and chops)	
Medium-rare	145°
Medium	160°
Well-done	170°
Leftovers	165°
Pork, fresh	
Medium	160°
Well-done	170°
Stuffing (cooked alone or in bird)	165°
Turkey	
Ground	170°
Whole	180°

According to the National Cattlemen's Beef Association, beef roasts can be removed from the oven when the thermometer registers about 5°F below the desired doneness and allowed to stand for about 15 minutes. The outside layers will continue to transfer heat to the center of the roast until it reaches the desired doneness.

–courtesy Food Safety and Inspection Service, USDA

TEMPERATURE CONVERSION

■ To convert Fahrenheit to Celsius, subtract 32 from the Fahrenheit number, multiply by 5, and divide by 9.

THE BIG CHILL

■ Almost any food can be frozen. Exceptions are eggs in shells and food in cans. (Once food is out of a can, it may be frozen.) To retain vitamin content, color, flavor, and texture, freeze items at peak freshness, and store at 0°F or lower. Food stored constantly at 0°F will always be safe to thaw and eat; only quality suffers with lengthy freezer storage—although freshness and quality at the time of freezing will affect the condition of frozen foods.

When freezing food, consider these tips:

Label foods for easy identification. Write the dish name/contents, number of servings (1 quart = 4 servings; 1 pint = 2 servings), and date on containers or bags.

To prevent sticking, spread food to be frozen (berries, hamburgers, cookies, etc.) on a cookie sheet and freeze until solid. Then place in plastic bags and into the freezer.

Most cookies freeze well and thaw quickly, a convenience when entertaining. Simply cover a plate of assorted cookies with plastic wrap or aluminum foil and put it into the freezer.

Freeze foods as quickly as possible by placing them directly against the side of the freezer.

Arrange the contents of the freezer by each food category.

If power is interrupted or if the freezer is not operating normally, do not open the freezer door. Food in a loaded freezer will usually stay frozen for 2 days.

–courtesy Food Safety and Inspection Service, USDA

HOW LONG WILL IT KEEP?

These times assume that the freezer temperature is maintained at 0°F (–18°C) or colder. The storage times are for quality only. Frozen foods remain safe almost indefinitely.

PRODUCT	MONTHS IN FREEZER
CHEESE (except those listed below)	6
Cottage cheese, cream cheese, feta, goat, fresh mozzarella, Neufchâtel, Parmesan, processed cheese (opened)	Not recommended
DAIRY PRODUCTS	
Butter	6 to 9
Cream, half-and-half	4
Ice cream	1 to 2
Margarine (not diet)	12
Milk	3
Yogurt	1 to 2
FISH AND SEAFOOD	
Clams, mussels, oysters, scallops, shrimp	3 to 6
Fatty fish (bluefish, mackerel, perch, salmon)	2 to 3
Lean fish (flounder, haddock, sole)	6
FRESH FRUIT (PREPARED FOR FREEZING)	
All fruit except those listed below	10 to 12
Avocados, bananas	3
Citrus fruit	4 to 6
Juices	8 to 12
FRESH VEGETABLES (PREPARED FOR FREEZING)	
Artichokes, eggplant	6 to 8
Asparagus, rutabagas, turnips	8 to 10
Bamboo shoots, cabbage, celery, cucumbers, endive, radishes, salad greens, watercress	Not recommended
Beans, beets, bok choy, broccoli, brussels sprouts, carrots, cauliflower, corn, greens, kohlrabi, leeks, mushrooms, okra, onions, parsnips, peas, peppers, soybeans, spinach, summer squash	10 to 12
Tomatoes (overripe or sliced)	2
MEAT	
Cooked	2 to 3
Ham, hot dogs, and lunch meats	1 to 2
Sausage, bacon	1 to 2
Uncooked, ground	3 to 4
Uncooked roasts, steaks, or chops	4 to 12
Wild game, uncooked	8 to 12

PRODUCT	MONTHS IN FREEZER

POULTRY

Cooked	4
Giblets, uncooked	3 to 4
Uncooked	12
Uncooked parts	9

MISCELLANEOUS

Cakes	4 to 6
Casseroles	2 to 3
Cookie dough	2
Cookies	3
Fruit pies, baked	2 to 4
Fruit pies, unbaked	8
Pastry, unbaked	2
Pumpkin or chiffon pies	1
Quick breads	2
Raw egg yolks, whites	12
Soups and stews	2 to 3
Yeast breads	6
Yeast dough	2 weeks

Note: When freezing liquids or foods with liquid, be sure to leave space in the container for expansion.

–adapted from Food Safety and Inspection Service, USDA

REFREEZING

▨ Once food has thawed in the refrigerator, it is safe to refreeze it without cooking, although there may be a loss of quality due to the moisture lost through defrosting. After cooking raw foods which were previously frozen, it is safe to freeze the cooked foods. And if previously cooked foods are thawed in the refrigerator, you may refreeze the unused portion.

▨ If you purchase previously frozen meat, poultry or fish at a retail store, you can refreeze if it has been handled properly and kept at 40°F or below at all times.   —*courtesy Food Safety and Inspection Service, USDA*

UNSAFE AT ANY TEMPERATURE

▨ Canned food that has frozen accidentally, such as a can left in a car or cold basement, can present health problems. If the can's seams have rusted or burst, discard it immediately. If the can is swollen and you are certain that the swelling was caused by freezing (not spoilage), the food may still be edible. Thaw the can in the refrigerator before opening. If, after thawing, the food inside looks and/or smells bad, discard it. Do not taste it!

—*courtesy Food Safety and Inspection Service, USDA*

EFFECTS OF FREEZING

▨ If frozen, the quality of some foods will suffer. Here are some examples:

THIS FOOD . . .	WHEN THAWED . . .
Canned ham	will become watery and soft
Cottage cheese, sour cream, cooked eggs, yogurt, mayonnaise	texture will suffer
Crumb toppings	will become soggy
Fried foods	may become rancid
Home-stuffed whole poultry on carcass	may become contaminated due to freezing or thawing
Lettuce, cabbage, radishes, green onions, celery	will become mushy
Milk, cream, custard and meringue fillings	will separate
Sauces heavy in fat	may separate or curdle
Whipping cream	may not whip

BECOME A HUMAN VACUUM!

▨ Here's how to make your own freezer "vacuum pack." Place food into a plastic zipper bag, insert a straw in the corner of the bag, and seal the bag as far as possible. Suck the air out of the bag with the straw. Then quickly remove the straw and completely seal the bag.

STORING HERBS AND SPICES

■ **FRESH HERBS:** Dill and parsley will keep for about 2 weeks with stems immersed in a glass of water tented with a plastic bag. Most other fresh herbs (and greens) will keep for short periods unwashed and refrigerated in tightly sealed plastic bags with just enough moisture to prevent wilting. For longer storage, use moisture- and gas-permeable paper and cellophane. Plastic cuts off oxygen to the plants and promotes spoilage.

■ **SPICES AND DRIED HERBS:** Store in a cool, dry place, not above the stove or right next to the burners, where heat and steam will cause them to lose flavor dramatically.

THREE SPICE MIXES FOR GOOD HOT CHILI

Mix the spices, store in an airtight jar, and use as needed when cooking chili.

MIX #1:

¼ cup chili powder

2 teaspoons ground cumin

1½ teaspoons salt

½ teaspoon ground cayenne
    pepper

1 teaspoon dried oregano

1 teaspoon garlic powder

1 teaspoon red pepper flakes

MIX #2:

¼ cup chili powder

1 tablespoon ground cumin

1½ teaspoons salt

½ teaspoon ground cayenne
    pepper

¼ cup paprika

1 teaspoon freshly ground black
    pepper

1 teaspoon garlic powder

MIX #3:

¼ cup chili powder

1 teaspoon ground cumin

½ teaspoon salt

pinch of ground cayenne pepper

1 tablespoon paprika

1 teaspoon ground cinnamon

1 teaspoon garlic powder

1 teaspoon sugar

½ teaspoon ground turmeric

½ teaspoon ground coriander

¼ teaspoon ground allspice

A GUIDE TO HERBS AND SPICES

■ Herbs are the leaves of plants (fresh or dried); spices are the seeds, flesh, flowers, bark, roots, or berries of specific plants (almost always dried).

HERB/SPICE	FLAVOR	USES
ALLSPICE	a blend of cinnamon, nutmeg, and cloves	in pot roasts, stuffings, cakes, pies, biscuits, and relishes
ANISE SEED	sweet licorice	in cookies, cakes, fruit fillings, and breads; with cottage cheese, shellfish, and spaghetti dishes
BASIL, SWEET	mild, mint-licorice	in tomato dishes, pesto, sauces, and salad dressings
BAY LEAVES	woodsy, pleasantly bitter	with meat, fish, poultry, sauces, and stews
CARAWAY SEED	sharp, pungent	in rye breads, cheese dips and rarebits, soups, applesauce, salads, and coleslaw; over pork and sauerkraut
CARDAMOM (ground)	mild ginger	in cakes, breads, pastries, curries, jellies, and sweet potatoes; to replace nutmeg in pumpkin pie
CAYENNE (red) PEPPER	blend of hot chile peppers	in sauces, soups, curries, and stews; with meat and seafood
CELERY SEED	celery	with vegetables, eggs, meat, fish, and poultry
CHERVIL	mild parsley	with soups, salads, sauces, eggs, fish, veal, lamb, and pork
CHILE PEPPERS (whole and powdered) (see also Cayenne pepper)	chili powder is usually a blend of sweet and/or hot hot chiles and other spices	in Mexican dishes, gravies, stews, and scrambled eggs; with shellfish
CHIVES	delicate onion	in vegetable dishes, casseroles, dressings, rice, eggs, cheese dishes, sauces, gravies, and dips
CILANTRO (fresh)	mild parsley	in soups, salads, and curries; as a garnish
CINNAMON (ground)	warm, spicy	in baked goods, stewed fruits, and vegetable dishes; in spiced teas and coffees
CLOVES (whole and ground)	hot spice	in baked goods, curries, baked beans, and stews; as a pickling spice
CORIANDER SEED (whole and ground)	pleasant, orange-lemon	with curries, meat pies, sausage, fish, breads, cream or pea soups, and artichokes
CUMIN SEED (whole and ground)	fresh, salty-sweet	use whole in yogurt dishes, soups, and breads; use ground in pork, rice, sausage, and chili and curry dishes

HERB/SPICE	FLAVOR	USES
DILL (fresh and seed)	mild, sweetly aromatic	use fresh with green beans, potato dishes, cheese, soups, salads, seafood, and sauces; use seed for pickles, and to enhance cauliflower, cabbage, and turnips
FENNEL SEED	mild licorice	in pastries, confectionery, sweet pickles, sausage, tomato dishes, and soups; as a flavoring for vinegars, oils, and curries
FENUGREEK (ground and seed)	bitterly aromatic	use ground in soups, stews, gravies, and sauces; use seeds in pickles and chutneys
GARLIC	pungent, aromatic	in tomato dishes, garlic bread, soups, dips, sauces, and marinades; with meat, poultry, fish, and vegetables
GINGER (ground)	sweet, spicy	in pies, pickles, puddings, cookies, cakes, cheese dishes, salad dressings, and soups; an important ingredient in Chinese, Indian, and Arabian dishes
JUNIPER BERRIES	bitter, tart	in sauerkraut dishes; marinades for game
LOVAGE	lemon-scented celery	in soups, stews, salad dressings, and potato dishes
MACE	soft, sweet, spicy	in doughnuts, baked goods, sauces; with chicken, creamed fish, seafood, and fruits
MARJORAM	delicate, flowery	in meat, fish, dairy, and vegetable dishes; in soups
MINT LEAVES (fresh and dried)	fruity, aromatic	with roast lamb or fish; in salads, jellies, and teas
MUSTARD (ground)	sharp, hot, spicy	in a dip for fried shrimp or shrimp or chicken tempura; with ham, corned beef, cold cuts, and hot dogs; to enliven gingerbread and cheese sauces
MUSTARD SEED	spicy	in tomato and vegetable dishes; for pickling; use crushed in salads, coleslaw, spiced meats, boiled and corned beef, and curries
NUTMEG (ground)	sweet, spicy	in cakes, applesauce and apple dishes, eggnog, soufflés, pies, custards; in meat and vegetable dishes

(continued on next page)

HERB/SPICE	FLAVOR	USES
OREGANO	pungent, zesty	in tomato and Italian dishes; with summer squash, potato, and mushroom dishes; in a marinade for lamb or game; use a pinch with baked or sautéed fish
PAPRIKA	spicy-sweet	in stews, omelets, and salad dressings; with fish and seafood
PARSLEY	sweet, clean	use fresh in soups, sauces, and salads; as a garnish
PEPPERCORNS, BLACK	hot, pungent, aromatic	freshly ground, can be used in almost any dish; use cracked in sauces
PEPPERCORNS, WHITE	hotter, less pungent than black peppercorns	in sauces, soups, and potato dishes; with fish and poultry
POPPY SEED	nutlike, sweet	in breads, cakes, pastries, and salad dressings; with vegetables and noodles
ROSEMARY	sweet, resinous	in poultry, lamb, and tomato dishes; in soups, stews, and vegetables; finely chopped in breads and custards
SAFFRON	exotic, bittersweet	in rice and seafood dishes, breads, pastries, cream soups, and sauces
SAGE	warm, pungent	in stuffings, cheese dishes, soups, pickles, and salads; with poultry, beans, and peas
SAVORY, SUMMER	aromatic, peppery	in soups, stews, and stuffings; with fish, chicken, green beans, and eggs
SESAME SEED	nutlike, when toasted	use the white seeds in breads, rolls, and cookies; use the black seeds in Asian cooking to coat meat and fish and to season rice and noodle dishes
STAR ANISE	spicy licorice	in Chinese cooking and marinades, teas, and coffees
TARRAGON	slightly bitter, anise-licorice	with meats, eggs, poultry, and seafood; in salad dressings, marinades and sauces
THYME	pleasant, pungent clove	in casseroles, stews, soups, and ragouts; with eggs, potatoes, fish, and green vegetables
TURMERIC	aromatic, mild	in chutneys, relishes, pickles, and rice and bean dishes; with eggs
VANILLA BEAN	sweet, rich	in custards, ice cream, and pastries; to flavor sauces

■ **BOUQUET GARNI** is usually made with bay leaves, thyme, and parsley tied with string or wrapped in cheesecloth. Use to flavor casseroles and soups. Remove after cooking.

■ **FINES HERBES** uses equal amounts of fresh parsley, tarragon, chives, and chervil chopped fine. Commonly used in French cooking, they make a fine omelet or add zest to soups and sauces. Add to salads and butter sauces, or sprinkle on noodles, soups, and stews.

■ **HERB BOUQUETS** are used to flavor soups, stews, and chowders as well as poached chicken and fish. Tie sprigs of fresh herbs together with twine or put dried herbs in a 4-inch square of cheesecloth and tie securely. Always remove bouquet before serving. The following recipes each make one bag of dried herbs.

CHICKEN:

1 bay leaf
1 tablespoon tarragon
1 tablespoon parsley
1 teaspoon rosemary
1 teaspoon thyme

BEEF:

1 teaspoon black peppercorns
2 whole cloves
1 broken bay leaf
2 teaspoons thyme
2 teaspoons marjoram
2 teaspoons savory
1 tablespoon parsley
½ teaspoon crushed lovage

FISH:

1 bay leaf
2 black peppercorns
1 teaspoon thyme
1 teaspoon fennel weed
1 teaspoon lovage
1 tablespoon parsley

■ **SIMPLE CURRY POWDER**

A blend of many spices, curry powder traditionally depends heavily on coriander for tone, turmeric for color, and red pepper and chiles for heat. Blend ingredients and store in an airtight jar. This recipe makes about 1 cup.

4 tablespoons ground coriander
3 tablespoons ground turmeric
2 tablespoons ground cumin
1 tablespoon pepper
1 tablespoon ground ginger
1 teaspoon ground fennel
1 teaspoon chili powder
½ teaspoon cayenne pepper

SUBSTITUTIONS FOR COMMON INGREDIENTS

ITEM	QUANTITY	SUBSTITUTION
Allspice	1 teaspoon	½ teaspoon cinnamon plus ⅛ teaspoon ground cloves
Arrowroot, as thickener	1½ teaspoons	1 tablespoon flour
Baking powder	1 teaspoon	¼ teaspoon baking soda plus ⅝ teaspoon cream of tartar
Bread crumbs, dry	¼ cup	1 slice bread
Bread crumbs, soft	½ cup	1 slice bread
Buttermilk	1 cup	1 cup plain yogurt
Chocolate, unsweetened	1 ounce	3 tablespoons cocoa plus 1 tablespoon butter or fat
Cracker crumbs	¾ cup	1 cup dry bread crumbs
Cream, heavy	1 cup	¾ cup milk plus ⅓ cup melted butter (this will not whip)
Cream, light	1 cup	⅞ cup milk plus 3 tablespoons melted butter
Cream, sour	1 cup	⅞ cup buttermilk or plain yogurt plus 3 tablespoons melted butter
Cream, whipping	1 cup	⅔ cup well-chilled evaporated milk, whipped; or 1 cup nonfat dry milk powder whipped with 1 cup ice water
Egg	1 whole	2 yolks
Flour, all-purpose	1 cup	1⅛ cups cake flour; or ⅝ cup potato flour; or 1¼ cups rye or coarsely ground whole grain flour; or 1 cup cornmeal
Flour, cake	1 cup	1 cup minus 2 tablespoons sifted all-purpose flour
Flour, self-rising	1 cup	1 cup all-purpose flour plus 1¼ teaspoons baking powder plus ¼ teaspoon salt
Garlic	1 small clove	⅛ teaspoon garlic powder; or ½ teaspoon instant minced garlic
Herbs, dried	½ to 1 teaspoon	1 tablespoon fresh, minced and packed
Honey	1 cup	1¼ cups sugar plus ½ cup liquid
Lemon	1	1 to 3 tablespoons juice plus 1 to 1½ teaspoons grated rind
Lemon juice	1 teaspoon	½ teaspoon vinegar
Lemon rind, grated	1 teaspoon	½ teaspoon lemon extract
Milk, skim	1 cup	⅓ cup instant nonfat dry milk plus about ¾ cup water
Milk, to sour	1 cup	Add 1 tablespoon vinegar or lemon juice to 1 cup milk minus 1 tablespoon. Stir and let stand 5 minutes.
Milk, whole	1 cup	½ cup evaporated milk plus ½ cup water; or 1 cup skim milk plus 2 teaspoons melted butter
Molasses	1 cup	1 cup honey
Mustard, prepared	1 tablespoon	1 teaspoon ground mustard
Onion, chopped	1 small	1 tablespoon instant minced onion; or 1 teaspoon onion powder; or ¼ cup frozen chopped onion

ITEM	QUANTITY	SUBSTITUTION
Sugar, granulated	1 cup	1 cup firmly packed brown sugar; or 1¾ cups confectioners' sugar (do not substitute in baking); or 2 cups corn syrup; or 1 cup superfine sugar
Tomatoes, canned	1 cup	½ cup tomato sauce plus ½ cup water; or 1⅓ cups chopped fresh tomatoes, simmered
Tomato juice	1 cup	½ cup tomato sauce plus ½ cup water plus dash each salt and sugar; or ¼ cup tomato paste plus ¾ cup water plus salt and sugar
Tomato ketchup	½ cup	½ cup tomato sauce plus 2 tablespoons sugar, 1 tablespoon vinegar, and ⅛ teaspoon ground cloves
Tomato purée	1 cup	½ cup tomato paste plus ½ cup water
Tomato soup	1 can (10¾ oz.)	1 cup tomato sauce plus ¼ cup water
Vanilla	1-inch bean	1 teaspoon vanilla extract
Yeast	1 cake (⅗ oz.)	1 package active dried yeast (1 scant tablespoon)
Yogurt, plain	1 cup	1 cup buttermilk

SUBSTITUTIONS FOR UNCOMMON INGREDIENTS

ITEM	SUBSTITUTION
Balsamic vinegar, 1 tablespoon	1 tablespoon red-wine vinegar plus ½ teaspoon sugar
Bamboo shoots	Asparagus (in fried dishes)
Bergamot	Mint
Cilantro	Parsley (for color only; flavor cannot be duplicated)
Delicata squash	Butternut squash or sweet potato
Green mangoes	Sour, green cooking apples
Habanero peppers	5 jalapeño or serrano peppers
Italian seasoning	Equal parts basil, marjoram, oregano, rosemary, sage, and thyme
Lemongrass	Lemon zest (zest from 1 lemon equals 2 stalks lemongrass)
Limes or lime juice	Lemons or lemon juice
Lo mein noodles	Egg noodles
Rice wine	Pale, dry sherry or white vermouth
Red peppers	Equal amount pimientos
Saffron	Turmeric (for color; flavor is different)
Shallots	Red onions or Spanish onions
Shrimp paste	Anchovy paste

Index

INDEX

INDEX